Collins

QUIZ MASTER

Published by Collins
An imprint of HarperCollins Publishers
Westerhill Road
Bishopbriggs
Glasgow G64 2QT
www.harpercollins.co.uk

First Edition 2014

10 9 8 7 6 5 4 3 2 1

© HarperCollins Publishers 2014

ISBN 978-0-00-757877-1

www.harpercollins.co.uk

Typeset by Davidson Publishing
Solutions, Glasgow

Printed in Great Britain by Clays Ltd,
St Ives plc

A catalogue record for this book is
available from the British Library.

If you would like to comment on any
aspect of this book, please contact
us at the above address or online.
E-mail: puzzles@harpercollins.co.uk

AUTHOR
Chris Bradshaw

Introduction

What makes a good quiz? A witty and amusing host and a choice of interesting categories are good places to start.

You could combine the hosting talents of Stephen Fry, Alexander Armstrong, and Jeremy Paxman, but if the questions are no good, the chances are that the quiz will fall flat. For singer Jessie J it was 'all about the money'; for quizzers, it's all about the questions.

That's where *Collins Quiz Master* comes in. We've taken the hassle out of creating the perfect quiz by providing 4000 great questions on all manner of subjects in an easy-to-use format.

There's something on offer for everyone, too, from easy questions for those taking their first tentative steps from quizzing base camp right up to super-tricky testers for those experienced trivia travellers heading for the highest peaks of general knowledge.

Let's get going.

The quizzes

The book is divided into 200 different categories. Half of them are based on classic quizzing categories ranging from films to football, nature to numbers, religion to Russia, and pretty much anything you could imagine in between. The other 100 quizzes are pot luck and contain a little bit of everything.

The quizzes are grouped together depending on how tricky they are. The easy ones come first, followed by medium and finally difficult.

Easy

Think of the questions in the easy quizzes as a nice, gentle stroll in the country. There's nothing too strenuous or taxing, but we've thrown the odd obstacle in just to keep you on your toes.

Medium

The medium questions will require a bit more effort as the trivia terrain gets a little more testing. The answers won't be quite so obvious and you'll get a good general knowledge workout tackling these.

Difficult

If the easy questions are like a gentle Sunday-afternoon meander, the difficult questions are more akin to a trek in the Himalayas. The quest to conquer the trivia summit will be tough, but think of the sense of achievement upon reaching these giddy heights. Get all of these toughies right and you'll have reached the quizzing equivalent of conquering Everest.

The answers

The answers to each quiz are printed at the bottom of the following one. For example, the answers to Quiz 1 appear at the bottom of Quiz 2. The exception to this rule is the last quiz in every level. The answers to these quizzes appear at the bottom of the very first quiz of the level.

Running a quiz

'By failing to prepare, you are preparing to fail,' said American statesman, scientist, and inventor Benjamin Franklin. While a quiz night may not be an earth-shattering event, there's still a great sense of satisfaction to be had in doing a job well, and a little bit of effort beforehand will go a long way to making sure that your quiz goes without a hitch.

❖ Rehearse: don't just pick this book up and read out the questions cold. Go through all the quizzes you're going to be asking by yourself beforehand. Check for any potentially tricky pronunciations. Note down all the questions (notes look better in a quiz environment than reading from a book) and answers. Every effort has been made to ensure that all the answers in *Collins Quiz Master* are correct. Despite our best endeavours, mistakes may still appear. If you see an answer you are not sure is right, or if you think there is more than one possible answer, then check.

❖ Paper and writing implements: do yourself a favour and prepare enough sheets of paper for everyone to write on. The aim of the game here is to stop the mad impulse certain people feel to 'help'. They will spend ten minutes running around looking for 'scrap' paper, probably ripping up your latest novel in the process. The same problem applies to pens. Ideally, have enough for everyone. Remember, though, that over half of them will be lost forever if you give them out.

❖ Prizes: everyone likes a prize. No matter how small, it's best to have one on offer. An egg cup will do nicely.

Good luck! We hope you enjoy *Collins Quiz Master*!

Contents

Easy Quizzes

Medium Quizzes

Difficult Quizzes

EASY QUIZZES

Quiz 1: Pot Luck

1. What do the initials NHS stand for?

2. Which legendary castle is also the name of the company that runs the UK National Lottery?

3. Katniss Everdeen is the central character in which film series?

4. Which two countries compete for the sporting competition known as 'The Ashes'?

5. According to the proverb, what are 'the windows to the soul'?

6. What name is shared by a fruit and a technology company that produces the iPhone?

7. Which member of the royal family gave birth to a daughter called Mia in January 2014?

8. What are the four American states whose name starts with the letter A?

9. Which comedy duo won the Best Presenter category at the British Television Awards for the thirteenth time in 2014?

10. How many pawns does each player start with in a game of chess?

11. The WBA, IBF and WBO are governing bodies in which sport?

12. Salt Lake City is the capital of which American state?

13. A cricket team is made up of how many players?

14. Prior to becoming manager of Manchester United, David Moyes was the boss at which club?

15. A person who is competent in many areas but is not outstanding in any particular one is said to be a what of all trades?

16. Sochi was the venue for which major 2014 sporting event?

17. Halley's and Hale-Bopp are examples of what type of celestial object?

18. In which reality TV series do competitors compete in 'Bush Tucker Trials'?

19. What was the name of the winner of the Best Animation at the 2014 Oscars?
a) Brass Monkeys
b) Chilly
c) Frozen

20. World Championship boxing matches are contested over how many rounds?
a) 10
b) 12
c) 15

Answers to Quiz 67: Pot Luck

1. 14
2. Eastern Central
3. Gareth Bale
4. Notting Hill
5. Pennines
6. The Mona Lisa
7. December
8. Kenya
9. Greg Dyke
10. Pulp Fiction
11. Barack Obama
12. Four
13. Jean-Claude Van Damme
14. Princess Margaret
15. Checkers
16. 1918
17. Goodwood
18. January
19. A tree
20. Wear it (it's a hat)

Quiz 2: Television part 1

1. Bob Monkhouse, Max Bygraves, Les Dennis and Vernon Kay have all hosted which game show?

2. Jon Snow and Krishnan Guru-Murthy read the news on which TV channel?

3. Which TV soap featured a week-long pub siege during 2013?

4. What is the name of the Saturday-night dating show hosted by Paddy McGuinness?

5. Who is the host of the game show 'Deal or No Deal'?

6. The short-lived TV soap 'Eldorado' was set in which country?

7. Complete the title of the BBC3 wedding show – 'Don't Tell the ...'?

8. Detective drama 'Taggart' is set in which city?

9. In which game show are players invited to 'say what you see'?

10. Who was the original host of TV quiz show 'Bullseye'?

11. René Artois was the central character in which popular 1980s sitcom?

12. The comedy 'Blackadder Goes Forth' was set during which conflict?

13. Which TV comedy followed the trials and tribulations of Liverpool's Boswell family?

14. Which bespectacled comic is the host of the chat show 'Chatty Man'?

15. Frank Burnside, Bob Cryer and June Ackland were characters in which police drama?

16. Suburban snob Hyacinth Bucket was the central character in which sitcom?

17. Who was the host of the snooker-inspired game show, 'Big Break'?

18. Terry Wogan, Les Dawson and Lily Savage all hosted which TV game show?

19. In the TV quiz 'Eggheads', each team is made up of how many players?
    a) 3
    b) 4
    c) 5

20. Leah Totton was the winner of which 2013 reality TV show?
    a) The Apprentice
    b) Big Brother
    c) Britain's Got Talent

Answers to Quiz 1: Pot Luck

1. National Health Service
2. Camelot
3. The Hunger Games
4. England and Australia
5. Eyes
6. Apple
7. Zara Phillips
8. Alabama, Alaska, Arizona and Arkansas
9. Ant and Dec
10. Eight
11. Boxing
12. Utah
13. 11
14. Everton
15. Jack
16. The Winter Olympics
17. Comet
18. I'm a Celebrity ... Get Me Out of Here
19. Frozen
20. 12

Quiz 3: Pot Luck

1. Which notorious American gangster had the nickname 'Scarface'?

2. What is the only South American country whose name starts and ends with the same letter?

3. In commerce, what do the initials B2B stand for?

4. What are the four African countries whose name starts with the letter E?

5. 'The Star Spangled Banner' is the national anthem of which country?

6. England's footballers won the World Cup in which year?

7. Which medical condition is abbreviated to SAD?

8. Which sport is played at grounds called Lord's and Trent Bridge?

9. ABTA is a trade association for people in which occupation?

10. In Internet slang, what do the initials NSFW stand for?

11. In which sport are Vitali and Wladimir Klitschko world champions?

12. Yom Kippur is a religious holy day marked by followers of which religion?

13. What does the MI in MI5 stand for?

14. What nationality is the tennis superstar Rafael Nadal?

15. Mount Fuji is an active volcano in which country?

16. 'He's not the Messiah. He's a very naughty boy' is a line from which film comedy?

17. The name of which Greek god was also the name of the American space programme that took man to the Moon?

18. 'Barnacle Bill' is the theme tune to which long-running children's TV show?

19. Which American sport is played on a pitch called a diamond?
    a) American football
    b) baseball
    c) basketball

20. Violinist Vanessa-Mae represented Thailand in the 2014 Winter Olympics in which sport?
    a) bobsleigh
    b) curling
    c) skiing

Answers to Quiz 2: Television part 1

1. Family Fortunes
2. Channel 4
3. Emmerdale
4. Take Me Out
5. Noel Edmonds
6. Spain
7. Bride
8. Glasgow
9. Catchphrase
10. Jim Bowen
11. 'Allo, 'Allo!
12. The First World War
13. Bread
14. Alan Carr
15. The Bill
16. Keeping Up Appearances
17. Jim Davidson
18. Blankety Blank
19. 5
20. The Apprentice

Quiz 4: Sport part 1

1. The 2014 World Cup was held in which country?

2. Who succeeded Sir Alex Ferguson as manager of Manchester United?

3. Bodyline was a controversial tactic used in which sport?

4. Who was the first British cyclist to win the Tour de France?

5. Which driver won his fourth consecutive Formula One Drivers' Championship in 2013?

6. Which footballer scored the infamous 'hand of God' goal?

7. Who won gold in the 5000m and the 10,000m at the 2013 World Athletics Championships?

8. Which Indian batsman called time on an illustrious career in November 2013 after scoring 15,921 runs in 200 Test matches?

9. Torvill and Dean famously won Olympic gold skating to which piece of music by Ravel?

10. Which jockey rode his 4000th winner in November 2013?

11. What sport is played at venues in Troon, Muirfield and Sandwich?

12. In which sport do the top two teams of the season compete in the Super Bowl?

13. A cricket Test match is played over a maximum of how many days?

14. Ben Watson scored the winner in 2013 to help which team to a shock FA Cup final win over Manchester City?

15. Which British middle-distance runner won gold in the 800m and the 1500m in the Athens Olympics in 2004?

EASY

16. Which German football team won the 2013 Champions League?

17. Which Gloucestershire town plays host to a famous horse-racing festival each March?

18. Which English golfer bloomed to take the US Open in 2013?

19. In which sport do teams compete for the Solheim Cup?
    a) golf
    b) rugby union
    c) tennis

20. Briton Phillips Idowu was a world champion in which athletics event?
    a) high jump
    b) pole vault
    c) triple jump

Answers to Quiz 3: Pot Luck

1. Al Capone
2. Argentina
3. Business to business
4. Egypt, Equatorial Guinea, Eritrea and Ethiopia
5. USA
6. 1966
7. Seasonal Affective Disorder
8. Cricket
9. Travel agents
10. Not safe for work
11. Boxing
12. Judaism
13. Military Intelligence
14. Spanish
15. Japan
16. Life of Brian
17. Apollo
18. Blue Peter
19. Baseball
20. Skiing

Quiz 5: Pot Luck

1. In the UK military, what do the initials SAS stand for?

2. What are the two members of the European Union whose names start and end with the same letter?

3. In aviation, what is the common language used by all pilots?

4. What is the only South American country whose name is made up of five letters?

5. According to the proverb, whose wife must be above suspicion?

6. Which of TV's Teletubbies was green?

7. In which continent are the Atlas Mountains found?

8. What are members of the religious order the Society of Jesus commonly known as?

9. In which reality TV series do competitors visit the 'Diary Room'?

10. Someone born between 23 September and 23 October has which star sign?

11. In which Olympic sport can competitors use a foil, épée or sabre?

12. Which American technology entrepreneur and philanthropist returned to the top of Forbes magazine's list of the world's richest people in 2014?

13. Captain Matthew Webb was the first person to swim across which body of water?

14. Which broadcaster and 'Strictly Come Dancing' star left BBC Breakfast in 2014 to join ITV's early-morning programme?

15. What is sometimes described as 'show business for ugly people'?

16. Molly Smitten-Downes represented the United Kingdom in 2014 in which musical competition?

17. In relation to radio broadcasting, what do the initials DJ stand for?

18. In 'The Simpsons', what is the name of Marge and Homer's youngest child?

19. What religious festival immediately follows Shrove Tuesday?
    a) Ash Wednesday
    b) Elm Wednesday
    c) Oak Wednesday

20. Which country hosted football's World Cup in 1970 and 1986?
    a) Argentina
    b) England
    c) Mexico

Answers to Quiz 4: Sport part 1

1. Brazil
2. David Moyes
3. Cricket
4. Sir Bradley Wiggins
5. Sebastian Vettel
6. Diego Maradona
7. Mo Farah
8. Sachin Tendulkar
9. Bolero
10. Tony McCoy
11. Golf
12. American football
13. Five
14. Wigan Athletic
15. Kelly Holmes
16. Bayern Munich
17. Cheltenham
18. Justin Rose
19. Golf
20. Triple jump

Quiz 6: History

1. Which disastrous event started in a bakery in Pudding Lane in 1666?

2. Caledonia was the Roman name for which country?

3. The St Valentine's Day Massacre took place in 1929 in which American city?

4. Queen Victoria was the last British monarch from which royal house?

5. In which year did the Irish 'Easter Rising' take place?

6. 'Lionheart' was the nickname of which English king?

7. Who was the first British monarch from the House of Windsor?

8. By what name was the Russian leader Vladimir Ilyich Ulyanov better known?

9. The fleet known as the Spanish Armada were hoping to overthrow which English monarch?

10. Who was Henry VIII's first wife?

11. What was the name of the assassin who killed US president Abraham Lincoln?

12. In 1989, the Velvet Revolution saw the bloodless removal of Communist rule in which European country?

13. Which colour rose was the emblem of the House of York in their war against their Lancastrian rivals?

14. Which colour was the rose used as a symbol of the House of Lancaster?

15. In which year did Adolf Hitler die?

16. Umberto II was the last king of which European country?

17. In which year did Diana, Princess of Wales die?

18. In 1980, servicemen from the SAS stormed the London embassy of which country?

19. In 1946, who delivered a speech in Fulton, Missouri, warning of an 'Iron Curtain' dividing Europe?
    a) Winston Churchill
    b) John F Kennedy
    c) Richard Nixon

20. What was the name of the survey commissioned by King William I and completed in 1086?
    a) Armageddon Book
    b) Domesday Book
    c) Revelation Book

Answers to Quiz 5: Pot Luck

1. Special Air Service
2. Austria and Czech Republic
3. English
4. Chile
5. Caesar's
6. Dipsy
7. Africa
8. Jesuits
9. Big Brother
10. Libra
11. Fencing
12. Bill Gates
13. The English Channel
14. Susanna Reid
15. Politics
16. Eurovision Song Contest
17. Disc jockey
18. Maggie
19. Ash Wednesday
20. Mexico

Quiz 7: Pot Luck

EASY

1. What style of sunglasses were originally worn by aircraft pilots in the 1920s?

2. What do the initials FBI stand for?

3. Which was the last city in the USA to host the Summer Olympics?

4. In police work, what is a SOCO?

5. Which festive character is known in Portugal as 'Pai Natal'?

6. Which animal represents the star sign Aries?

7. Rosh Hashanah is a festival celebrated by followers of which religion?

8. Because of its unusual shape, which European country is sometimes informally known as 'the boot'?

9. The flags of Germany and Belgium are made up of which three colours?

10. Which former panel-show host plays teacher George Windsor in the TV drama 'Waterloo Road'?

11. Which famous film trilogy was based on an original novel by Mario Puzo?

12. 'Undisputed Truth' was the title of the autobiography of which controversial world heavyweight boxing champion?

13. Darjeeling and Earl Grey are varieties of which drink?

14. Which European country is associated with the House of Orange?

15. 'Well, here's another nice mess you've gotten me into' is a phrase associated with which comedy duo?

Answers – page 17

16. Which common condiment has the chemical formula NaCl?

17. What are the four swimming strokes allowed in Olympic competition?

18. Which Hollywood icon died during the filming of the 1962 film 'Something's Got to Give'?

19. Which place in England is known as the 'city of dreaming spires'?
    a) Birmingham
    b) Hull
    c) Oxford

20. The martial art judo originated in which country?
    a) Brazil
    b) Germany
    c) Japan

Answers to Quiz 6: History

1. The Great Fire of London
2. Scotland
3. Chicago
4. The House of Hanover
5. 1916
6. Richard I
7. George V
8. Lenin
9. Elizabeth I
10. Catherine of Aragon
11. John Wilkes Booth
12. Czechoslovakia
13. White
14. Red
15. 1945
16. Italy
17. 1997
18. Iran
19. Winston Churchill
20. Domesday Book

Quiz 8: Crime and Punishment

1. Which criminal, who took part in 1963's Great Train Robbery and spent many years exiled in Brazil, died in January 2014?

2. In the British police, what rank is represented by the initials DCI?

3. Which doctor was Britain's most prolific serial killer?

4. Who was assassinated by Jack Ruby in 1963?

5. True or false – actor Tim Allen spent time in jail for drug trafficking?

6. 'The Ballad of Reading Gaol' was written by which author?

7. What were the first names of the Kray twins?

8. The prison formerly known as Winson Green is in which British city?

9. Nelson Mandela spent 18 years behind bars in which jail?

10. In English law enforcement, what is a PCSO?

11. Alcatraz Prison was located just offshore of which city?

12. 'The Last Gangster: My Final Confession' was the title of the 2014 autobiography by which London gangland boss?

13. Parker and Barrow were the surnames of which pair of American outlaws?

14. The notorious American gangster Al Capone was eventually jailed for which offence?

15. In 1981, John Hinckley attempted to assassinate which public figure?

16. In the Metropolitan Police, two 'pips' on an epaulette indicates which rank?

17. In the Bible, what was the name of the bandit released by Pontius Pilate in place of Jesus?

18. Which British prisoner was the subject of a 2008 film biopic starring Tom Hardy?

19. Which method of execution was used for the first time in Carson City, Nevada in February 1924?
    a) electric chair
    b) gas chamber
    c) lethal injection

20. Actor Dominic West played which serial killer in the TV drama 'Appropriate Adult'?
    a) Ian Brady
    b) Peter Sutcliffe
    c) Fred West

Answers to Quiz 7: Pot Luck

1. Aviators
2. Federal Bureau of Investigation
3. Atlanta
4. Scene of Crime Officer
5. Father Christmas
6. Ram
7. Judaism
8. Italy
9. Red, black and yellow
10. Angus Deayton
11. The Godfather
12. Mike Tyson
13. Tea
14. The Netherlands
15. Laurel and Hardy
16. Salt
17. Backstroke, breaststroke, butterfly and freestyle (front crawl)
18. Marilyn Monroe
19. Oxford
20. Japan

Quiz 9: Pot Luck

1. In economics, what do the initials GNP stand for?

2. 'I Dreamed a Dream' was a million-selling album in 2009 for which Scottish singer?

3. Which star of TV show 'The Apprentice' was appointed CBE for her services to entrepreneurship in the 2014 New Years Honours list?

4. Edgbaston cricket ground is in which English city?

5. The bull is used to represent which sign of the zodiac?

6. On a bottle of tanning lotion, what do the initials SPF stand for?

7. Which football manager's autobiography was the biggest selling book of 2013?

8. Which three colours appear on the flag of Italy?

9. The number one hit 'What Makes You Beautiful' was the debut single from which boy band?

10. Suiyobi, Mokuyobi and Kinyobi are days of the week in which language?

11. Complete the title of the classic Alfred Hitchcock film – 'Strangers on a ...'?

12. Which country is sometimes known as 'The Lucky Country'?

13. In the 'Chronicles of Narnia' books, what type of animal was Aslan?

14. Which international rugby team plays its home matches at the Stadio Flaminio?

15. In snooker, which ball is worth four points?

16. 'And now for something completely different' is a phrase associated with which comedy team?

17. What is the speed limit for cars on a UK motorway?

18. True or false – the UK House of Commons is also known as 'the Upper House'?

19. What is the name of the implement used to strike the ball in a game of croquet?
a) hammer
b) mallet
c) mashie

20. Which of the following was the title of a classic novel by Dostoevsky?
a) The Boozer
b) The Gambler
c) The Philanderer

Answers to Quiz 8: Crime and Punishment

1. Ronnie Biggs
2. Detective Chief Inspector
3. Harold Shipman
4. Lee Harvey Oswald
5. True
6. Oscar Wilde
7. Ronnie and Reggie
8. Birmingham
9. Robben Island
10. Police Community Support Officer
11. San Francisco
12. Charlie Richardson
13. Bonnie and Clyde
14. Tax evasion
15. President Ronald Reagan
16. Inspector
17. Barrabas
18. Charles Bronson
19. Gas chamber
20. Fred West

Quiz 10: The Good, the Bad and the Ugly

EASY

1. Which fairy tale tells the story of an abused little bird who turns into a beautiful swan?

2. Ray Liotta played gangster Henry Hill in which classic 1990 crime drama?

3. What is the home ground of Premier League football club Everton?

4. In which sport would competitors use a shuttlecock?

5. 'Goodbye Yellow Brick Road' was a 1973 hit for which British singer?

6. In which pantomime do the characters known as the ugly sisters appear?

7. What was the Beach Boys' first UK number-one single?

8. On which day of the year do Christians commemorate the crucifixion of Jesus Christ?

9. Which actress played Bet Lynch in the TV soap 'Coronation Street'?

10. Sanjeev Bhaskar, Kulvinder Ghir, Meera Syal and Nina Wadia starred in which TV comedy sketch show?

11. Which controversial singer topped the album charts in 2007 with 'Good Girl Gone Bad'?

12. Who is the head judge on the TV show 'Strictly Come Dancing'?

13. Bradford Meade, Wilhelmina Slater and Hilda Suarez were characters in which US drama set in the world of fashion?

14. Richard Briers played Tom and Felicity Kendal played Barbara in which 1970s TV sitcom?

15. Alfie Wickers, Simon Fraser, Isobel Pickwell and Rosie Gulliver are characters in which school-set BBC sitcom?

16. Halitosis is another name for what?

17. What name is given to someone who helps a person in need without wanting any recognition or reward?

18. According to the proverb 'one good turn deserves ...'?

19. A dishonest and troublemaking person is known as a bad?
    a) apple   b) orange   c) pear

20. Complete the title of Little Richard's 1958 hit – 'Good Golly Miss ...'?
    a) Dolly   b) Holly   c) Molly

Answers to Quiz 9: Pot Luck

1. Gross National Product	11. Train
2. Susan Boyle	12. Australia
3. Karren Brady	13. Lion
4. Birmingham	14. Italy
5. Taurus	15. Brown
6. Sun Protection Factor	16. Monty Python
7. Sir Alex Ferguson	17. 70mph
8. Green, white and red	18. False
9. One Direction	19. Mallet
10. Japanese	20. The Gambler

Quiz 11: Pot Luck

1. In a game of chess, each player starts with how many rooks?

2. What is the capital city of Poland?

3. True or false – cricketer Michael Vaughan and broadcaster Johnny Vaughan are brothers?

4. In commerce what do the initials B2C stand for?

5. What are the five American states whose names end with the letter S?

6. The famous Trevi Fountain is in which Italian city?

7. Who played the title character in the 2013 film 'Captain Phillips'?

8. Which comedy duo host 'The Great British Bake Off'?

9. Which was the first Canadian city to host the Summer Olympics?

10. What is the capital city of the US state of Colorado?

11. Which American city is nicknamed 'Motor City'?

12. What is the largest of the Canary Islands?

13. Which British Olympic gold medallist wrote the 2013 autobiography 'Twin Ambition'?

14. Which eponymous sitcom character wished his listeners 'good mental health'?

15. Which Northern Irish city was the UK's City of Culture for 2013?

16. The flag of the Netherlands is made up of which three colours?

17. In Internet slang, what do the initials ICYMI stand for?

18. The word sitcom is an amalgamation of which two words?

19. The city of Exeter is in which English county?
    a) Devon
    b) Dorset
    c) Somerset

20. Mount Vesuvius is in which European country?
    a) France
    b) Italy
    c) Spain

Answers to Quiz 10: The Good, the Bad and the Ugly

1. The Ugly Duckling	11. Rihanna
2. Goodfellas	12. Len Goodman
3. Goodison Park	13. Ugly Betty
4. Badminton	14. The Good Life
5. Elton John	15. Bad Education
6. Cinderella	16. Bad breath
7. Good Vibrations	17. Good Samaritan
8. Good Friday	18. Another
9. Julie Goodyear	19. Apple
10. Goodness Gracious Me	20. Molly

Quiz 12: Colours

EASY

1. Complete the title of Chris de Burgh's 1986 chart topper: 'The Lady in ...'?

2. What is the nickname of Manchester United football club?

3. Which colour jersey is worn by the leader of the Tour de France cycle race?

4. Which boy band represented the UK in the 2011 Eurovision Song Contest?

5. Jake and Elwood are the first names of which musical film siblings?

6. What was the full name of Jennifer Aniston's character in the hit sitcom 'Friends'?

7. Which snooker player lost six World Championship finals between 1984 and 1994?

8. Which author wrote the best-selling books 'The Da Vinci Code', 'The Lost Symbol' and 'Inferno'?

9. The bumbling French detective Inspector Clouseau appears in which series of films?

10. Craig Charles, Chris Barrie and Danny John-Jules starred in which TV comedy?

11. 'American Idiot' was the biggest UK hit by which American rock band?

12. In 2013, Lindsey Russell became the 36th presenter of which long-running TV show?

13. Roger Waters, Richard Wright, Syd Barrett, David Gilmour and Nick Mason were members of which British rock band?

14. Which actor enjoyed surprise success in the pop charts in partnership with Jerome Flynn?

15. Which American soul singer was known as 'the hardest-working man in showbusiness'?

16. Which bergamot-flavoured tea is named after a 19th-century British prime minister?

17. Which actor starred alongside Paul Newman in the movie classics 'The Sting' and 'Butch Cassidy and the Sundance Kid'?

18. What is the informal name for the identity card that allows holders to gain permanent residency in the USA?

19. Which 1971 film was based on a novel by Anthony Burgess?
    a) A Clockwork Orange   b) A Clockwork Lime
    c) A Clockwork Lemon

20. What is the name of the actress who plays Dot Cotton in the TV soap 'EastEnders'?
    a) June Black   b) June Brown   c) June White

Answers to Quiz 11: Pot Luck

1. Two
2. Warsaw
3. False
4. Business to customer
5. Arkansas, Illinois, Kansas, Massachusetts, Texas
6. Rome
7. Tom Hanks
8. Mel Giedroyc and Sue Perkins
9. Montreal
10. Denver
11. Detroit
12. Tenerife
13. Mo Farah
14. Dr Frasier Crane
15. Derry / Londonderry
16. Red, white and blue
17. In case you missed it
18. Situation comedy
19. Devon
20. Italy

Quiz 13: Pot Luck

1. Which branch of the British armed forces has an officer training college in Dartmouth?

2. What are the three member countries of the European Union whose names are made up of five letters?

3. Mittwoch is the German word for which day of the week?

4. According to the proverb, what 'is the thief of time'?

5. Who wrote the popular children's book 'Fantastic Mr Fox'?

6. In 2012, Justin Timberlake married which actress, singer and model?

7. What sporting activity is known in French as 'la natation'?

8. In business, what do the intitals SME stand for?

9. 'How Did All This Happen?' is the title of which Liverpudlian comedian's 2013 autobiography?

10. In cricket, what do the initials ODI stand for?

11. Which film trilogy was nominated for 30 Oscars, winning 17?

12. Which American state takes its name from the Spanish for mountain?

13. By what name is the British magician Steven Frayne more commonly known?

14. Which athletics event features a planting box?

15. Only one state in the USA starts with the letter L. Which one?

16. Which author lived in a Jamaican house called 'Goldeneye'?

17. Which playing card is also known as a knave?

18. Which actress played Cindy Beale in 'EastEnders' and 'Stella Price' in 'Coronation Street'?

19. Set during the First World War, what is the title of the famous novel by Erich Maria Remarque?
a) All Quiet on the Eastern Front
b) All Quiet on the Northern Front
c) All Quiet on the Western Front

20. In Greek mythology, a centaur had the head, arms and torso of a human and the body of which animal?
a) horse
b) lion
c) tiger

EASY

Answers to Quiz 12: Colours

1. Red
2. The Red Devils
3. Yellow
4. Blue
5. The Blues Brothers
6. Rachel Green
7. Jimmy White
8. Dan Brown
9. The Pink Panther
10. Red Dwarf
11. Green Day
12. Blue Peter
13. Pink Floyd
14. Robson Green
15. James Brown
16. Earl Grey
17. Robert Redford
18. Green card
19. A Clockwork Orange
20. June Brown

Quiz 14: Alias Smith and Jones

1. Which Welsh actress won her first, and so far only, Oscar in the 2002 musical 'Chicago'?

2. Which high street newsagent was founded in 1792?

3. 'It's Not Unusual' was the first number-one single from which singer?

4. Whom did Tony Blair succeed as leader of the Labour Party?

5. Which of the Dragons on TV show 'Dragons' Den' shares his name with a London department store?

6. Which Welsh presenter replaced Christine Bleakley as host of 'The One Show'?

7. Which actress played Rudi in 'Gavin & Stacey', Janet in 'Two Pints of Lager and a Packet of Crisps Please' and magician's assistant Joey Ross in 'Jonathan Creek'?

8. Granny Smith is a variety of which fruit?

9. 'Men in Black', 'Gettin' Jiggy With It' and 'Wild Wild West' were top-five hits for which actor and rapper?

10. Which actor won his only Oscar for the 1993 film 'The Fugitive'?

11. John 'Hannibal' Smith was the leader of which gang of 1980s TV fugitives?

12. Harrison Ford made his debut appearance as which archaeologist in 'Raiders of the Lost Ark'?

13. Which famous fictional diarist was played on the big screen by Renée Zellweger?

14. Winston Smith is the central character in which novel by George Orwell?

EASY

15. Which American actor provided the voice of Darth Vader in the original Star Wars films?

16. Which Radio 2 DJ first found fame singing 'Walking in the Air' in the film 'The Snowman'?

17. Which actor appeared as Doctor Who for the last time on Christmas Day 2013?

18. Edward J Smith was the captain of which ill-fated ship?

19. Complete the title of a 1939 film starring James Stewart: 'Mr Smith Goes to ...'
    a) Warrington   b) Washington   c) Wolverhampton

20. Chef Delia Smith is a major shareholder of which football club?
    a) Ipswich Town   b) Norwich City   c) West Ham United

Answers to Quiz 13: Pot Luck

1. The Royal Navy
2. Italy, Malta and Spain
3. Wednesday
4. Procrastination
5. Roald Dahl
6. Jessica Biel
7. Swimming
8. Small and medium enterprises
9. John Bishop
10. One-day international
11. The Lord of the Rings
12. Montana
13. Dynamo
14. Pole vault
15. Louisiana
16. Ian Fleming
17. Jack
18. Michelle Collins
19. All Quiet on the Western Front
20. Horse

Quiz 15: Pot Luck

1. Which European mountain is known in Italy as 'Monte Bianco'?

2. In the zodiac, which animal represents the star sign Cancer?

3. Honshu is the largest island of which country?

4. Sir Ben Ainslie is a multiple Olympic gold medal winner in which sport?

5. Which two football teams compete in the 'Old Firm' derby?

6. A violin has how many strings?

7. Which sculptor, best known for 'The Angel of the North', was knighted in 2014?

8. Which fictional character drove a car with the number plate JBZ6007?

9. In 'The Wizard of Oz', which character wanted a heart?

10. What was the pseudonym of the murderer who killed five women in Whitechapel, London in 1888?

11. According to the proverb, a wonder lasts how many days?

12. In Britain, spring officially begins in which month?

13. Which popular activity is known in French as 'le jardinage'?

14. Howard Webb and Mark Halsey are match officials in which sport?

15. Contract bridge is a card game for how many players?

16. What is the name of the thin layer about 15 miles above the Earth's surface that protects life from harmful ultraviolet radiation from the sun?

17. The phrase 'throw a curveball', meaning to surprise someone with something unexpected, derives from which sport?

18. After 25 years in the hot seat, who stepped down as the presenter of 'Newsnight' in 2014?

19. What is the name of the official office of the president of the USA?
a) Oval Office
b) Round Office
c) Square Office

20. Allen Ginsberg and Jack Kerouac were poets associated with which movement?
a) Beat Generation
c) Drum Generation
c) New Generation

Answers to Quiz 14: Alias Smith and Jones

1. Catherine Zeta-Jones
2. WH Smith
3. Tom Jones
4. John Smith
5. Peter Jones
6. Alex Jones
7. Sheridan Smith
8. Apple
9. Will Smith
10. Tommy Lee Jones
11. The A Team
12. Indiana Jones
13. Bridget Jones
14. 1984
15. James Earl Jones
16. Aled Jones
17. Matt Smith
18. The Titanic
19. Washington
20. Norwich City

Quiz 16: Connections part 1

1. By what name is the disease rubella more commonly known?

2. Michael Caine starred as Charlie Croker in which classic 1969 crime comedy?

3. Which actress plays Carrie Mathison in the hit US TV drama 'Homeland'?

4. What is the name of the cylindrical sponge dessert that is filled with a spiral filling of jam or cream?

5. 'Dear Fatty' was the title of the autobiography of which British comedienne?

6. Which Scottish author's works include 'Trainspotting', 'Skagboys' and 'Filth'?

7. Hawthorn Hawks, Essendon Bombers and Fremantle Dockers are teams that play which sport?

8. What was the name of the 2001 crime film starring Brad Pitt and Julia Roberts, who search for a valuable antique gun?

9. By what name is the Shakespeare play 'Macbeth' often referred to by actors wishing to avoid bad luck?

10. Which war ended with the Parliamentarian victory at the Battle of Worcester on 3 September 1651?

11. Complete the title of the 2010 film comedy starring Russell Brand and Jonah Hill – 'Get Him to the …'?

12. 'That'll do nicely' was a catchphrase associated with which credit card company?

13. Which Premiership rugby union team, known as the Exiles, plays its home games at the Madejski Stadium?

14. A pandemic of which virus killed millions of people in 1918 and 1919?

15. Aneka had a number one single in the UK in 1981 singing about what type of boy?

16. David Yip starred as Detective Sergeant John Ho in which 1980s police drama?

17. What is the vegetable called rutabaga in the USA more commonly known as in the UK?

18. Which ska band's only UK hit single was 'Train To Skaville'?
    a) The Ethiopians
    b) The Kenyans
    c) The Nigerians

19. If a couple want to split the bill at a restaurant, they're said to go ...?
    a) Belgian
    b) French
    c) Dutch

20. What is the connection between the answers?

Answers to Quiz 15: Pot Luck

1. Mont Blanc
2. Crab
3. Japan
4. Sailing
5. Celtic and Rangers
6. Four
7. Sir Antony Gormley
8. James Bond
9. The Tin Man
10. Jack the Ripper
11. Nine
12. March
13. Gardening
14. Football
15. Four
16. Ozone layer
17. Baseball
18. Jeremy Paxman
19. Oval Office
20. Beat Generation

Quiz 17: Pot Luck

EASY

1. Bombay is the former name of which Indian city?

2. In a hospital, what do the initials A&E stand for?

3. In which reality TV show is the winner crowned King or Queen of the Jungle?

4. What are the three African countries whose names start with the letter N?

5. Which nursery rhyme character 'sat among the cinders, warming her pretty little toes'?

6. In which month does the Wimbledon tennis championship start?

7. Are the stripes on the flag of Germany horizontal or vertical?

8. Glyndebourne is a venue associated with which type of music?

9. In which sport do teams compete for the America's Cup?

10. Chelsea is the only child of which former US president?

11. Which word, that can be used as a farewell, also means a run scored in cricket where the ball has not hit the bat or the batsman's body?

12. According to the proverb, what 'is better than cure'?

13. Stud, draw and Omaha are variations of which card game?

14. Which Scandinavian capital city gives its name to a condition where hostages bond with their kidnappers?

15. In relation to tempo, what do the initials BPM stand for?

16. Which medical condition is known colloquially as 'kissing disease'?

17. By what name is the Alsatian dog also known?

18. Birkbeck College is based in which British city?

19. How many strings does a banjo have?
    a) four
    b) six
    c) eight

20. What was the first name of TV's Sergeant Bilko?
    a) Arnie
    b) Bernie
    c) Ernie

Answers to Quiz 16: Connections part 1

1. German measles
2. The Italian Job
3. Claire Danes
4. Swiss roll
5. Dawn French
6. Irvine Welsh
7. Australian Rules Football
8. The Mexican
9. The Scottish Play
10. The English Civil War
11. Greek
12. American Express
13. London Irish
14. Spanish flu
15. Japanese Boy
16. The Chinese Detective
17. Swede
18. The Ethiopians
19. Dutch
20. They all contain a nationality

Quiz 18: Reality TV

1. Who are the hosts of 'Britain's Got Talent'?

2. Who was the only judge to appear in all of the first 11 series of 'The X Factor'?

3. 2012 'Dancing on Ice' winner Matthew Wolfendon plays David Metcalfe in which TV soap?

4. Which veteran radio DJ was the first winner of 'I'm a Celebrity ... Get Me Out of Here'?

5. In which musical TV talent show can the voting result in 'Deadlock'?

6. Which actress, best known for playing Janine in 'EastEnders' won 'I'm a Celebrity ... Get Me Out of Here' in 2012?

7. Which bald fruit and veg expert is a judge on culinary TV talent show 'Masterchef'?

8. Which DJ and broadcaster is the presenter of 'The X Factor'?

9. Craig Phillips, Brian Dowling and Kate Lawler were the first three winners of which show?

10. Which actor and comedian joined the judging panel of 'Britain's Got Talent' in 2012?

11. Kian Egan, the winner of 'I'm a Celebrity ... Get Me Out of Here' was a member of which boy band?

12. 'How Do You Solve a Problem Like Maria?' was a TV talent show to find a performer to star in which stage musical?

13. 2013 'Dancing on Ice' winner Beth Tweddle was an Olympic medallist in which sport?

14. Francis Boulle, Cheska Hull and Binky Felstead appear in which scripted reality series?

15. Which dance troupe pipped Susan Boyle to victory in the 2009 series of 'Britain's Got Talent'?

16. 'The Only Way Is Up' by Yazz is the theme tune to which scripted reality show?

17. What is the name of the bespectacled choirmaster who helped tune up the teams in the 2013 series 'Sing While You Work'?

18. Will Young was the first winner of which TV talent show?

19. Which member of Take That has won 'Celebrity Big Brother'?
    a) Gary Barlow
    b) Mark Owen
    c) Robbie Williams

20. Who was the original female host of 'Dancing on Ice'?
    a) Zoe Ball
    b) Tess Daly
    c) Holly Willoughby

Answers to Quiz 17: Pot Luck

1. Mumbai
2. Accident and Emergency
3. I'm a Celebrity ... Get Me Out of Here
4. Namibia, Niger and Nigeria
5. Little Polly Flinders
6. June
7. Horizontal
8. Opera
9. Sailing
10. Bill Clinton
11. Bye
12. Prevention
13. Poker
14. Stockholm
15. Beats per minute
16. Glandular fever
17. German Shepherd
18. London
19. Six
20. Ernie

Quiz 19: Pot Luck

EASY

1. Arg, Lauren Pope, Sam Faiers and Nanny Pat are regulars in which scripted reality TV show?

2. According to the proverb, what shouldn't you cut off to spite your face?

3. What name is shared by a Yorkshire town and the mascot for the charity 'Children in Need'?

4. The opera 'The Magic Flute' was written by which composer?

5. At UK cinemas a film can be given a U certificate. What does the 'U' stand for?

6. 'Vert' is the French word for which colour?

7. In which sport would a competitor use a manoeuvre called a 'Boston crab'?

8. In the zodiac, the lion represents which star sign?

9. Ligue 1 is the name of the top-flight football league in which European country?

10. What is the UK's biggest-selling daily newspaper?

11. In a game of rugby union, how long does each half last?

12. Slalom, downhill and freestyle are disciplines in which winter sport?

13. 'Vertigo', 'Psycho' and 'North by Northwest' were directed by which filmmaker?

14. Which island country lies 40 miles off the south-east coast of India?

15. GM are the initials of which American car manufacturer?

16. In which year did David Cameron become the British prime minister?

17. If something is described as 'feline', it refers to which family of animals?

18. An atheist is someone that does not believe in what?

19. On a golf course, a hole that bends sharply to one side is known as?
    a) cat leg
    b) dog leg
    c) rabbit leg

20. Which mythical spirit is said to be the personification of winter?
    a) Jack Frost
    b) Jack Ice
    c) Jack Snow

Answers to Quiz 18: Reality TV

1. Ant and Dec	11. Westlife
2. Louis Walsh	12. The Sound of Music
3. Emmerdale	13. Gymnastics
4. Tony Blackburn	14. Made in Chelsea
5. The X Factor	15. Diversity
6. Charlie Brooks	16. The Only Way Is Essex
7. Gregg Wallace	17. Gareth Malone
8. Dermot O'Leary	18. Pop Idol
9. Big Brother	19. Mark Owen
10. David Walliams	20. Holly Willoughby

Quiz 20: Religion

1. In Christianity, which feast celebrates the birth of Jesus?

2. Mecca, the holiest city in Islam, is in which country?

3. The Vatican City is an enclave of which Italian city?

4. Which saint was the first Pope?

5. In Islam, Eid-ul-Fitr is a religious holiday that marks the end of which month of fasting?

6. Lambeth Palace is the official London residence of which religious figure?

7. In which 40-day period do Christians traditionally give something up?

8. The Islamic holy book the Quran is written in which language?

9. In Christianity, what is the name of the cup or goblet in which communion wine is served?

10. Shinto is a religion native to which Asian country?

11. Chanukah is a festival celebrated by the followers of which religion?

12. The Bishop of Rome is more commonly known by what title?

13. Which Hindu festival of light translates into English as 'rows of lighted lamps'?

14. Which three religions are known as the 'Abrahamic' religions?

15. In the 2011 UK census, 176,632 people identified themselves as followers of which religion, based on 'Star Wars'?

16. In which religion do followers wear the five Ks?

17. The Four Noble Truths are the central doctrine of which religion?

18. The Hindu god Ganesh has the head of which animal?

19. In Islam, which day is the sabbath?
    a) Friday
    b) Saturday
    c) Sunday

20. Which religion was founded first?
    a) Hinduism
    b) Islam
    c) Sikhism

EASY

Answers to Quiz 19: Pot Luck

1. The Only Way Is Essex
2. Your nose
3. Pudsey
4. Mozart
5. Universal
6. Green
7. Wrestling
8. Leo
9. France
10. The Sun
11. 40 minutes
12. Skiing
13. Alfred Hitchcock
14. Sri Lanka
15. General Motors
16. 2010
17. Cat
18. God
19. Dog leg
20. Jack Frost

Quiz 21: Pot Luck

1. In which pantomime does a boy exchange a cow for some magic beans?

2. Serie A is the name of the top-flight football league in which European country?

3. Which name is shared by a popular Welsh singer and the title character in a novel by Henry Fielding?

4. 'Cry – God for Harry! England and Saint George!' is a famous line from which play by Shakespeare?

5. In slang, which animal is used to describe a sum of £25?

6. What nickname is shared by golfer Ernie Els and the city of New Orleans?

7. Which animal features on the badge of the motor manufacturer Porsche?

8. True or false – the Earth is a pefect sphere?

9. 'Ich bin ein Star – Holt mich hier raus!' is the German version of which reality TV show?

10. Which boy's name is also a document outlining what happens to a person's estate after they have died?

11. Tiger, basking and hammerhead are types of which marine creature?

12. Jimmy Rabbitte is the central character in which film musical, which later hit the West End stage?

13. What number is represented by XV in Roman numerals?

14. What is the seventh planet from the Sun?

15. The cathedral known informally as 'Paddy's Wigwam' is in which British city?

16. In the nursery rhyme, why did Jack and Jill go up the hill?

17. Which word can mean something put in soil to grow or a type of snooker shot involving two touching balls?

18. Which game is known in France as 'échecs'?

19. If someone is feeling blissfully happy they are said to be on what?
    a) cloud seven
    b) cloud eight
    c) cloud nine

20. How often does the World Athletics Championships take place?
    a) every year
    b) every two years
    c) every four years

Answers to Quiz 20: Religion

1. Christmas
2. Saudi Arabia
3. Rome
4. St Peter
5. Ramadan
6. The Archbishop of Canterbury
7. Lent
8. Arabic
9. Chalice
10. Japan
11. Judaism
12. The Pope
13. Diwali
14. Judaism, Christianity and Islam
15. Jedi
16. Sikhism
17. Buddhism
18. Elephant
19. Friday
20. Hinduism

Quiz 22: Movies

All of the films listed below have at least one number in their title. Fill in the blanks.

1.   '____ Day' (2011)

2.   '____ Fast ____ Furious' (2003)

3.   '____ Leagues Under the Sea' (1954)

4.   '____ Amigos' (1986)

5.   '____ Flew Over the Cuckoo's Nest' (1975)

6.   '____ Going On ____' (2004)

7.   '____mm' (1999)

8.   '____ Samurai' (1954)

9.   '____ Again' (2009)

10. '____ Men Out' (1988)

11. '____ Psychopaths' (2012)

12. '____ Hrs.' (1982)

13. '____ Squadron' (1964)

14. '____ Days of Night' (2007)

15. '____ Days' (2000)

16. '___ Weeks Later' (2007)

17. 'United ___' (2006)

18. '___ Blocks' (2006)

19. 'The ___ Blows' (1959)

20. 'Stalag ___' (1953)

Answers to Quiz 21: Pot Luck

1. Jack and the Beanstalk
2. Italy
3. Tom Jones
4. Henry V
5. Pony
6. The Big Easy
7. Horse
8. False
9. I'm a Celebrity ... Get Me Out of Here
10. Will
11. Shark
12. The Commitments
13. 15
14. Uranus
15. Liverpool
16. To fetch a pail of water
17. Plant
18. Chess
19. Cloud nine
20. Every two years

Quiz 23: Pot Luck

EASY

1. In UK cinemas, what does the certificate PG stand for?

2. According to the proverb, what 'abhors a vacuum'?

3. Which nursery rhyme character 'could eat no fat'?

4. In which year did the First World War begin?

5. Oddjob was henchman for which James Bond baddie?

6. In which sport does the leader wear the 'maillot jaune'?

7. Premier League football clubs enter the FA Cup in which round?

8. Which veteran British pop star released his 100th album in 2013?

9. What number comes next in this list – 19, 23, 29, 31?

10. Which planet was downgraded to a dwarf planet by astronomers in 2006?

11. What famous sporting venue was originally known as the Empire Stadium?

12. A nicker is slang for how much money?

13. What are the six teams whose name begins with the letter W to have played in football's Premier League?

14. True or false – Olympic gold medals are made out of solid gold?

15. 'Total Recall' was the title of which Hollywood star's 2012 autobiography?

16. Which word meaning a robot with human features is also the name of a popular mobile-phone operating system?

17. Ceylon orange pekoe is a variety of which drink?

18. Which sign of the zodiac is represented by an archer?

19. According to Forbes magazine, the richest British person in 2014 was the Duke of where?
    a) Kent
    b) York
    c) Westminster

20. The Bundesliga is the name of the premier football league in which country?
    a) Belgium
    b) Germany
    c) The Netherlands

EASY

Answers to Quiz 22: Movies

1.	One	11.	Seven
2.	2 Fast 2 Furious	12.	48
3.	20,000	13.	633
4.	Three	14.	30
5.	One	15.	Thirteen
6.	13 Going On 30	16.	28
7.	8	17.	93
8.	Seven	18.	16
9.	17	19.	400
10.	Eight	20.	17

Quiz 24: Sport part 2

1. The Davis Cup is a team competition in which sport?

2. Which football team won the Premier League for the 13th time in 2012/13?

3. Which English county cricket team plays its home matches at Headingley?

4. What is the nationality of Chelsea manager Jose Mourinho?

5. The IPL and the Big Bash are competitions in which sport?

6. In rugby union, what number shirt is worn by the hooker?

7. What nationality is tennis star Roger Federer?

8. In which month does the Grand National take place?

9. The Lakeside in Frimley Green is the venue for a world championship in which sport?

10. Which Spanish football team won the first five European Cup competitions?

11. English football's Premier League is made up of how many teams?

12. The MCG, the SCG and the Gabba are cricket grounds in which country?

13. Eldrick is the real first name of which golfing legend?

14. How many professional golf tournaments are known as 'majors'?

15. The horse-racing classics The Oaks and The Derby are held at which course?

16. Who are the two players with the initials BB to have won the men's singles at Wimbledon?

17. Who won the BBC Sports Personality of the Year award in 2013?

18. The Australian Formula One Grand Prix is held in which city?

19. The Giro is a cycle race that takes place in which country?
    a) France
    b) Italy
    c) Spain

20. In which year were football's European Championships hosted in England?
    a) 1992
    b) 1996
    c) 2000

Answers to Quiz 23: Pot Luck

1. Parental guidance
2. Nature
3. Jack Sprat
4. 1914
5. Goldfinger
6. Cycling
7. Third
8. Sir Cliff Richard
9. 37 (prime numbers)
10. Pluto
11. Wembley Stadium
12. £1
13. Watford, West Bromwich Albion, West Ham, Wigan, Wimbledon and Wolverhampton Wanderers
14. False
15. Arnold Schwarzenegger
16. Android
17. Tea
18. Sagittarius
19. Westminster
20. Germany

Quiz 25: Pot Luck

1. Which baker and TV talent-show judge was named 'Oldie of the Year' by magazine 'The Oldie' in February 2014?

2. Colonel Gaddafi was the long-time leader of which Arab country?

3. The MLS is a football league in which two countries?

4. What is the capital city of Switzerland?

5. During the First World War, what were 'conchies'?

6. Which instrument is larger – a viola or a violin?

7. Venison meat comes from which animal?

8. Who are the three people to have regularly hosted the TV quiz show 'A Question of Sport'?

9. In the board game Monopoly, what colour are the miniature hotels?

10. It takes the earth just over how many days to orbit the sun?

11. True or false – more people are killed each year by lions than by crocodiles?

12. Which type of golf club is also an alternative name for a chauffeur?

13. Which team reached the FA Cup final for the first time in 2014?

14. The Formula One circuit Hockenheim is in which country?

15. Which animal represents the star sign Pisces?

16. Which nursery rhyme character 'called for his pipe and he called for his bowl and he called for his fiddlers three'?

17. Which is the only South American country whose name is made up of four letters?

18. In Texas hold 'em poker, each player is dealt how many cards?

19. By what name was the German First World War fighter pilot Manfred von Richthofen also known?
    a) The Blue Baron
    b) The Green Baron
    c) The Red Baron

20. How long in feet is a full-size snooker table?
    a) 10ft
    b) 11ft
    c) 12ft

EASY

Answers to Quiz 24: Sport part 2

1. Tennis
2. Manchester United
3. Yorkshire
4. Portuguese
5. Cricket
6. 2
7. Swiss
8. April
9. Darts
10. Real Madrid
11. 20
12. Australia
13. Tiger Woods
14. Four
15. Epsom
16. Bjorn Borg and Boris Becker
17. Andy Murray
18. Melbourne
19. Italy
20. 1996

Quiz 26: Transport and Travel

EASY

1. Which motorway links Exeter with Birmingham?

2. Schiphol airport serves which European city?

3. The home ground of Manchester City football club is named after which airline?

4. Olympic Airlines was the national flag carrier airline of which country?

5. The SNCF is the national railway of which country?

6. Longbridge, the site of a former massive car factory is in which city?

7. 'Driving in My Car' was a number four hit in 1982 for which band?

8. Which area of London gives its name to a type of taxi?

9. The National Railway Museum is in which English city?

10. The motor manufacturer Daewoo is based in which country?

11. Heathrow Airport is now home to how many terminals?

12. Which Italian luxury car maker started life as a manufacturer of tractors?

13. Which animal appears on the badge of the motor manufacturer Peugeot?

14. The Metropolitana is the name of the underground railway system in which European capital?

15. CDG is the code for which European airport?

16. In 1580, which English explorer circumnavigated the globe on a ship called 'The Golden Hind'?

EASY

17. Which city is served by La Guardia airport?

18. What was the name of Horatio Nelson's flagship at the battle of Trafalgar?

19. On a ship, what is kept in a binnacle?
    a) ship's compass
    b) flares
    c) life jackets

20. Paragon railway station serves which Yorkshire city?
    a) Hull
    b) Bradford
    c) Sheffield

Answers to Quiz 25: Pot Luck

1. Mary Berry
2. Libya
3. USA and Canada
4. Berne
5. Conscientious objectors
6. Viola
7. Deer
8. David Vine, David Coleman and Sue Barker
9. Red
10. 365
11. False
12. Driver
13. Hull City
14. Germany
15. Fish
16. Old King Cole
17. Peru
18. Two
19. The Red Baron
20. 12ft

Quiz 27: Pot Luck

1. Which team won English football's Premier League for the second time in 2014?

2. If the days of the week were listed alphabetically which day would be last on the list?

3. 'Meet the gang 'cos the boys are here, the boys to entertain you' was the theme tune to which sitcom?

4. What is the most common surname in Wales?

5. Which city hosts the World Snooker Championship?

6. What is 40% of 2000?

7. 'My very educated mother just served us noodles' is a mnemonic used to remember what?

8. What type of animal was Willy in the 'Free Willy' film series?

9. The TV panel show 'Room 101' takes its name from which famous novel?

10. Which long-running drama features investigations by the 'Unsolved Crime and Open-case Squad'?

11. In games of pool, what colour is the 8 ball?

12. In the children's TV show 'Teletubbies', which Teletubby was yellow?

13. 'Jaune' is the French word for which colour?

14. In which sport do competitors use a puck?

15. 'Miércoles' is the Spanish word for which day of the week?

16. Which American city is nicknamed 'The Windy City'?

EASY

17. In which decade of the 20th century was the United Nations founded?

18. How many rings are on the Olympic flag?

19. Which team was the subject of the 2009 film 'The Damned United'?
    a) Leeds United
    b) Manchester United
    c) Newcastle United

20. What is the occupation of Norman Foster, Richard Rogers and Terry Farrell?
    a) architects
    b) fashion designers
    c) hairdressers

Answers to Quiz 26: Transport and Travel

1. M5
2. Amsterdam
3. Etihad
4. Greece
5. France
6. Birmingham
7. Madness
8. Hackney (carriage)
9. York
10. South Korea
11. Five
12. Lamborghini
13. Lion
14. Rome
15. Charles de Gaulle (in Paris)
16. Francis Drake
17. New York City
18. HMS Victory
19. A ship's compass
20. Hull

Quiz 28: I'm All Right Jack

EASY

1. Bill Tarmey played which character in the TV soap 'Coronation Street'?

2. In which sport do players aim at a target called a jack?

3. Which Scot won the Formula One World Drivers' Championship in 1969, 1971 and 1973?

4. Which British Home Secretary was preceded by Michael Howard and succeeded by David Blunkett?

5. Jack Bauer was the central character in which action-packed TV drama?

6. What was the name of the inspector played by John Thaw in the classic 1970s cop drama 'The Sweeney'?

7. 'The Golden Bear' is the nickname of which record-breaking golfer?

8. Who was the president of France from 1995 to 2007?

9. Who won the Best Director Oscar in 2004 for 'The Lord of the Rings: The Return of the King'?

10. Which abstract expressionist painter was famous for his 'drip' technique?

11. Which famous brand of alcoholic drink is produced in Lynchburg, Tennessee?

12. Which Australian actor received his first Oscar nomination in 2013 for his portrayal of Valjean in 'Les Miserables'?

13. What was Jackie Kennedy Onassis' maiden name?

14. Who wrote the 1957 novel 'On the Road'?

15. Who starred alongside Chris Tucker in the 1998 martial-arts adventure 'Rush Hour'?

16. Which actor voiced the title role in the hit film animation 'Kung Fu Panda'?

17. 'The Manassa Mauler' was the nickname of which world heavyweight boxing champion?

18. Who was Britain's first female Home Secretary?

19. 'The Call of the Wild' and 'White Fang' are novels by which American author, who died in 1916?
    a) Jack London
    b) Jack Manchester
    c) Jack Oxford

20. Which actor played Jack Frost in the British detective drama 'A Touch of Frost'?
    a) David Jason
    b) John Nettles
    c) John Thaw

Answers to Quiz 27: Pot Luck

1. Manchester City
2. Wednesday
3. It Ain't Half Hot, Mum
4. Jones
5. Sheffield
6. 800
7. The order of the planets from the sun
8. Whale
9. George Orwell's '1984'
10. New Tricks
11. Black
12. Laa-Laa
13. Yellow
14. Ice hockey
15. Wednesday
16. Chicago
17. 1940s
18. Five
19. Leeds United
20. Architects

Quiz 29: Pot Luck

1. A blue plaque was unveiled in Stoke-on-Trent in February 2014 as part of the 40th birthday celebrations of which singer?

2. Bratislava is the capital city of which European country?

3. What was the first name of the composer Vivaldi?

4. The Fosbury Flop is a technique used in which athletics event?

5. La Liga is the name of the football league of which European country?

6. What is the most common surname in Scotland?

7. 'Kiwi' is a slang term used to describe someone from which country?

8. H_2SO_4 is the chemical formula for which acid?

9. The first Champions League final to feature two teams from the same city took place in 2014. Which city were the teams from?

10. The island of Tonga lies in which ocean?

11. In English football, the division known as the Championship is made up of how many teams?

12. Which country is the largest democracy in the world?

13. In which month does football's FA Cup final traditionally take place?

14. The cult US drama 'Mad Men' is set in which city?

15. Which Soviet leader was associated with the policies of 'glasnost' and 'perestroika'?

16. The detective drama 'Magnum, PI' was set in which American state?

17. In the nursery rhyme, who 'kissed the girls to make them cry'?

18. What colour scarf does the cartoon character Rupert Bear wear?

19. County Mayo is on which coast of Ireland?
    a) east
    b) south
    c) west

20. In tournament darts, players start on what score?
    a) 500
    b) 501
    c) 502

Answers to Quiz 28: I'm All Right Jack

1.	Jack Duckworth	11.	Jack Daniel's
2.	Bowls	12.	Hugh Jackman
3.	Jackie Stewart	13.	Bouvier
4.	Jack Straw	14.	Jack Kerouac
5.	24	15.	Jackie Chan
6.	Jack Regan	16.	Jack Black
7.	Jack Nicklaus	17.	Jack Dempsey
8.	Jacques Chirac	18.	Jacqui Smith
9.	Peter Jackson	19.	Jack London
10.	Jackson Pollock	20.	David Jason

Quiz 30: The Four Seasons

1. Which season is known in America as the fall?

2. 'Springtime for Hitler' is a song from which hit West End musical?

3. Which season is known in French as 'l'hiver'?

4. Summer Bay is the setting for which long-running TV drama?

5. 'Summer Nights' was a number one hit in 1978 for which duo?

6. Which duo wrote and recorded the original version of the song 'A Hazy Shade of Winter'?

7. Complete the title of the 1997 horror film: 'I Know What You Did Last ...'?

8. Autumn bliss is a variety of which berry?

9. 'A Winter's Tale' was a number two hit in 1982 for which singer?

10. 'I Only Want to Be With You' was the debut hit from which British singer?

11. 'Autumnsong' was a top-ten hit in 2007 for which Welsh band?

12. 'The Rite of Spring' is a famous work by which Russian-born classical composer?

13. 'Printemps' is the name of a large department store in Paris. What does the name means in English?

14. A dog called Schnorbitz was the sidekick of which comedian, who died in 1991?

15. True or false – 'Summer of 69' by Bryan Adams failed to reach the UK top 40?

EASY

16. Which Hollywood A-lister received her first Oscar nomination for her performance in the 2010 film 'Winter's Bone'?

17. Which season is known in Germany as 'der Herbst'?

18. 'High Hopes' was a number-one album released in 2014 by which veteran rock star?

19. Which band had a number three hit in 1983 singing about the 'Long Hot Summer'?
    a) Dexys Midnight Runners
    b) Haircut 100
    c) The Style Council

20. The line 'Now is the winter of our discontent' appears in which play by Shakespeare?
    a) Hamlet
    b) Richard III
    c) Romeo and Juliet

Answers to Quiz 29: Pot Luck

1.	Robbie Williams	11.	24
2.	Slovakia	12.	India
3.	Antonio	13.	May
4.	High jump	14.	New York
5.	Spain	15.	Mikhail Gorbachev
6.	Smith	16.	Hawaii
7.	New Zealand	17.	Georgie Porgie
8.	Sulphuric acid	18.	Yellow
9.	Madrid	19.	West
10.	Pacific	20.	501

Quiz 31: Pot Luck

EASY

1. Are the stripes on the flag of Italy horizontal or vertical?

2. Which former British prime minister lost an eye as a youth after an accident playing rugby?

3. Emerald, racing and Lincoln are shades of which colour?

4. Clean and jerk, and snatch are disciplines in which Olympic sport?

5. Which former footballer's Twitter biography reads 'Once kicked a ball about. Now talk about kicking a ball about. Still flogging spuds'?

6. 'Yank' is a slang term used to describe someone from which country?

7. In which TV show do competitors compete for the Glitterball Trophy?

8. The Toon Army is a name used to describe the followers of which football team?

9. Detroit is the largest city in which American state?

10. According to the nursery rhyme 'Monday's Child', which day's child 'is full of woe'?

11. On a standard dartboard, which number lies between 5 and 1?

12. Who was the first Labour prime minister to win three successive general elections?

13. Which male name can also mean 'a beam of light'?

14. Jason Gardiner, Karen Barber and Katarina Witt have all been judges on which TV talent show?

15. The name of which TV Teletubby is also the name of a major Italian river?

16. What are the three American states whose names contain only four letters?

17. According to the nursery rhyme, what was stolen by 'Tom, Tom the piper's son'?

18. How many teams take part in cricket's County Championship?

19. In which sport do teams compete for the Mosconi Cup?
a) darts
b) pool
c) snooker

20. Which room in a house is known in France as 'la salle de bains'?
a) bathroom
b) bedroom
c) dining room

Answers to Quiz 30: The Four Seasons

1. Autumn
2. The Producers
3. Winter
4. Home and Away
5. John Travolta and Olivia Newton John
6. Simon and Garfunkel
7. Summer
8. Raspberry
9. David Essex
10. Dusty Springfield
11. Manic Street Preachers
12. Igor Stravinsky
13. Spring
14. Bernie Winters
15. True
16. Jennifer Lawrence
17. Autumn
18. Bruce Springsteen
19. The Style Council
20. Richard III

Quiz 32: Famous Eds

1. Who succeeded Gordon Brown as leader of the Labour Party?

2. Which actor provided the voice of the donkey in the 'Shrek' film franchise?

3. Jennifer Saunders plays Edina Monsoon in which British sitcom?

4. Which British monarch abdicated in 1936?

5. A Jack Russell called Eddie was a central character in which long-running US sitcom?

6. 'The Eagle' was the nickname of which British Winter Olympian?

7. Edward Cullen is a central character in which series of vampire-themed books and films by Stephanie Meyer?

8. Which haulage company is the subject of the Channel 5 documentary series 'Trucks and Trailers'?

9. Who was the British prime minister between 1970 and 1974?

10. 'I Don't Wanna Dance' and 'Electric Avenue' were hit singles in the 1980s for which reggae star?

11. Which English composer appeared on the £20 note from 1999 until 2010?

12. Which American inventor created the phonograph and the first practical electric light bulb?

13. What is the home ground of English county cricket team Warwickshire?

14. Which athlete set the world record for the triple jump while winning the 1995 World Championship?

15. Hibernian football club is based in which British city?

16. Which painter, who died in 1967, is best known for his works showing everyday scenes of American life?

17. Prince Edward Island is a province of which Commonwealth country?

18. Which actor and comedian ran 43 marathons in 51 days for Sport Relief in 2009?

19. What was the name of Rowan Atkinson's character in the TV comedy 'Blackadder'?
    a) Edgar Blackadder
    b) Edmund Blackadder
    c) Edward Blackadder

20. Ade Edmondson played Eddie Elizabeth Hitler in which slapstick comedy from the 1990s?
    a) Bottom
    b) Middle
    c) Top

Answers to Quiz 31: Pot Luck

1. Vertical
2. Gordon Brown
3. Green
4. Weightlifting
5. Gary Lineker
6. USA
7. Strictly Come Dancing
8. Newcastle United
9. Michigan
10. Wednesday's
11. 20
12. Tony Blair
13. Ray
14. Dancing on Ice
15. Po
16. Iowa, Ohio and Utah
17. A pig
18. 18
19. Pool
20. Bathroom

Quiz 33: Pot Luck

1. What martial art featured in the title of a UK number-one single for Carl Douglas?

2. What connects a chocolate bar and the a ship on which Fletcher Christian led a famous mutiny?

3. 'Canuck' is a slang term for someone from which country?

4. Which author wrote the sci-fi classic 'The War of the Worlds'?

5. True or false – the Tropic of Capricorn is south of the equator?

6. Complete the title of a 1965 number one for the Rolling Stones: 'Get Off My ...'?

7. Pesto sauce is traditionally made using which herb?

8. The ghostly figure of Jacob Marley appears in which story by Charles Dickens?

9. Which planet is named after the Roman god of war?

10. What is a fandango?

11. What are the two teams to have won English football's top flight whose name ends in a vowel?

12. In 2010, who became the first jockey to win the BBC Sports Personality of the Year Award?

13. What vegetable is the main ingredient in the eastern European soup borscht?

14. 'Sunny Jim' was the nickname of which British prime minister?

15. The name of which Central American country translates into English as 'The Saviour'?

16. Which chat-show host played Father Noel Furlong in the sitcom 'Father Ted'?

17. In American politics, which animal is the emblem of the Republican Party?

18. What are the four corner squares on a 'Monopoly' board?

19. How many tiles are in a full set of dominoes?
    a) 20
    b) 24
    c) 28

20. What was the title of the 1994 hit for Tori Amos?
    a) Branflake Girl
    b) Cornflake Girl
    c) Porridge Girl

Answers to Quiz 32: Famous Eds

1. Ed Miliband
2. Eddie Murphy
3. Absolutely Fabulous
4. Edward VIII
5. Frasier
6. Eddie Edwards
7. Twilight
8. Eddie Stobart
9. Edward Heath
10. Eddy Grant
11. Edward Elgar
12. Thomas Edison
13. Edgbaston
14. Jonathan Edwards
15. Edinburgh
16. Edward Hopper
17. Canada
18. Eddie Izzard
19. Edmund Blackadder
20. Bottom

Quiz 34: Science and Nature

1. The left and right ventricle and left and right atrium are parts of which organ of the human body?

2. By what name is deoxyribonucleic acid more commonly known?

3. Molars, incisors and canines are types of what?

4. Which organ of the human body controls water and salt levels and removes waste?

5. What element of the periodic table has the symbol H and the atomic number 1?

6. The famous equation $E = mc^2$ first appeared in a paper written by which German-born scientist?

7. By what acronym is the underwater communication technique known as sound navigation and ranging more commonly known?

8. In relation to lighting, what do the initials LED stand for?

9. Scurvy is a disease caused by a deficiency of which vitamin?

10. Igneous, sedimentary and metamorphic are types of what?

11. What is the only element of the periodic table that starts with the letter K?

12. Which branch of science is concerned with the study of the earth and its interior?

13. What is the only metal that is a liquid at room temperature?

14. Cardiology is the branch of medicine that deals with which organ of the body?

15. Which grow faster, fingernails or toenails?

16. What is the most common gas in the earth's atmosphere?

17. Haematology is the scientific study of which substance?

18. In which part of the body can the metatarsal bones be found?

19. Which of the following is a unit used to measure temperature?
a) Keith
b) Kevin
c) Kelvin

20. What type of charge does a neutron have?
a) positive
b) negative
c) no charge

Answers to Quiz 33: Pot Luck

1. Kung Fu (Fighting)
2. Bounty
3. Canada
4. HG Wells
5. True
6. Cloud
7. Basil
8. A Christmas Carol
9. Mars
10. A type of dance
11. Aston Villa and Chelsea
12. Tony McCoy
13. Beetroot
14. James Callaghan
15. El Salvador
16. Graham Norton
17. Elephant
18. Go, Jail/Just Visiting, Free Parking and Go to Jail
19. 28
20. Cornflake Girl

Quiz 35: Pot Luck

1. In an American hospital, what do the initials ER stand for?

2. What is the name of the imaginary line that separates the northern and southern hemispheres?

3. By what Hebrew name is the Jewish festival the Day of Atonement also known?

4. What does the Latin phrase 'Corpus Christi' mean in English?

5. Which British prime minister quipped that 'I have taken more out of alcohol than alcohol has taken out of me'?

6. What is the only country in Africa whose name starts with the letter D?

7. Which of the Earth's continents has the largest population?

8. On a standard dartboard, what number lies between 3 and 7?

9. Pandora Braithwaite was the love interest of which fictional teenage diarist?

10. Halloumi cheese originates from which country?

11. Zammo Maguire, Danny Kendall and Gripper Stebson were pupils at which fictional school?

12. Which area of London has the postcode prefix SW19?

13. Which day of the week is an anagram of the word 'dynamo'?

14. The vernal equinox marks the start of which season?

15. On a bottle of wine, what do the initials ABV stand for?

16. Which French band recorded the best-selling 2013 album 'Random Access Memories'?

17. Cd is the chemical symbol for which element?

18. What Hollywood actress has the same name as the wife of William Shakespeare?

19. In which century did the Black Death pandemic sweep through Europe?
    a) 12th
    b) 13th
    c) 14th

20. How many teams took part in the 2014 World Cup finals?
    a) 16
    b) 24
    c) 32

Answers to Quiz 34: Science and Nature

1. Heart
2. DNA
3. Teeth
4. Kidney
5. Hydrogen
6. Albert Einstein
7. Sonar
8. Light emitting diode
9. Vitamin C
10. Rock
11. Krypton
12. Geology
13. Mercury
14. Heart
15. Fingernails
16. Nitrogen
17. Blood
18. Foot
19. Kelvin
20. No charge

Quiz 36: Numbers

1. One million is a 1 followed by how many zeroes?

2. At the start of a frame of snooker, how many red balls are on the table?

3. Which aircraft is known informally as the Jumbo Jet?

4. A leap year is made up of how many days?

5. Which motorway links Leeds and London?

6. Two of England's classic horse races are open to fillies only. The Oaks is one; what is the other?

7. What size of paper measures 297mm by 420mm?

8. Oxbridge General Hospital was the setting for which medical TV drama that ran from 1957 until 1967?

9. 18.29m is the world record for which athletics event?

10. Dennis Haysbert plays President David Palmer in which TV series?

11. 0151 is the telephone dialling code for which English city?

12. The 49ers are an American football team based in which American city?

13. Which group of literary youngsters owned a dog called Timmy?

14. Since joining Manchester United, Wayne Rooney has had which squad number?

15. 90210 is the zip code for which American city?

16. 'I got my head checked / By a jumbo jet / It wasn't easy / But nothing is' are lyrics from which song by indie popsters Blur?

17. What was the title of Paul Hardcastle's only UK number-one single?

18. A sonnet is a poem that contains how many lines?

19. What was the only UK top-ten single by the Barenaked Ladies?
a) One Day
b) One Week
c) One Year

20. The tropics lie approximately how many degrees north and south of the equator?
a) 19
b) 21
c) 23

Answers to Quiz 35: Pot Luck

1. Emergency room
2. Equator
3. Yom Kippur
4. The Body of Christ
5. Sir Winston Churchill
6. Djibouti
7. Asia
8. 19
9. Adrian Mole
10. Cyprus
11. Grange Hill
12. Wimbledon
13. Monday
14. Spring
15. Alcohol by volume
16. Daft Punk
17. Cadmium
18. Anne Hathaway
19. 14th century
20. 32

Quiz 37: Pot Luck

1. In the northern hemisphere, the summer solstice occurs in which month?

2. Who was the only one of Snow White's seven dwarfs not to have a beard?

3. Who was the last politician to have non-consecutive spells as British prime minister?

4. What is the last word of the Bible?

5. FIQQ 1ZZ is the postcode for which British Overseas Territory?

6. Which British actress took her stage name from the third wife of Henry VIII?

7. Which year is marked by the Roman numerals MLXVI?

8. How many minutes are in a day?

9. The disease rickets is caused by a deficiency of which vitamin?

10. What is the oldest tennis tournament in the world?

11. The Japanese flag is made up of which two colours?

12. Which vegetable has all five vowels in its name?

13. The Falls Road and the Shankill Road are famous thoroughfares in which city?

14. Often used to clean feet, what is the only rock that will float in water?

15. What are the Yeoman Warders at the Tower of London more commonly known as?

16. As the crow flies, which city is closer to London – Moscow or Washington DC?

17. Which of the acting Affleck brothers is older, Ben or Casey?

18. Which radio drama was broadcast for the first time on 1 January 1951?

19. Thomas Chippendale was a notable maker of what?
    a) clothes
    b) furniture
    c) hats

20. Where in the UK are the Cambrian Mountains?
    a) Northern Ireland
    b) Scotland
    c) Wales

Answers to Quiz 36: Numbers

1. Six
2. 15
3. Boeing 747
4. 366
5. M1
6. The 1000 Guineas
7. A3
8. Emergency – Ward 10
9. Triple jump
10. 24
11. Liverpool
12. San Francisco
13. The Famous Five
14. 10
15. Beverly Hills
16. Song 2
17. 19
18. 14
19. One Week
20. 23

Quiz 38: Connections part 2

EASY

1. Which Hollywood actress made her big-screen debut on the 1994 film 'The Mask'?

2. 'The Ox' is the nickname of which Arsenal and England footballer?

3. What name is given to a person who builds and maintains roofs made from straw?

4. Which Australian actor played The Joker in the 2008 film 'The Dark Knight'?

5. What is the Dutch city Den Haag known as in English?

6. What was the name of the character played by Peter Sallis in the sitcom 'Last of the Summer Wine'?

7. Which sprinter was stripped of the 100m gold medal at the 1988 Olympics after failing a drug test?

8. What is the name of the biblical garden described in the book of Genesis?

9. What do the initials CNN in the name of the TV station stand for?

10. The Kentucky Derby horse race is held at which American racecourse?

11. In the British Army, which rank comes between Captain and Lieutenant Colonel?

12. Which actor played Rusty Ryan in 'Ocean's Eleven' and its sequels?

13. What was the name of the character played by Johnny Briggs in the TV soap 'Coronation Street'?

14. Who was the lead singer with the indie band The Stone Roses?

Answers – page 79

15. Who did the explorer Sir Henry Morton Stanley famously meet near Lake Tanganyika in Africa in October 1871?

16. Which contemporary charity was founded in 1911 as the 'Society for the Prevention and Relief of Cancer'?

17. Which 1999 horror film featured three film students who vanished after travelling into a Maryland forest?

18. What was the title of the ITV game show hosted by Jasper Carrott where players had to decide whether to 'Share or Steal' the prize money?

19. 'Mustang Sally', 'In The Midnight Hour' and 'Land of 1000 Dances' were hits in the 1960s for which soul singer?

20. What is the connection between the answers?

EASY

Answers to Quiz 37: Pot Luck

1. June
2. Dopey
3. Harold Wilson
4. Amen
5. Falkland Islands
6. Jane Seymour
7. 1066
8. 1440
9. D
10. Wimbledon
11. White and red
12. Cauliflower
13. Belfast
14. Pumice
15. Beefeaters
16. Moscow
17. Ben
18. The Archers
19. Furniture
20. Wales

Quiz 39: Pot Luck

1. The official start of summer is in which month?

2. What is the only UK airport to be named after a footballer?

3. What does the 'I' in the name of political party UKIP stand for?

4. Which is the only US state whose name ends in the letter G?

5. Conkers come from which tree?

6. The niqab is worn by adherents to which religion?

7. George Lazenby made his only appearance as 007 in which James Bond film?

8. The renminbi is the currency of which Asian country?

9. Which legume is the main ingredient in the Middle Eastern dip hummus?

10. Which classic soul song features the line 'Watching the ships roll in, then I watch them roll away again'?

11. What is the only European country whose name in English begins with the letter D?

12. Who was the original host of the TV quiz show 'Countdown'?

13. Blood, navel and Seville are varieties of which fruit?

14. What is the only sign of the zodiac that is represented by an inanimate object?

15. What is the largest two-digit prime number?

16. In darts, how many points are scored for hitting the bullseye?

17. Which three colours appear on the flag of Jamaica?

18. 'Matilda' and 'James and the Giant Peach' were written by which popular children's author?

19. How many league games does each team play in a Premier League season?
    a) 38
    b) 42
    c) 46

20. Clarice Cliff was a famous designer of what?
    a) clothes
    b) pottery
    c) shoes

Answers to Quiz 38: Connections part 2

1. Cameron Diaz
2. Alex Oxlade-Chamberlain
3. Thatcher
4. Heath Ledger
5. The Hague
6. Norman Clegg
7. Ben Johnson
8. Eden
9. Cable News Network
10. Churchill Downs
11. Major
12. Brad Pitt
13. Mike Baldwin
14. Ian Brown
15. David Livingstone
16. Macmillan Cancer Support
17. The Blair Witch Project
18. Golden Balls
19. Wilson Pickett
20. They all contain the surname of a British politician

Quiz 40: Chart Toppers of the 1960s

EASY

Which singer or band topped the UK singles charts with the songs below?

1. 'It's Now or Never' (1960)

2. 'The Young Ones' (1962)

3. 'From Me to You' (1963)

4. 'How Do You Do It?' (1963)

5. 'Sweets For My Sweet' (1963)

6. '(There's) Always Something There to Remind Me' (1964)

7. 'Oh Pretty Woman' (1964)

8. 'I'm Into Something Good' (1964)

9. 'Tired of Waiting for You' (1965)

10. 'The Sun Ain't Gonna Shine Anymore' (1966)

11. 'Distant Drums' (1966)

12. 'Something Stupid' (1967)

13. 'Massachusetts' (1967)

14. 'This Is My Song' (1967)

15. 'What a Wonderful World' (1968)

16. 'Do It Again' (1968)

17. 'The Israelites' (1969)

18. 'Honky Tonk Women' (1969)

19. 'Je T'Aime ... Moi Non Plus' (1969)

20. 'Dizzy' (1969)

Answers to Quiz 39: Pot Luck

1. June
2. George Best Belfast City Airport
3. Independence
4. Wyoming
5. Horse chestnut
6. Islam
7. On Her Majesty's Secret Service
8. China
9. Chickpea
10. (Sittin' On) The Dock of the Bay' by Otis Redding
11. Denmark
12. Richard Whiteley
13. Orange
14. Libra
15. 97
16. 50
17. Green, yellow and black
18. Roald Dahl
19. 38
20. Pottery

Quiz 41: Pot Luck

1. Tartan is associated with which country?

2. Which letter appears on the most tiles in the English version of Scrabble?

3. In the original 'Band Aid' record, who sang the line 'Well, tonight thank God it's them instead of you'?

4. Greendale was the setting for which popular children's TV programme?

5. Which actor plays the Earl of Grantham in the TV drama 'Downton Abbey'?

6. 'Domingo' is the Spanish word for which day of the week?

7. 'Deutschland' is the native name for which country?

8. What is 2015 in Roman numerals?

9. The balti is a curry dish most commonly associated with which English city?

10. What is the capital city of Lebanon?

11. An internet address ending in the letters .cn is from which country?

12. Australian Ian Thorpe was a multiple Olympic gold medallist in which sport?

13. In relation to transport, what do the initials HS2 stand for?

14. Fauntleroy is the middle name of which Disney cartoon character?

15. Actors Damian Lewis and Dominic West both attended which famous school?

16. In Indian cuisine, what is 'kulfi'?

17. Which English city is home to a rugby league team called the Bulls?

18. Hydroponics is a method of growing plants without the use of what?

19. What is the most common surname in Ireland?
    a) Byrne
    b) Murphy
    c) Sullivan

20. Which country's flag is made up of a pale blue band above a yellow band?
    a) Bulgaria
    b) Russia
    c) Ukraine

EASY

Answers to Quiz 40: Chart Toppers of the 1960s

1. Elvis Presley
2. Cliff Richard and the Shadows
3. The Beatles
4. Gerry and the Pacemakers
5. The Searchers
6. Sandie Shaw
7. Roy Orbison
8. Herman's Hermits
9. The Kinks
10. The Walker Brothers
11. Jim Reeves
12. Frank and Nancy Sinatra
13. The Bee Gees
14. Petula Clark
15. Louis Armstrong
16. The Beach Boys
17. Desmond Dekker and the Aces
18. The Rolling Stones
19. Serge Gainsbourg and Jane Birkin
20. Tommy Roe

Quiz 42: North, South, East and West

1. Which band recorded 26 UK top ten singles over a 14-year career that stretched from 1998 until 2012?

2. Which TV soap is set in the fictional E20 postcode area?

3. Slieve Donard is the highest mountain in which country?

4. Which country won the Rugby World Cup in 1995 and 2007?

5. Which American rapper got engaged to Kim Kardashian in late 2013?

6. In 2011, Kim Jong-un became the supreme leader of which country?

7. Sydney is the capital city of which Australian state?

8. 'Stay Another Day' was a Christmas number one in 1994 for which boy band?

9. Which Christian festival celebrates the resurrection of Jesus Christ?

10. What is the name of the massive shopping centre in White City, West London?

11. The Hawthorns is the home ground of which English football club?

12. The film director John Ford is most commonly associated with which movie genre?

13. Stan, Kyle, Kenny and Cartman are the main characters in which animated comedy?

14. Martin Sheen played President Jed Bartlet in which long-running political drama?

15. In relation to the military alliance, what do the initials NATO stand for?

16. 'Carry On Up the Charts' was a massive-selling album for which Hull-based band?

17. Based on Shakespeare's 'Romeo and Juliet', which musical features gangs called the Jets and the Sharks?

18. St Mary's is the home ground of which English football team?

19. By what name is the astronomical phenomenon Aurora Borealis also known?
a) Northern Lights   b) Southern Lights   c) Western Lights

20. Stars from which constellation appear on the flags of Australia and New Zealand?
a) Eastern Cross   b) Southern Cross   c) Western Cross

Answers to Quiz 41: Pot Luck

1. Scotland
2. E
3. Bono
4. Postman Pat
5. Hugh Bonneville
6. Sunday
7. Germany
8. MMXV
9. Birmingham
10. Beirut
11. China
12. Swimming
13. High Speed 2
14. Donald Duck
15. Eton
16. Ice cream
17. Bradford
18. Soil
19. Murphy
20. Ukraine

Quiz 43: Pot Luck

1. Which three colours appear on the flag of Bulgaria?

2. The Summer Olympics takes place every how many years?

3. What are the first three words of the Old Testament of the Bible?

4. What are the four American states whose name starts with the letter W?

5. Blue, crested and great are types of which bird?

6. According to the nursery rhyme, what are made from 'snips and snails and puppy dog tails'?

7. 0203 is a telephone dialling code for which British city?

8. The giant panda is native to which country?

9. Which three colours make up the flag of Norway?

10. According to the proverb, what 'have ears'?

11. 'The Potters' is the nickname of which English football team?

12. 'Prisoner and Escort' was the title of the pilot episode of which TV comedy?

13. In which sport do players stand at the oche?

14. Which colour is associated with envy?

15. What is the name of the river that flows through the centre of the city of Dublin?

16. 'Freitag' is the German word for which day of the week?

17. Which sport did the playwright Harold Pinter describe as 'the greatest thing that God created on earth'?

EASY

18. A chess board is made up of how many squares?

19. What was the title of the huge 2014 hit by Avicii?
    a) Hey Brother
    b) Hey Mother
    c) Hey Sister

20. A speedway race usually features how many riders?
    a) three
    b) four
    c) five

Answers to Quiz 42: North, South, East and West

1. Westlife
2. EastEnders
3. Northern Ireland
4. South Africa
5. Kanye West
6. North Korea
7. New South Wales
8. East 17
9. Easter
10. Westfield
11. West Bromwich Albion
12. Westerns
13. South Park
14. The West Wing
15. North Atlantic Treaty Organization
16. The Beautiful South
17. West Side Story
18. Southampton
19. Northern Lights
20. Southern Cross

Quiz 44: Chart Toppers of the 1970s

Which singer or band topped the UK singles charts with the songs below?

1. 'Tears of a Clown' (1970)

2. 'Get It On' (1971)

3. 'Grandad' (1971)

4. 'I'd Like to Teach the World to Sing' (1972)

5. 'Mama Weer All Crazee Now' (1972)

6. 'Tiger Feet' (1974)

7. 'Billy Don't Be a Hero' (1974)

8. 'Annie's Song' (1974)

9. 'Sugar Baby Love' (1974)

10. 'Bye Bye Baby' (1975)

11. 'I'm Not in Love' (1975)

12. 'Stand By Your Man' (1975)

13. 'Don't Go Breaking My Heart' (1976)

14. 'If You Leave Me Now' (1976)

15. 'I Love to Love' (1976)

EASY

16. 'Don't Give Up on Us' (1977)

17. 'Chanson d'Amour' (1977)

18. 'Wuthering Heights' (1978)

19. 'Ring My Bell' (1979)

20. 'Sunday Girl' (1979)

Answers to Quiz 43: Pot Luck

1. Red, white and green
2. Four
3. In the beginning
4. Washington, West Virginia, Wisconsin and Wyoming
5. Tit
6. Little boys
7. London
8. China
9. Red, white and blue
10. Walls
11. Stoke City
12. Porridge
13. Darts
14. Green
15. River Liffey
16. Friday
17. Cricket
18. 64
19. Hey Brother
20. Four

Quiz 45: Pot Luck

1. The Rhinos are a rugby league team based in which northern English city?

2. Which city in Italy is home to a famous leaning tower?

3. In which month does winter officially start?

4. In Olympic athletics relay races each team comprises how many runners?

5. Which cartoon character owns a dog called Muttley?

6. St Stephen's Green, Grafton Street and Temple Bar are areas of which city?

7. What is the first name of the Christmas curmudgeon Scrooge?

8. Yellow-eyed, Emperor and Rockhopper are types of which bird?

9. Which three sporting activities make up an Olympic triathlon?

10. According to the proverb, all roads lead where?

11. Which colour helmets are worn by United Nations peacekeeping soldiers?

12. The Gorbals is an area of which British city?

13. True or false – the Rolling Stones never had a UK number-one hit single?

14. Mel Gibson played which Scottish patriot in the film 'Braveheart'?

15. The Empire State Building is in which city?

Answers – page 93

16. Which footballer released a brand of perfume called 'Instinct'?

17. What is the only European capital city whose name starts with the letter O?

18. In a game of darts, what is the highest score that can be finished in two darts?

19. The composer Edward Elgar is associated with which English county?
a) Hampshire
b) Worcestershire
c) Yorkshire

20. La Mancha is a region of which country?
a) France
b) Italy
c) Spain

Answers to Quiz 44: Chart Toppers of the 1970s

1. Smokey Robinson and the Miracles
2. T Rex
3. Clive Dunn
4. The New Seekers
5. Slade
6. Mud
7. Paper Lace
8. John Denver
9. The Rubettes
10. The Bay City Rollers
11. 10cc
12. Tammy Wynette
13. Elton John and Kiki Dee
14. Chicago
15. Tina Charles
16. David Soul
17. Manhattan Transfer
18. Kate Bush
19. Anita Ward
20. Blondie

Quiz 46: World War Two

EASY

1. In which year did World War Two begin?

2. What was the animal-inspired nickname of the British Seventh Armoured Division?

3. Who was the British monarch during World War Two?

4. Who was the British prime minister at the start of World War Two?

5. What German military tactic translates into English as 'lightning war'?

6. Who was the British prime minister at the end of World War Two?

7. In which year did the USA enter the war?

8. The Americans joined the war following an attack on which naval base?

9. Who was the US president when the US entered World War Two?

10. The Japanese surrendered after atomic bombs were dropped on which two cities?

11. Britain and France entered the war after Germany invaded which country?

12. The Battle of Midway was a naval battle fought in which ocean?

13. Which general led the Free French movement that fought against the occupation of France by Axis powers?

14. In June 1940, hundreds of ships evacuated thousands of British servicemen from which French port?

EASY

15. In which year did World War Two end?

16. Who was the US president at the end of World War Two?

17. What was the name of the famous battleship named after Germany's so-called 'Iron Chancellor'?

18. The D-Day landings took place in which French region?

19. What was the first name of the Italian fascist leader Mussolini?
a) Benito
b) Bernardo
c) Giovanni

20. The Luftwaffe was the name of the German
a) air force
b) army
c) navy

Answers to Quiz 45: Pot Luck

1. Leeds
2. Pisa
3. December
4. Four
5. Dick Dastardly
6. Dublin
7. Ebenezer
8. Penguin
9. Swimming, cycling and running
10. To Rome
11. Pale blue
12. Glasgow
13. False
14. William Wallace
15. New York
16. David Beckham
17. Oslo
18. 110 (treble 20 followed by bullseye)
19. Worcestershire
20. Spain

Quiz 47: Pot Luck

1. By what name is the gas-extraction process of hydraulic fracturing more commonly known?

2. In June 2014, who announced that he would be abdicating as the King of Spain after 40 years on the throne?

3. The Ballon d'Or is awarded to the leading player in the world in which sport?

4. Piccadilly, Victoria and Oxford Road are railway stations in which English city?

5. DCI John Barnaby is the central character in which TV detective drama?

6. TV presenter Vernon Kay is married to which fellow broadcaster?

7. What is the national speed limit for vehicles in built-up areas?

8. @wossy is the Twitter handle of which broadcaster?

9. 'Liberty, equality, fraternity' is the motto of which European country?

10. The flag of Denmark is made up of which two colours?

11. The name of which chocolate bar is also the name of the galaxy in which our solar system is located?

12. What type of health resort takes its name from a town near Liège in Belgium?

13. The first modern Olympic Games were held in which European capital?

14. Describing something outrageous, what do the initials OTT stand for?

15. In rugby league, how many points are awarded for scoring a try?

16. In 2014, which rock band's Greatest Hits became the first album to sell over six million copies in the UK?

17. Which flower is worn in the run-up to Remembrance Sunday?

18. Which famous TV family lives at 742 Evergreen Terrace?

19. The novelist John Le Carré is associated with which genre of fiction?
    a) espionage
    b) romance
    c) science fiction

20. Which New York thoroughfare is synonymous with finance?
    a) Broadway
    b) Fifth Avenue
    c) Wall Street

Answers to Quiz 46: World War Two

1. 1939
2. The Desert Rats
3. King George VI
4. Neville Chamberlain
5. Blitzkrieg
6. Winston Churchill
7. 1941
8. Pearl Harbor
9. Franklin D Roosevelt
10. Hiroshima and Nagasaki
11. Poland
12. Pacific
13. Charles de Gaulle
14. Dunkirk
15. 1945
16. Harry S Truman
17. Bismarck
18. Normandy
19. Benito
20. Air force

Quiz 48: Anagrams part 1

EASY

Rearrange the letters to make the name of an animal:

1. Braze

2. Toga

3. Dyke No

4. As Ken

5. Fag Fire

6. The Arms

7. Leg Rib

8. The Panel

9. Pine Gun

10. Log Rail

11. Was Eel

12. Key Rut

13. Cop Cake

14. Snore Choir

15. The Ache

EASY

16. A Pearl Orb
17. Limo Fang
18. Paroled
19. Tire Soot
20. Lean Poet

Answers to Quiz 47: Pot Luck

1. Fracking
2. King Juan Carlos I
3. Football
4. Manchester
5. Midsomer Murders
6. Tess Daly
7. 30mph
8. Jonathan Ross
9. France
10. Red and white
11. Milky Way
12. Spa
13. Athens
14. Over the top
15. Four
16. Queen
17. Poppy
18. The Simpsons
19. Espionage
20. Wall Street

Quiz 49: Pot Luck

1. The 2016 Olympic Games will be hosted in which city?

2. If the days of the week were listed alphabetically, which would be first on the list?

3. Which chess piece is also the name of a bird in the crow family?

4. Which is larger – a cricket ball or a tennis ball?

5. Which British composer is best known for 'The Planets' suite?

6. Which planet orbits closest to the sun?

7. Which jazz singer was known as 'Lady Day'?

8. Which middle-distance athletics track event is known as the metric mile?

9. Which are the three teams to have played in football's Premier League whose name starts and ends with the same letter?

10. Which conflict is also known as 'The Great War'?

11. In a game of darts, what is the highest score that can be finished in three darts?

12. The poet Andrew 'Banjo' Paterson wrote the words to which famous Antipodean song?

13. Which was launched first – Channel 5 or Sky TV?

14. Who is the only American artist to feature in the list of the UK's top ten biggest-selling albums of all time?

15. In a game of chess, each player starts with how many pieces?

16. 'We Will Rock You' and 'Another One Bites the Dust' were hits for which rock band?

17. The Spirit of Ecstasy is a badge used by which motor manufacturer?

18. The IRB is the global governing body of which sport?

19. In the Bible, to whom were the Ten Commandments given?
    a) Elijah
    b) John the Baptist
    c) Moses

20. What type of food is a 'wurst'?
    a) fruit
    b) sausage
    c) vegetable

Answers to Quiz 48: Anagrams part 1

1. Zebra
2. Goat
3. Donkey
4. Snake
5. Giraffe
6. Hamster
7. Gerbil
8. Elephant
9. Penguin
10. Gorilla
11. Weasel
12. Turkey
13. Peacock
14. Rhinoceros
15. Cheetah
16. Polar bear
17. Flamingo
18. Leopard
19. Tortoise
20. Antelope

Quiz 50: Music

1. Which former Take That star recorded the album 'Since I Saw You Last'?

2. 'The Boss' is the nickname of which American rock star?

3. 'At first I was afraid I was petrified' is the opening line to which karaoke classic?

4. Which veteran rock band takes its name from the Latin for 'the existing state of affairs'?

5. 'Wannabe' was the debut 1996 single from which female quintet?

6. The 2014 album 'Kiss Me Once' was the 12th album from which Antipodean singer?

7. 'Sex Bomb' was a hit in 2000 for which veteran singer?

8. Which controversial song by Robin Thicke featuring TI and Pharrell Williams was the biggest-selling single in the UK in 2013?

9. Ziggy Stardust was the alter ego of which pop star?

10. Which band holds the record for the most weeks spent at the top of the UK album charts?

11. 'Someone Like You' was a million-selling single in 2011 for which British singer?

12. Which legendary rock band went on an 'Exile on Main St' in 1972?

13. 'Wake Me Up' was a million-selling single in 2013 for which Scandinavian DJ and producer?

14. Which girl's name appeared in the title of a 1982 number one by Dexys Midnight Runners?

15. The song 'Blue Is the Colour' was recorded by the players of which football team?

16. Which former 'X Factor' star was in the 'Right Place, Right Time' in 2013?

17. Who said, 'I've always maintained I'm the most radical rock 'n' roll singer Britain has ever seen. I was the only one who didn't spit or swear or sleep around'?

18. Which condiment appears in the title of an album by The Beatles?

19. Complete the title of the 1976 chart topper by Julie Covington: 'Don't Cry For Me ...'
a) Argentina
b) America
c) Australia

20. 'Let Her Go' was a huge hit in 2013 for which artist?
a) Driver
b) Passenger
c) Pedestrian

Answers to Quiz 49: Pot Luck

1. Rio de Janeiro
2. Friday
3. Rook
4. Cricket ball
5. Gustav Holst
6. Mercury
7. Billie Holiday
8. 1500m
9. Aston Villa, Charlton Athletic and Liverpool
10. World War One
11. 170
12. Waltzing Matilda
13. Sky TV
14. Michael Jackson
15. 16
16. Queen
17. Rolls-Royce
18. Rugby union
19. Moses
20. Sausage

Quiz 51: Pot Luck

1. In which month is Remembrance Sunday observed?

2. What was the maiden name of Catherine, Duchess of Cambridge?

3. Which Pope resigned from office in February 2013?

4. IOC are the initials of which sporting organization?

5. What is the earth's only natural satellite?

6. On which date is St George's Day celebrated?

7. Which planet is named after the Roman goddess of love?

8. What type of animal is a John Dory?

9. Which English monarch was known as 'The Virgin Queen'?

10. Which cartoon character owns a dog called Pluto?

11. Which mountain range is known as 'the backbone of England'?

12. Which smelly animal is also the name of a potent form of the drug cannabis?

13. Land's End, the most westerly point in England, is in which county?

14. Andre Marriner, Phil Dowd and Martin Atkinson are match officials in which sport?

15. Sushi is a type of cuisine associated with which country?

16. The ANC is the governing party of South Africa. What do the initials ANC stand for?

17. Which national newspaper is printed on pink paper?

18. If an event is biennial, how often does it take place?

19. In which month does autumn officially begin?
    a) August
    b) September
    c) October

20. How many dogs take part in a standard greyhound race?
    a) four
    b) five
    c) six

Answers to Quiz 50: Music

1. Gary Barlow
2. Bruce Springsteen
3. 'I Will Survive' by Gloria Gaynor
4. Status Quo
5. The Spice Girls
6. Kylie Minogue
7. Tom Jones
8. Blurred Lines
9. David Bowie
10. The Beatles
11. Adele
12. The Rolling Stones
13. Avicii
14. Eileen
15. Chelsea
16. Olly Murs
17. Cliff Richard
18. Pepper
19. Argentina
20. Passenger

Quiz 52: Places

EASY

1. With a population of less than 1000 and covering an area of just 0.2 miles, what is the world's smallest state?

2. Houston is the largest city in which American state?

3. Munich is the capital city of which German province?

4. The Royal Mile is a feature of which British city?

5. The Alhambra Palace is in which Spanish city?

6. The prison formerly known as Strangeways is in which British city?

7. True or false – the Czech Republic is a landlocked country?

8. What is the largest of the world's oceans?

9. Which English county is sometimes abbreviated as Salop?

10. Piedmont and Umbria are regions of which European country?

11. Which European country is known in its own language as Magyarország?

12. Which canal connects the Atlantic Ocean and the Pacific Ocean?

13. The Rocky Mountains are situated in which two countries?

14. Niagara Falls marks the border between which American state and which Canadian province?

15. Aquitaine is a region of which country?

16. Toxteth, Broad Green and Fazakerley are areas of which British city?

Answers – page 107

EASY

17. Which range of mountains is known as 'the backbone of Italy'?

18. Which world-famous landmark is located just outside the town of Keystone in the US state of South Dakota?

19. What is the capital of the Scilly Isles?
    a) Hugh Town
    b) Pugh Town
    c) Barney McGrew Town

20. The Patagonia area of Argentina is associated with speakers of which language?
    a) Gaelic
    b) Manx
    c) Welsh

Answers to Quiz 51: Pot Luck

1. November
2. Middleton
3. Benedict XVI
4. International Olympic Committee
5. The Moon
6. 23rd April
7. Venus
8. Fish
9. Elizabeth I
10. Mickey Mouse
11. The Pennines
12. Skunk
13. Cornwall
14. Football
15. Japan
16. African National Congress
17. Financial Times
18. Every two years
19. September
20. Six

Quiz 53: Pot Luck

1. Steve Brookstein was the first winner of which TV talent show?

2. Tigers are native to which continent?

3. The maple leaf is a symbol of which country?

4. 'Dancing with the Stars' is the American equivalent of which British TV show?

5. The All Blacks is the nickname of the rugby team of which country?

6. The name of which sport is also used to describe browsing on the internet?

7. What colour are the stars on the flag of the European Union?

8. Pope Francis comes from which South American country?

9. The Charleston, waltz and American smooth are types of what?

10. True or false – a wasp can sting only once?

11. Which part of the body is removed in a hysterectomy operation?

12. What does the 'C' in the name of the BBC stand for?

13. Which former British prime minister died on 8 April 2013?

14. Which British actor made his big-screen debut playing Hans Gruber in the thriller 'Die Hard'?

15. Which comedy duo collaborated with the Lightning Seeds on the football song 'Three Lions'?

16. Thelonius Monk and Chet Baker are associated with which genre of music?

17. What was the first name of the German composer Wagner?

18. Who is the eldest of Queen Elizabeth's children?

19. Russell Crowe played which Biblical character in a 2014 film?
    a) Jesus
    b) Moses
    c) Noah

20. In which month do Americans celebrate Thanksgiving Day?
    a) October
    b) November
    c) December

Answers to Quiz 52: Places

1. Vatican City	11. Hungary
2. Texas	12. Panama Canal
3. Bavaria	13. Canada and the USA
4. Edinburgh	14. New York and Ontario
5. Granada	15. France
6. Manchester	16. Liverpool
7. True	17. Apennines
8. Pacific	18. Mount Rushmore
9. Shropshire	19. Hugh Town
10. Italy	20. Welsh

Quiz 54: On Stage

1. The Royal Shakespeare Company is based in which English town?

2. Sally Bowles is the central character in which musical?

3. When wishing an actor good luck, it's customary to hope that they break what?

4. 'The Mousetrap' has played in London for thousands of performances. Who wrote it?

5. 'Viva Forever!' was a musical featuring the songs of which band?

6. The musical 'Charlie and the Chocolate Factory' is based on a novel by which author?

7. The jukebox musical 'We Will Rock You' was written by which comedian and author?

8. Fill in the missing word from this play by Tennessee Williams – 'A Streetcar Named ____'

9. True or false – the musical 'Blood Brothers' is set in Birmingham?

10. The Three Witches are characters who appear in which play by Shakespeare?

11. Which pop star wrote the music for the stage version of 'Billy Elliot'?

12. Theatre impresario Bill Kenwright is also the chairman of which Premier League football club?

13. 'Waiting for Godot' is the best-known work by which Irish playwright?

14. Which musical features the songs 'Cell Block Tango', 'Me and My Baby' and 'All That Jazz'?

15. 'The Sound of Music' was the last musical written by which duo?

16. Which playwright was married to Marilyn Monroe?

17. By what name is the Antoinette Perry Award for Excellence in Theatre better known?

18. 'All the Fun of the Fair' is a musical based on the songs of which British singer?

19. Which of the following was the title of an Andrew Lloyd Webber musical?
    a) Sunset Avenue
    b) Sunset Boulevard
    c) Sunset Street

20. Which musical was based upon George Bernard Shaw's play 'Pygmalion'?
    a) Cabaret
    b) My Fair Lady
    c) The King and I

Answers to Quiz 53: Pot Luck

1. The X Factor
2. Asia
3. Canada
4. Strictly Come Dancing
5. New Zealand
6. Surfing
7. Gold (yellow)
8. Argentina
9. Dance
10. False
11. Womb (uterus)
12. Corporation
13. Margaret Thatcher
14. Alan Rickman
15. Baddiel and Skinner
16. Jazz
17. Richard
18. Prince Charles
19. Noah
20. November

Quiz 55: Pot Luck

1. What does the J in the name Homer J Simpson stand for?

2. Who was South Africa's first black president?

3. Who was stripped of his seven Tour de France victories after admitting doping offences?

4. Which animal also means 'to talk incessantly'?

5. The drachma was the former currency of which European country?

6. On which TV show may you see 'a star in a reasonably-priced car'?

7. In February 2014, Matteo Renzi became the youngest prime minister of which country?

8. Which letter of the alphabet is also the title of a British national daily newspaper?

9. What is the only athletics event that features a water jump?

10. What is the smallest denomination euro banknote?

11. How many ounces make one pound?

12. Which four-letter word can mean 'remaining' or 'went'?

13. Which children's animation series features a pony called Pedro, a zebra called Zoe and a fox called Freddy?

14. In cricket, which animal is used to describe a score of nought?

15. Which boy's name is also a slang term for a police officer?

16. What is the only country in the world that starts with the letter Q?

17. Actor Tom Hiddleston, Olympian Matthew Pinsent and Prime Minister David Cameron all attended which public school?

18. Bouncer, long hop and jaffa are terms used in which sport?

19. The London street Savile Row is associated with which industry?
    a) electricals
    b) newspapers
    c) tailoring

20. In which year was the law legalizing gay marriage in England and Wales passed?
    a) 1993
    b) 2003
    c) 2013

Answers to Quiz 54: On Stage

1. Stratford-upon-Avon
2. Cabaret
3. A leg
4. Agatha Christie
5. The Spice Girls
6. Roald Dahl
7. Ben Elton
8. Desire
9. False
10. Macbeth
11. Elton John
12. Everton
13. Samuel Beckett
14. Chicago
15. Rodgers and Hammerstein
16. Arthur Miller
17. Tony Award
18. David Essex
19. Sunset Boulevard
20. My Fair Lady

Quiz 56: Chart-Toppers of the 1980s

Which singer or band topped the UK singles charts with the songs below?

1. 'Geno' (1980)

2. 'The Tide Is High' (1980)

3. 'Don't You Want Me' (1981)

4. 'House of Fun' (1982)

5. 'Total Eclipse of the Heart' (1983)

6. 'Let's Dance' (1983)

7. 'The Reflex' (1984)

8. 'Two Tribes' (1984)

9. 'I Want to Know What Love Is' (1985)

10. 'You Spin Me Round (Like a Record)' (1985)

11. 'A Good Heart' (1985)

12. 'Chain Reaction' (1986)

13. 'Rock Me Amadeus' (1986)

14. 'Don't Leave Me This Way' (1986)

15. 'Respectable' (1987)

16. 'Never Gonna Give You Up' (1987)

17. 'I Owe You Nothing' (1988)

18. 'I Think We're Alone Now' (1988)

19. 'Orinoco Flow' (1988)

20. 'Eternal Flame' (1989)

Answers to Quiz 55: Pot Luck

1.	Jay	11.	16
2.	Nelson Mandela	12.	Left
3.	Lance Armstrong	13.	Peppa Pig
4.	Rabbit	14.	Duck
5.	Greece	15.	Bobby
6.	Top Gear	16.	Qatar
7.	Italy	17.	Eton
8.	I	18.	Cricket
9.	Steeplechase	19.	Tailoring
10.	€ 5	20.	2013

Quiz 57: Pot Luck

1. The Caribbean island of Guadeloupe is an overseas territory of which European country?

2. The flag of Pakistan is made up of which two colours?

3. At the Olympic Games, what is the shortest track athletics event?

4. How many humps does a Bactrian camel have?

5. The 'Mary Rose' was the flagship of which English monarch?

6. What was the name of the coffee shop in the TV sitcom 'Friends'?

7. In Argentina they're known as the 'Islas Malvinas'. What are they known as in Britain?

8. Which is the only one of the Seven Wonders of the Ancient World that is still standing?

9. What does the 'H' in the medical condition ADHD stand for?

10. Which four letter word can mean 'a large piece, usually of food' and 'a well-built, handsome man'?

11. Which board game features a character called Jake the Jailbird?

12. In online slang, what do the initials WYWH stand for?

13. The phrase 'touch base' derives from which sport?

14. What is the only country whose name doesn't appear on its postage stamps?

15. The popular holiday resort of Sharm el-Sheikh is in which country?

16. Which British monarch was the father of Queen Elizabeth II?

17. Which planet is named after the Roman god of the sea?

18. In the TV quiz show 'University Challenge', each team is made up of how many contestants?

19. What is the name of the magazine produced by the Consumers' Association?
    a) What?
    b) Where?
    c) Which?

20. In cricket, what name is given to a delivery aimed at a batsman's toes?
    a) Lanker
    b) Warker
    c) Yorker

Answers to Quiz 56: Chart-Toppers of the 1980s

1. Dexys Midnight Runners
2. Blondie
3. The Human League
4. Madness
5. Bonnie Tyler
6. David Bowie
7. Duran Duran
8. Frankie Goes to Hollywood
9. Foreigner
10. Dead or Alive
11. Feargal Sharkey
12. Diana Ross
13. Falco
14. The Communards
15. Mel and Kim
16. Rick Astley
17. Bros
18. Tiffany
19. Enya
20. The Bangles

Quiz 58: Television part 2

1. Who is the host of the anarchic comedy show 'TV Burp'?

2. Ned Flanders is the next door neighbour of which fictional family?

3. The last episode of which BBC comedy, featuring the fictional Brockman family, aired in March 2014?

4. In which game show did contestants have to choose 'top, middle or bottom' and avoid 'hot spots'?

5. Which soap was set in the fictional district of King's Oak, near Birmingham?

6. Complete the title of the TV property show: 'Homes under the ...'?

7. John Craven, Julia Bradbury and Matt Baker have all presented which rural affairs show?

8. In the TV comedy 'Gavin & Stacey', what is the name of the man-eating character played by Ruth Jones?

9. Experts Philip Serrell, Mark Stacey and Catherine Southon regularly appear on TV shows on what subject?

10. TV duo Ant and Dec first found fame appearing in which children's TV drama?

11. Which high-profile politician made a guest appearance in 'EastEnders' in 2009?

12. Which long-running sports programme aired for the first time on 22 August 1964?

13. Which daytime TV show, originally broadcast from Liverpool, celebrated its 25th anniversary in October 2013?

14. Hosted by Gordon Burns and later by Ben Shephard, which TV programme was dubbed 'Britain's toughest quiz'?

15. Grace Brothers department store was the setting for which classic 1970s TV comedy?

16. Which crime drama is set on the fictional Caribbean island of Sainte Marie?

17. The Chatsworth estate was the setting for which long-running Channel 4 drama?

18. Who are the two property experts tasked with finding a couple a home in 'Location, Location, Location'?

19. Which chat-show host made his TV debut in an advert for Rice Krispies?
a) Graham Norton   b) Michael Parkinson
c) Jonathan Ross

20. Which quiz-show host plays DS Ronnie Brooks in the TV drama 'Law and Order UK'?
a) Alexander Armstrong   b) Nick Knowles
c) Bradley Walsh

Answers to Quiz 57: Pot Luck

1. France
2. Green and white
3. 100m
4. Two
5. Henry VIII
6. Central Perk
7. The Falkland Islands
8. The Great Pyramid of Giza
9. Hyperactivity
10. Hunk
11. Monopoly
12. Wish you were here
13. Baseball
14. The United Kingdom
15. Egypt
16. George VI
17. Neptune
18. Four
19. Which?
20. Yorker

Quiz 59: Pot Luck

1. Which two teams scored over 100 goals in the Premier League in 2013/14?

2. Majorca and Menorca are part of which island group?

3. Which size of paper is larger – A3 or A4?

4. Sam Bailey won which TV talent show in 2013?

5. In measurement, how many feet make up one yard?

6. Britain's Rebecca Adlington won Olympic gold in which sport?

7. 'And so as Tiny Tim observed, "God Bless Us, Every One!"' is the last line of which story by Charles Dickens?

8. Truro is the only city in which English county?

9. A nonagon is a shape with how many sides?

10. Which whiskery sailor was dropped as a brand by a frozen-food company in March 2014?

11. Which band recorded the hit album 'Definitely Maybe'?

12. Myopia is a condition that affects which part of the body?

13. The volcanic Mount Etna is on which Mediterranean island?

14. Graphology is the study of what?

15. 'A Time to Kill' was the first novel by which prolific American thriller writer?

16. In 2014, who became only the third person to top the charts with the same song on three separate occasions with his hit 'Happy'?

17. 'Wuthering Heights' was the only novel written by which author?

18. What bird is sometimes known as a sea parrot?

19. What is the English equivalent of the Italian name Giacomo?
    a) James
    b) John
    c) Joseph

20. In which year was the American Declaration of Independence proclaimed?
    a) 1676
    b) 1776
    c) 1876

Answers to Quiz 58: Television part 2

1. Harry Hill
2. The Simpsons
3. Outnumbered
4. Strike It Lucky (later renamed 'Strike It Rich')
5. Crossroads
6. Hammer
7. Countryfile
8. Nessa
9. Antiques
10. Byker Grove
11. Boris Johnson
12. Match of the Day
13. This Morning
14. The Krypton Factor
15. Are You Being Served?
16. Death in Paradise
17. Shameless
18. Phil Spencer and Kirstie Allsopp
19. Jonathan Ross
20. Bradley Walsh

Quiz 60: Chart Toppers of the 1990s

EASY

Which singer or band topped the UK singles charts with the songs below?

1. 'Vogue' (1990)

2. 'Ice, Ice Baby' (1990)

3. 'The One and Only' (1991)

4. 'The Shoop Shoop Song (It's in His Kiss)' (1991)

5. 'I Will Always Love You' (1992)

6. 'I'd Do Anything for Love (But I Won't Do That)' (1993)

7. 'Dreams' (1993)

8. 'Things Can Only Get Better' (1994)

9. 'Love Is All Around' (1994)

10. 'Never Forget' (1995)

11. 'Some Might Say' (1995)

12. 'Spaceman' (1996)

13. 'Firestarter' (1996)

14. 'Ooh Aah ... Just a Little Bit' (1996)

15. 'Block Rockin' Beats' (1997)

Answers – page 123

16. 'I Believe I Can Fly' (1997)

17. 'Barbie Girl' (1997)

18. 'My Heart Will Go On' (1998)

19. 'Millennium' (1998)

20. 'Genie in a Bottle' (1999)

Answers to Quiz 59: Pot Luck

1. Manchester City and Liverpool
2. Balearic Islands
3. A3
4. The X Factor
5. Three
6. Swimming
7. A Christmas Carol
8. Cornwall
9. Nine
10. Captain Birdseye
11. Oasis
12. The eye
13. Sicily
14. Handwriting
15. John Grisham
16. Pharrell Williams
17. Emily Bronte
18. Puffin
19. James
20. 1776

Quiz 61: Pot Luck

1. In which part of the UK is Plaid Cymru a major political force?

2. Which is the only US state whose name ends with the letter D?

3. Which actor and politician is nicknamed 'The Governator'?

4. Which are the two US states that do not share a border with any other American states?

5. The Matildas is the nickname of the women's football team from which country?

6. Detective drama 'Luther' is set in which city?

7. Who was the first cricketer to score 100 international centuries?

8. Which word can mean 'a stopper for closing a hole in a container' or 'a bribe, especially in the world of sport'?

9. Ronnie Scott's is a nightclub associated with which genre of music?

10. Which classic sitcom starring David Jason, which ran from 1973 to 1985, was revived in 2014?

11. RHS are the initials of which green-fingered organization?

12. If you were tuning in to a radio programme called 'TMS', which sport sould you be listening to?

13. The Blades is the nickname of which English football team?

14. A single lap of an Olympic-sized athletics track is how many metres?

15. Which metric measurement is equal to 2.205lb?

16. 'Fuzz' and 'plod' are slang terms for people in which job?

17. The MOBOs is a music awards ceremony. What do the initials MOBO stand for?

18. What are the three African countries whose names start with the letter T?

19. What is the boiling point of water in degrees Fahrenheit?
    a) 100°F
    b) 220°F
    c) 340°F

20. Which period came first?
    a) Bronze age
    b) Iron age
    c) Stone age

Answers to Quiz 60: Chart Toppers of the 1990s

1. Madonna
2. Vanilla Ice
3. Chesney Hawkes
4. Cher
5. Whitney Houston
6. Meat Loaf
7. Gabrielle
8. D:Ream
9. Wet Wet Wet
10. Take That
11. Oasis
12. Babylon Zoo
13. The Prodigy
14. Gina G
15. The Chemical Brothers
16. R Kelly
17. Aqua
18. Celine Dion
19. Robbie Williams
20. Christina Aguilera

Quiz 62: Connections part 3

1. Who was re-elected Mayor of London for a second term in May 2012?

2. George Cole played which dodgy dealer in the TV drama 'Minder'?

3. The Fiesta, Ka and Focus are cars produced by which manufacturer?

4. Norma Jeane Mortenson was the real name of which Hollywood icon?

5. Ross Kemp played which character in the TV soap 'EastEnders'?

6. Which American state is located north of Oregon, west of Idaho and south of the Canadian province of British Columbia?

7. Who played James Bond for the last time in the 2002 film 'Die Another Day'?

8. Who captained the England football team at the Euro 96 competition?

9. Which domestic-appliance manufacturer was founded in 1908 and built its first UK factory in Perivale, Middlesex in 1932?

10. Who was Britain's prime minister from 1964 to 1970 then again from 1974 until 1976?

11. Which snooker player won his only World Championship title after beating Steve Davis in 1985?

12. Bill Murray provided the voice of which animated cat in a 2004 film and its 2006 sequel?

13. Which New York sporting venue regularly hosts basketball and ice hockey and has staged many World Championship boxing bouts?

14. Which 1998 film starred Jim Carrey as an insurance salesman who discovered that his whole life was in fact a TV programme?

15. Which veteran Welsh singer represented the United Kingdom at the 2013 Eurovision Song Contest?

16. Which US city is home to an American football team called the Browns?

17. Which actor starred as Han Solo in the Star Wars films?

18. The 1981 single 'One Day In Your Life' was the first UK number-one single for which legendary singer?

19. Which British actor played Egg in 'This Life', Simon in 'Teachers' and is now best known for playing Rick Grimes in the US vampire drama 'The Walking Dead'?

20. What is the connection between the answers?

EASY

Answers to Quiz 61: Pot Luck

1. Wales
2. Rhode Island
3. Arnold Schwarzenegger
4. Alaska and Hawaii
5. Australia
6. London
7. Sachin Tendulkar
8. Bung
9. Jazz
10. Open All Hours
11. Royal Horticultural Society
12. Cricket (Test Match Special)
13. Sheffield United
14. 400m
15. 1kg
16. Police officer
17. Music of Black Origin
18. Tanzania, Togo and Tunisia
19. 220°F
20. Stone age

Quiz 63: Pot Luck

1. Crack is an especially potent form of which drug?

2. The DUP, SDLP and Sinn Féin are political parties in which country of the UK?

3. The fictional secret agent James Bond was created by which author?

4. Which sporting competition was founded by the Frenchman Baron Pierre de Coubertin?

5. What are the four South American countries whose names end with a consonant?

6. Gryffindor, Hufflepuff, Ravenclaw and Slytherin are the names of the houses at which fictional school?

7. What name is shared by a famous castle in Northern Ireland and a football ground in Yorkshire?

8. CAMRA is an organization that campaigns for what?

9. The ICC is the global governing body for which sport?

10. What is the largest country that is solely in the southern hemisphere?

11. 'Supermatch Game' and the 'Head to Head' were rounds in which popular TV game show?

12. Which name is shared by a southern English port and the capital of the US state of Delaware?

13. The Black Cats is the nickname of which English football team?

14. Which UK department store chain celebrated its 150th anniversary in 2014?

15. What are the four American states that start with the letter I?

EASY

16. Who was the first cricketer to score a Test match quadruple century?

17. Who won his only acting Oscar for his performance in the 1957 film 'The Bridge on the River Kwai'?

18. Val Kilmer, Adam West and George Clooney have all played which superhero on the big screen?

19. Which of the following is the title of a popular music magazine?
    a) O   b) P   c) Q

20. Complete the title of the long-running radio panel show –
    'I'm Sorry I Haven't a ...'?
    a) Clue   b) Joke   c) Sound

Answers to Quiz 62: Connections part 3

1. Boris Johnson
2. Arthur Daley
3. Ford
4. Marilyn Monroe
5. Grant Mitchell
6. Washington
7. Pierce Brosnan
8. Tony Adams
9. Hoover
10. Harold Wilson
11. Dennis Taylor
12. Garfield
13. Madison Square Garden
14. The Truman Show
15. Bonnie Tyler
16. Cleveland
17. Harrison Ford
18. Michael Jackson
19. Andrew Lincoln
20. They all contain the surname of an American president

Quiz 64: Chart-Toppers of the 2000s

EASY

Which singer or band topped the UK singles charts with the songs below?

1. 'Can We Fix It' (2000)

2. 'Don't Stop Movin'' (2001)

3. 'Just Like a Pill' (2002)

4. 'Are You Ready For Love' (2003)

5. 'Leave Right Now' (2003)

6. 'Toxic' (2004)

7. 'Vertigo' (2004)

8. 'Like Toy Soldiers' (2005)

9. 'Don't Cha' (2005)

10. 'Push the Button' (2005)

11. 'I Bet You Look Good on the Dancefloor' (2005)

12. 'You Raise Me Up' (2005)

13. 'Hips Don't Lie' (2006)

14. 'A Moment Like This' (2006)

15. 'Mercy' (2008)

16. 'Sex on Fire' (2008)

17. 'Viva la Vida' (2008)

18. 'If I Were a Boy' (2008)

19. 'The Fear' (2009)

20. 'Poker Face' (2009)

Answers to Quiz 63: Pot Luck

1. Cocaine
2. Northern Ireland
3. Ian Fleming
4. The Olympic Games
5. Brazil, Ecuador, Paraguay and Uruguay
6. Hogwarts
7. Hillsborough
8. Real ale
9. Cricket
10. Australia
11. Blankety Blank
12. Dover
13. Sunderland
14. John Lewis
15. Idaho, Illinois, Indiana, Iowa
16. Brian Lara
17. Sir Alec Guinness
18. Batman
19. Q
20. Clue

Quiz 65: Pot Luck

1. In online slang, what do the initials TTFN stand for?

2. M10 9KC is the postcode for which fictional thoroughfare?

3. Who was the sidekick of the cartoon character Yogi Bear?

4. Which US president is the father of daughters called Barbara and Jenna?

5. A futon is a bed that originates from which Asian country?

6. What is the subject of the weekly magazine 'Kerrang!'?

7. CR7 is a range of underwear launched by which sportsman?

8. In horse racing, 'Burlington Bertie' is slang for what odds?

9. Enrico is the Italian equivalent of which English name?

10. Which distance is equal to 0.621 miles?

11. 'Something is rotten in the state of Denmark' is a line from which Shakespeare play?

12. Shiitake and king oyster are varieties of which food?

13. Golden spire, King's Acre Pippin and Kentish Fillbasket are varieties of which fruit?

14. Which five countries are permanent members of the United Nations Security Council?

15. 'Smudger' is a common nickname for people with which surname?

16. 'Houston, we have a problem' was a tagline to which 1995 film?

17. Anchorage is the largest city in which American state?

18. What two-word Latin phrase means 'in the year of our Lord'?

19. In which year did Prince William get married?
    a) 2010
    b) 2011
    c) 2012

20. Which of the following is a type of fish?
    a) Dover sole
    b) Folkestone sole
    c) Portsmouth sole

Answers to Quiz 64: Chart-Toppers of the 2000s

1. Bob the Builder
2. S Club 7
3. Pink
4. Elton John
5. Will Young
6. Britney Spears
7. U2
8. Eminem
9. Pussycat Dolls
10. Sugababes
11. Arctic Monkeys
12. Westlife
13. Shakira
14. Leona Lewis
15. Duffy
16. Kings of Leon
17. Coldplay
18. Beyonce
19. Lily Allen
20. Lady Gaga

Quiz 66: Anagrams part 2

Rearrange the letters to make the name of a city in the UK:

1. Owls Gag

2. Viler Loop

3. Stab Elf

4. Fox Rod

5. Be Dry

6. Chin Row

7. Held Fifes

8. Nervy Cot

9. Tree Ex

10. The Recs

11. Nude Ed

12. Behind Rug

13. Lost Rib

14. Lumpy Hot

15. A New Ass

16. Man Tonight
17. Elect Sire
18. Tense March
19. Ma Bring Him
20. Grab Medic

Answers to Quiz 65: Pot Luck

1. Ta-ta for now
2. Coronation Street
3. Boo-Boo
4. George W Bush
5. Japan
6. Rock music
7. Cristiano Ronaldo
8. 100 to 30
9. Henry
10. One kilometre
11. Hamlet
12. Mushroom
13. Apple
14. China, France, Russia, UK and USA
15. Smith
16. Apollo 13
17. Alaska
18. Anno Domini
19. 2011
20. Dover sole

Quiz 67: Pot Luck

EASY

1. One stone is equal to how many pounds?

2. In London postcodes, what do the letters EC stand for?

3. 'Bagel Hater' is an anagram of the name of which footballer?

4. Which part of London is home to Europe's largest carnival?

5. Which range of hills stretches from the Peak District in the south to the Cheviot Hills on the Anglo-Scottish border?

6. What famous painting is known in French as 'La Joconde'?

7. In which month does the winter solstice occur?

8. Nairobi is the capital city of which African country?

9. Which TV executive was appointed Chairman of the Football Association in July 2013?

10. Samuel L Jackson received his first Oscar nomination for his appearance in which 1994 film?

11. Malia and Sasha are the names of the children of which politician?

12. A viola has how many strings?

13. 'The Muscles from Brussels' is the nickname of which actor?

14. Who was the only sibling of Queen Elizabeth II?

15. By what name is the board game draughts known in the USA?

16. In which year did the First World War finish?

17. Which racecourse is prefixed with the title 'Glorious'?

18. In which month does the Australian Open tennis championship take place?

19. What is a sequoia?
    a) an animal
    b) a fruit
    c) a tree

20. What would you do with a fedora?
    a) eat it
    b) play it
    c) wear it

EASY

Answers to Quiz 66: Anagrams part 2

1. Glasgow	11. Dundee
2. Liverpool	12. Edinburgh
3. Belfast	13. Bristol
4. Oxford	14. Plymouth
5. Derby	15. Swansea
6. Norwich	16. Nottingham
7. Sheffield	17. Leicester
8. Coventry	18. Manchester
9. Exeter	19. Birmingham
10. Chester	20. Cambridge

MEDIUM QUIZZES

Quiz 68: Pot Luck

1. Which city beat competition from Dundee, Leicester and Swansea to be named UK City of Culture for 2017?

2. Which cartoon couple had a daughter called Pebbles?

3. The Broncos are an American football team based in which city?

4. Highgrove House is the country home of which member of the royal family?

5. What was the first Asian city to host the Olympic Games?

6. The Bodleian Library is in which English city?

7. The Azteca Stadium is in which city?

8. In the board game Scrabble, the letter J is worth how many points?

9. 'Songs of Innocence' and 'Songs of Experience' are works by which English poet?

10. The majority of Bollywood films are made in which Indian city?

11. How many red balls are used in a game of billiards?

12. Which artist designed the sleeve for The Beatles' 'Sgt. Pepper' album?

13. Which politician was Vince Cable describing when he quipped that he had been transformed 'from Stalin to Mr Bean'?

14. Erich von Stalhein was the arch-enemy of which fictional flyer?

15. Which veteran British rock band won a Grammy in 2014 for their album 'Celebration Day'?

Answers – page 141

16. Who was the first cricketer to make 200 Test match appearances?

17. Which sport is named after the Gloucestershire home of the Duke of Beaufort?

18. Brock and bawson are alternative names for which creature?

19. Tennis star Rafael Nadal was born on which island?
    a) Lanzarote
    b) Majorca
    c) Tenerife

20. Green does not appear on the flag of which of these countries?
    a) Hungary
    b) Latvia
    c) Lithuania

MEDIUM

Answers to Quiz 134: Pot Luck

1.	Morocco	11.	Left
2.	Mexico	12.	1910s
3.	David Lloyd George	13.	Architect
4.	Atlantic	14.	Grayson Perry
5.	Manchester	15.	Saturn
6.	North Sea	16.	Steve McQueen
7.	14	17.	Hereford
8.	Mary Poppins	18.	British ruling royal houses
9.	John Stuart Mill	19.	Postcards
10.	Wall Street Journal	20.	Curry Mallet

Quiz 69: Silver and Gold

1. Christopher Lee played Francisco Scaramanga in which James Bond film?

2. A stretch of promenade known as 'The Golden Mile' can be found in which English seaside resort?

3. Which investment bank was founded in 1869 and is based in Lower Manhattan, New York?

4. Dorothy, Rose, Blanche and Sophia were the central characters in which long-running sitcom?

5. Which Welsh hip-hop band had hits with 'Guns Don't Kill People Rappers Do' and 'Your Missus Is a Nutter'?

6. On which TV quiz show could competitors win prizes for completing a 'Gold Run'?

7. On which TV show can competitors win a golden gavel?

8. Jennifer Lawrence won her first Oscar in 2013 for her performance in which Philadelphia-set film?

9. Which Hollywood actress, who starred in the 1995 film 'Clueless', also appeared in a number of videos with US rockers Aerosmith?

10. Irishman Henry Kelly was the host of which pan-European quiz show?

11. Who won the Best Actress in a Supporting Role Oscar in 1990 for her performance in 'Ghost'?

12. What is the actor and drum-and-bass musician Clifford Price more commonly known as?

13. Who had a 2005 UK number-two hit with the song 'Gold Digger'?

14. Writer and film-producer Jane Goldman is the wife of which British TV personality?

15. Which American actor's film credits include 'The Fly', 'Jurassic Park' and 'Independence Day'?

16. Who sang the theme song to the 1995 James Bond film 'GoldenEye'?

17. The 1953 children's book 'The Silver Chair' was written by which author?

18. Who won her only Oscar for her performance in the 1969 film 'Cactus Flower'?

19. On the children's TV show 'Blue Peter', what type of animal was Goldie?
a) cat   b) dog   c) tortoise

20. Golden Miller was a successful performer in which sport?
a) greyhound racing   b) horse racing   c) pigeon racing

MEDIUM

Answers to Quiz 68: Pot Luck

1. Hull
2. Fred and Wilma Flintstone
3. Denver
4. Prince of Wales
5. Tokyo
6. Oxford
7. Mexico City
8. Eight
9. William Blake
10. Mumbai
11. One
12. Peter Blake
13. Gordon Brown
14. Biggles
15. Led Zeppelin
16. Sachin Tendulkar
17. Badminton
18. Badger
19. Majorca
20. Latvia

Quiz 70: Pot Luck

1. The city of New York is located at the mouth of which river?

2. In July 2013, Mark Carney succeeded Mervyn King in which post?

3. The Pumas is the nickname of which international rugby union team?

4. Greg Rutherford won Olympic gold at the 2012 Games in which athletics event?

5. LS6 3DP is the postcode of which English sporting venue?

6. Prior to becoming president, Bill Clinton was the governor of which American state?

7. Who was Muhammad Ali's opponent in the fight known as 'The Thriller in Manila'?

8. On The Beatles' album 'Abbey Road', which member of the band crosses the road first?

9. 'In Old Bavaria', 'Der Guten Tag Hop-Clop' and 'Keep It Gay' are songs from which hit musical?

10. In which month does the Chelsea Flower Show take place?

11. Which county has won cricket's County Championship the most times?

12. What was the first name of the British composer Delius?

13. What type of creature is a bittern?

14. What is the name of the pub in the radio drama 'The Archers'?

15. De Montfort University is in which city?

16. Which spin bowler was the first man to take 800 wickets in Test cricket?

17. As the crow flies, which city is closer to London – Lille in France or Liverpool?

18. Name five African countries whose name ends in the letter N.

19. In which year was BBC 2 launched?
    a) 1964
    b) 1968
    c) 1972

20. King Baudouin Stadium is located in which European capital?
    a) Amsterdam
    b) Brussels
    c) Paris

MEDIUM

Answers to Quiz 69: Silver and Gold

1. The Man with the Golden Gun
2. Blackpool
3. Goldman Sachs
4. The Golden Girls
5. Goldie Lookin Chain
6. Blockbusters
7. Bargain Hunt
8. Silver Linings Playbook
9. Alicia Silverstone
10. Going for Gold
11. Whoopi Goldberg
12. Goldie
13. Kanye West
14. Jonathan Ross
15. Jeff Goldblum
16. Tina Turner
17. CS Lewis
18. Goldie Hawn
19. Dog
20. Horse racing

Quiz 71: Heaven and Earth

1. According to a song by Eddie Cochran, there are how many steps to heaven?

2. Maurice White is the lead singer with which band?

3. 'Planet Earth' was the first hit single by which new romantic band?

4. 'There's a lady who's sure all that glitters is gold' is the opening line to which classic rock song?

5. The TV series 'Life on Earth: A Natural History' was presented by which broadcaster?

6. 'Heaven Knows I'm Miserable Now' was a hit for which band?

7. Which actor, best known for his roles in horror films, played the Time Lord in the 1966 film 'Daleks – Invasion Earth: 2150 AD'?

8. Which Beatle had a top ten solo hit with 'Give Me Love (Give Me Peace On Earth)'?

9. Who played the title character in the 1976 film 'The Man Who Fell to Earth'?

10. Which 2005 film, directed by Ridley Scott and starring Orlando Bloom is set during the 12th century Crusades?

11. What was the 1995 UK Christmas number-one single?

12. Which Manchester band enjoyed 'One Night in Heaven' in 1993?

13. Which German philosopher said, 'In heaven, all the interesting people are missing'?

14. The Channel 4 show 'TV Heaven, Telly Hell' was presented by which bespectacled comedian?

15. The song 'Temptation' was a number-two hit in 1982 for which band?

Answers – page 147

16. Which actress and singer played Catwoman in the 1960s TV version of 'Batman'?

17. What was American singer Belinda Carlisle's only UK number-one single?

18. Thirty-nine members of which religious cult, who believed in unidentified flying objects, committed suicide in San Diego, California in 1997?

19. Fill in the missing word from the title of a best-selling book by Mitch Albom: 'The ____ People You Meet in Heaven'.
    a) Five   b) Six   c) Seven

20. Complete the title of a 1978 film starring Warren Beatty: 'Heaven Can ...'
    a) Come   b) Go   c) Wait

Answers to Quiz 70: Pot Luck

1. Hudson River
2. Governor of the Bank of England
3. Argentina
4. Long jump
5. Headingley Cricket Ground
6. Arkansas
7. Joe Frazier
8. John Lennon
9. The Producers
10. May
11. Yorkshire
12. Frederick
13. Bird
14. The Bull
15. Leicester
16. Muttiah Muralitharan
17. Lille
18. Benin, Cameroon, Gabon, South Sudan and Sudan
19. 1964
20. Brussels

MEDIUM

145

Quiz 72: Pot Luck

1. In which year did the Summer Games known as 'Hitler's Olympics' in Berlin take place?

2. NSA are the initials of which American intelligence organization?

3. A 'vaporetto' is a form of transport found in which Italian city?

4. The BBC TV drama 'Peaky Blinders' is set in which English city?

5. In which sport did the Brownlee brothers win Olympic medals in 2012?

6. The phrase 'step up to the plate' originates from which sport?

7. Prior to becoming president, John F Kennedy was a senator for which American state?

8. In which month does the famous horse race The Derby take place?

9. Who was the first Englishman to win golf's US Masters?

10. According to a poem by Philip Larkin, 'sexual intercourse began' in which year?

11. Which American holiday is observed each year on the final Monday in May?

12. What are the two African countries whose names end with the letter D?

13. Tucker Jenkins was a popular character in TV drama 'Grange Hill'. What was Tucker's actual first name?

14. What are the two countries in South America whose names are made up of six letters?

15. Who were the two Englishmen to win the World Snooker Championship in the 1980s?

16. Which Shakespearean knight was the subject of an opera by Verdi?

17. Soekarno–Hatta International Airport is in which Asian country?

18. In which sport is Sheikh Mohammed bin Rashid al-Maktoum a notable name?

19. Carthage, the site of an ancient civilization, is in which modern-day country?
    a) Algeria
    b) Morocco
    c) Tunisia

20. A baseball team is made up of how many players?
    a) 7
    b) 9
    c) 11

MEDIUM

Answers to Quiz 71: Heaven and Earth

1. Three
2. Earth, Wind and Fire
3. Duran Duran
4. Stairway to Heaven
5. David Attenborough
6. The Smiths
7. Peter Cushing
8. George Harrison
9. David Bowie
10. Kingdom of Heaven
11. Earth Song
12. M People
13. Friedrich Nietzsche
14. Sean Lock
15. Heaven 17
16. Eartha Kitt
17. Heaven Is a Place on Earth
18. Heaven's Gate
19. Five
20. Wait

Quiz 73: The First World War

1. The First World War was sparked following the assassination of which Austrian archduke?

2. In which city did this assassination take place?

3. Who was the British prime minister at the start of the First World War?

4. Gallipoli, the scene of a major First World War battle, is in which modern-day country?

5. What was the name of the ocean liner that was sunk by a German U-boat on 7 May 1917, resulting in the deaths of 1198 passengers and crew?

6. Which British monarch was on the throne during the First World War?

7. In which year did the USA enter the war?

8. The British and German fleets of dreadnought battleships came to blows only once in the First World War. In which famous naval battle?

9. Which First World War poet wrote 'Anthem for Doomed Youth'?

10. Who was the British prime minister at the end of the War?

11. Which English nurse was executed for helping Allied soldiers escape from German-occupied Belgium?

12. What type of animal was Cher Ami, who was awarded the 'Croix de Guerre' for his service during the First World War?

13. Who was the president of the USA throughout the duration of the First World War?

14. By what name was the Dutch exotic dancer Margaretha Geertruida Zelle, who was executed by France on spying charges, better known?

15. 'Little Willie' was a prototype in the development of which type of military vehicle?

16. Britain declared war on Germany following the German invasion of which country?

17. Which disease killed millions of soldiers and civilians during the latter stages of the war?

18. Which historian, diarist and Tory MP coined the phrase 'lions led by donkeys'?

19. If laid end-to-end, the trenches of the First World War would stretch approximately how many miles?
    a) 5000 miles   b) 15,000 miles   c) 25,000 miles

20. What was the name of the howitzer used by German forces during the First World War?
    a) Big Bella   b) Big Bertha   c) Big Bessie

MEDIUM

Answers to Quiz 72: Pot Luck

1. 1936
2. National Security Agency
3. Venice
4. Birmingham
5. Triathlon
6. Baseball
7. Massachusetts
8. June
9. Nick Faldo
10. 1963
11. Memorial Day
12. Chad and Swaziland
13. Peter
14. Brazil and Guyana
15. Steve Davis and Joe Johnson
16. Sir John Falstaff
17. Indonesia
18. Horse racing
19. Tunisia
20. 9

Quiz 74: Pot Luck

1. Tribeca is a neighbourhood in which American city?

2. What name connects the golfer who won the Open Championship in 2007 and 2008 and a style of jacket favoured by mods?

3. 'Gladness' is a type of beer produced by which UK pop band?

4. What is the area of Germany known locally as 'Schwarzwald' more commonly called in English?

5. Europe's largest public library opened in 2013 in which English city?

6. Which sport has the higher net – badminton or volleyball?

7. TDCU 1ZZ is the postcode for which British overseas territory?

8. What type of salad was also the title of an episode of the classic comedy 'Fawlty Towers'?

9. How many minutes are there in a week?

10. True or false – John Prescott is Britain's longest-serving deputy prime minister?

11. Who was America's first Roman Catholic president?

12. Which Shakespearean character utters the famous lines, 'Friends, Romans, countrymen, lend me your ears'?

13. Who starred in the classic 1926 silent film 'The General'?

14. What are the first names of the comedy duo Punt and Dennis?

15. What nationality was the Nobel Prize-winning scientist Niels Bohr?

16. Which planet of the Solar System has moons called Enceladus, Tethys, Dione and Mimas?

17. Which chemical element has the symbol Se and atomic number 34?

18. Who was the first female tennis player to win all four Grand Slam titles and an Olympic gold medal in the same year?

19. Complete the title of the Stephen Sondheim musical – 'Sunday in the Park with ...'?
    a) John
    b) Paul
    c) George

20. What type of creature is a rhea?
    a) bird
    b) monkey
    c) snake

MEDIUM

Answers to Quiz 73: The First World War

1. Franz Ferdinand
2. Sarajevo
3. Herbert Asquith
4. Turkey
5. RMS Lusitania
6. King George V
7. 1917
8. The Battle of Jutland
9. Wilfred Owen
10. David Lloyd George
11. Edith Cavell
12. Pigeon
13. Woodrow Wilson
14. Mata Hari
15. Tank
16. Belgium
17. Influenza
18. Alan Clark
19. 25,000 miles
20. Big Bertha

Quiz 75: Sherlock Holmes

1. Sherlock Holmes was created by which author?

2. The detective is famous for wearing what style of hat?

3. Which of Holmes' adversaries was described as being 'the Napoleon of crime'?

4. What is the name of Holmes' housekeeper?

5. Holmes was an accomplished player of which musical instrument?

6. In the modern-day BBC TV series 'Sherlock', the detective's flat is located above a café. What is the café's name?

7. What is the name of Sherlock's older brother?

8. What was the name of the group of street urchins who occasionally helped Holmes?

9. What is the name of the bumbling Scotland Yard inspector who often called for the help of Holmes?

10. Which actor played Holmes in the 1988 spoof film, 'Without a Clue'?

11. Dr Watson's middle name begins with which letter?

12. True or false – Sherlock Holmes was originally called Sheringham Holmes?

13. Who plays Dr Watson in the US TV series 'Elementary'?

14. Which British filmmaker directed the 2009 film 'Sherlock Holmes' and the 2011 sequel 'Sherlock Holmes: A Game of Shadows'?

15. Which Hollywood star played Holmes in both of the above films?

16. And who played Dr Watson?

17. After being killed off in 'The Final Problem', Holmes was resurrected in which story?

18. Which author wrote the 2012 Sherlock Holmes novel 'The House of Silk'?

19. Which character was accused of being a vampire in 'The Adventure of the Sussex Vampire'?
    a) Mrs Atkinson
    b) Mrs Ferguson
    c) Mrs Moyes

20. Sherlock Holmes featured in which of the following novels?
    a) The Sign of Three
    b) The Sign of Four
    c) The Sign of Five

MEDIUM

Answers to Quiz 74: Pot Luck

1. New York City
2. Harrington
3. Madness
4. The Black Forest
5. Birmingham
6. Volleyball
7. Tristan da Cunha
8. Waldorf salad
9. 10080
10. True
11. John F Kennedy
12. Mark Antony
13. Buster Keaton
14. Steve and Hugh
15. Danish
16. Saturn
17. Selenium
18. Steffi Graf
19. George
20. Bird

Quiz 76: Pot Luck

1. Which cinema organization has the initials BBFC?

2. What is the French motto of the British monarch?

3. True or false – boxer Mike Tyson, who once bit off part of an opponent's ear, is now a vegan?

4. Which contemporary politician is the grandson of former deputy prime minister Herbert Morrison?

5. Who was the first US President whose surname started with a vowel?

6. If something is galline, it relates to or resembles which creature?

7. In 1990, Namibia gained independence from which country?

8. The headquarters of the International Criminal Court are in which city?

9. 2014 marked the 100th anniversary of which Welsh poet and writer who is best known for 'Under Milk Wood'?

10. Which duo had the UK Christmas number one in 1982 with 'Save Your Love'?

11. What are the seven African countries whose names start with the letter M?

12. In how many James Bond films did Pierce Brosnan play 007?

13. Which pair of comic actors starred in the TV comedy drama 'The Trip'?

14. True or false – Queen Elizabeth II won a BAFTA award in 2013?

15. What nationality was the polar explorer Roald Amundsen?

16. In Olympic diving competitions, how high in metres is the high board?

17. Which British author wrote the series of romantic novels known as 'The Rutshire Chronicles'?

18. The volcanic island Stromboli lies off the coast of which Mediterranean island?

19. Which sport took place on a Good Friday for the first time in 2014?
    a) football
    b) horse racing
    c) rugby league

20. The Earth orbits the Sun at approximately what speed?
    a) 6700mph
    b) 67,000 mph
    c) 167,000mph

MEDIUM

Answers to Quiz 75: Sherlock Holmes

1. Arthur Conan Doyle
2. Deerstalker
3. Moriarty
4. Mrs Hudson
5. Violin
6. Speedy's
7. Mycroft
8. The Baker Street Irregulars
9. Lestrade
10. Michael Caine
11. H
12. False
13. Lucy Liu
14. Guy Ritchie
15. Robert Downey Jr
16. Jude Law
17. The Adventure of the Empty House
18. Anthony Horowitz
19. Mrs Ferguson
20. The Sign of Four

Quiz 77: Dark and Light

1. Who provided the voice of Buzz Lightyear in the 'Toy Story' film trilogy?

2. 'We skipped the light fandango / Turned cartwheels 'cross the floor' are the opening lines to which 1967 hit single?

3. The songs 'Money' and 'Time' appeared on which album by Pink Floyd?

4. The Light Programme was the precursor to which BBC radio station?

5. In the 'Star Wars' films, what is the weapon of choice of the Jedi?

6. Gary Lightbody is the lead singer with which Northern Irish rock band?

7. Which band recorded the hit 2003 festive single 'Christmas Time (Don't Let the Bells End)'?

8. What was the sequel to the 2005 film 'Batman Begins'?

9. Timothy Dalton made his debut as 007 in which James Bond film?

10. 'Livin' Thing', 'Don't Bring Me Down' and 'Mr Blue Sky' were top-ten hits for which band?

11. Trinity House is the body responsible for the provision and maintenance of what?

12. 'Dancing in the Dark' was a top-five hit in 1984 for which American rock star?

13. What distance is equal to just under 10 trillion kilometres?

14. 'Ocean Drive' and 'Postcards from Heaven' were top-ten albums in the 1990s for which band?

15. In Olympic men's boxing, with a maximum weight of 49kg, what is the lowest weight division?

16. Which controversial film won the Best Picture award at the 2013 Oscars?

17. Which American science-fiction series created by Rod Sterling first appeared on TV screens in 1959?

18. 'Red Light Spells Danger' was a number-two hit in 1977 for which singer?

19. Which British actor plays psychologist Cal Lightman in the US TV drama 'Lie To Me'?
a) Andrew Lincoln   b) Gary Oldman   c) Tim Roth

20. 'The Dark Destroyer' was the nickname of which British boxer?
a) Nigel Benn   b) Chris Eubank   c) Michael Watson

MEDIUM

Answers to Quiz 76: Pot Luck

1. British Board of Film Classification
2. Dieu et mon droit
3. True
4. Peter Mandelson
5. John Adams
6. Chicken
7. South Africa
8. The Hague
9. Dylan Thomas
10. Renée and Renato
11. Madagascar, Malawi, Mali, Mauritania, Mauritius, Morocco and Mozambique
12. Four
13. Steve Coogan and Rob Brydon
14. True
15. Norwegian
16. 10m
17. Jilly Cooper
18. Sicily
19. Horse racing
20. 67,000mph

Quiz 78: Pot Luck

1. Which American president was Lyndon Johnson describing when he said, 'He can't walk and chew gum at the same time'?

2. Gary Oldman and Sir Alec Guinness have both played which fictional spy?

3. The US presidential inauguration ceremony is held in front of which building?

4. In which century did the population of British people living in towns exceed those living in rural areas for the first time?

5. Who was the British prime minister when Elizabeth II became queen?

6. What pattern of fabric is also the name of a type of synthetic athletics track?

7. Which multinational company takes its name from the Greek goddess of victory?

8. 'It is better to light a candle than to curse the darkness' is the motto of which human rights organization?

9. In 2011, who became the first Manxman to win the BBC Sports Personality of the Year Award?

10. What is the square root of 289?

11. Which athlete, whose surname is that of a Biblical figure, won 122 consecutive 400m hurdle races between 1977 and 1987?

12. What are the first names of the film-making Coen brothers?

13. What is the official language of the African country Togo?

14. Colin Firth played which British monarch in the 2010 film 'The King's Speech'?

15. Which designer, born in Merthyr Tydfil, succeeded Alexander McQueen as the chief designer at fashion house Givenchy?

16. In which year did William Shakespeare die?

17. El Alamein, the scene of a famous World War Two battle, is a coastal town in which country?

18. Which was the first English team to lose in the final of football's European Cup?

19. In George Orwell's 'Animal Farm' what type of animal was Napoleon?
    a) dog   b) hen   c) pig

20. The 1908 Olympics were originally due to be held in Rome. What prevented that from happening?
    a) eruption of Mount Vesuvius   b) a flu epidemic
    c) political violence

MEDIUM

Answers to Quiz 77: Dark and Light

1. Tim Allen
2. 'A Whiter Shade of Pale' by Procul Harum
3. The Dark Side of the Moon
4. Radio 2
5. Lightsaber
6. Snow Patrol
7. The Darkness
8. The Dark Knight
9. The Living Daylights
10. Electric Light Orchestra
11. Lighthouses
12. Bruce Springsteen
13. A light year
14. Lighthouse Family
15. Light flyweight
16. Zero Dark Thirty
17. The Twilight Zone
18. Billy Ocean
19. Tim Roth
20. Nigel Benn

Quiz 79: World War Two

1. The Desert Fox was the nickname of which celebrated German Field Marshall?

2. What was the first name of Field Marshall Montgomery?

3. In which year was the aerial Battle of Britain fought?

4. The 1939 Molotov–Ribbentrop Pact was signed by which two countries?

5. What was the code name for the German invasion of the USSR during World War Two?

6. Who was the commander of the German Air Force during World War Two?

7. The Spitfire was made by which British aircraft manufacturer?

8. The 1940 Summer Olympic Games were cancelled because of the onset of war. Which Asian city was originally scheduled to have hosted them?

9. Which island was awarded the George Cross to mark the 'heroism' and 'devotion' of its people during a siege in the war?

10. Which British aeronautical engineer invented the bouncing bomb as used in the 'Dambusters' Raid?

11. Which Scandinavian country remained neutral during World War Two?

12. 'Old Blood and Guts' was the nickname of which American general?

13. VE Day was declared in which month of 1945?

14. In 1939, which two countries signed a treaty known as 'The Pact of Steel'?

15. Who was the leader of the USSR during World War Two?

16. The Maginot Line was a series of fortifications along which country's border with Germany in the 1930s?

17. In which month did the D-Day landings take place?

18. What were the names of the five beaches on which the D-Day landings took place?

19. The official Japanese surrender was signed on which American ship?
    a) USS California
    b) USS Missouri
    c) USS New York

20. What was the code name given to the Allied D-Day landing?
    a) Operation Kingpin
    b) Operation Overlord
    c) Operation Storm

MEDIUM

Answers to Quiz 78: Pot Luck

1. Gerald Ford
2. George Smiley
3. The Capitol
4. 19th century
5. Sir Winston Churchill
6. Tartan
7. Nike
8. Amnesty International
9. Mark Cavendish
10. 17
11. Ed Moses
12. Joel and Ethan
13. French
14. King George VI
15. Julien Macdonald
16. 1616
17. Egypt
18. Leeds United
19. Pig
20. Eruption of Mount Vesuvius

Quiz 80: Pot Luck

1. Between 1925 and 1961, by what name was the city of Volgograd known?

2. Which was the first Australian city to host the Olympic Games?

3. Who served longer as British prime minister – Gordon Brown or Sir Alec Douglas Home?

4. Which of TV's 'Teletubbies' carries a red bag?

5. Which 'brothers' topped the charts in 1965 with 'Make It Easy on Yourself'?

6. True or false – there is a village in Yorkshire called Great Fryup?

7. In 1979, Shah Mohammad Reza Pahlavi was overthrown as the ruler of which Asian country?

8. Who was the US president at the start of the 20th century?

9. In which year were the Olympic Games hosted in London for the first time?

10. Whose name is missing from this list – Roy Plomley, Michael Parkinson, ____, Kirsty Young?

11. The title of which opera by Verdi translates into English as 'The Troubadour'?

12. Which British prime minister was also awarded the Nobel Prize for Literature?

13. Which Asian country's flag is made up of two overlapping triangles?

14. Who is the patron saint of animals?

15. What is the highest decoration awarded for valour in the British armed forces?

16. Simon Peckingham is the real name of which contemporary British comic actor?

17. Between 2000 and 2010, who were the two female winners of the BBC Sports Personality of the Year Award?

18. In metres, how long is an Olympic rowing race?

19. Suvarnabhumi Airport and Don Mueang International Airport serve which Asian capital?
    a) Bangkok
    b) Jakarta
    c) Kuala Lumpur

20. What was the title of a 2014 film starring Nick Frost?
    a) Cuban Fiesta
    b) Cuban Frenzy
    c) Cuban Fury

MEDIUM

Answers to Quiz 79: World War Two

1. Erwin Rommel
2. Bernard
3. 1940
4. Germany and the USSR
5. Operation Barbarossa
6. Hermann Göring
7. Supermarine
8. Tokyo
9. Malta
10. Sir Barnes Wallis
11. Sweden
12. George Patton
13. May
14. Germany and Italy
15. Stalin
16. France
17. June
18. Gold, Juno, Omaha, Sword and Utah
19. USS Missouri
20. Operation Overlord

Quiz 81: Family Ties

MEDIUM

1. Which group won the Eurovision Song Contest in 1976 with 'Save Your Kisses for Me'?

2. Ted Mosby is the central character in which long-running US sitcom?

3. Craggy Island was the setting for which TV comedy?

4. American Napoleon Solo and Russian Illya Kuryakin were the central characters in which 1960s espionage drama?

5. Fir Park is the home ground of which Scottish football club?

6. What was the nun Anjezë Gonxha Bojaxhiu better known as?

7. 'We Are Family' was a top-ten hit in 1979 for which American band?

8. Lennard Pearce played which character in 'Only Fools and Horses'?

9. 'The Harder I Try' and 'He Ain't No Competition' were top-ten hits in the 1980s for which boy band?

10. The children's book 'Gangsta Granny' was written by which actor and comedian?

11. Which 2000 film directed by the Coen brothers was loosely based on Homer's epic poem 'The Odyssey'?

12. Which variety of apple was discovered in Ryde near Sydney in Australia in 1868?

13. Which annual celebration takes place in Britain on the fourth Sunday in Lent?

14. In the Bible, who said 'am I my brother's keeper'?

15. Steve Martin starred as George Banks in which 1991 marital comedy?

16. 'Uncle' is a slang term for someone in which occupation?

17. 'The Godfather of Soul' was the nickname of which singer?

18. Quahog, Rhode Island is the setting for which animated comedy?

19. What was the name of Frank Zappa's backing band?
    a) Brothers of Invention
    b) Mothers of Invention
    c) Sisters of Invention

20. What was the name of the nun who presented a series of TV documentaries on the history of art?
    a) Sister Cindy
    b) Sister Mandy
    c) Sister Wendy

MEDIUM

Answers to Quiz 80: Pot Luck

1. Stalingrad
2. Melbourne
3. Gordon Brown
4. Tinky Winky
5. The Walker Brothers
6. True
7. Iran
8. William McKinley
9. 1908
10. Sue Lawley (hosts of the radio programme 'Desert Island Discs')
11. Il Trovatore
12. Sir Winston Churchill
13. Nepal
14. St Francis of Assisi
15. The Victoria Cross
16. Simon Pegg
17. Paula Radcliffe and Zara Phillips
18. 2000m
19. Bangkok
20. Cuban Fury

Quiz 82: Pot Luck

1. What bird provided Fleetwood Mac with the title of a 1969 number one?

2. Which female British singer released the 2014 album 'Sheezus'?

3. Baja California, Campeche and Durango are states in which country?

4. 'Always There' by Marti Webb was a vocal version of the theme song to which 1980s TV drama?

5. Socks was the name of the pet cat owned by which American president?

6. Which name comes next on the list – Madeleine Albright, Colin Powell, Condoleezza Rice, ...?

7. Julie Hesmondhalgh played which long-serving character in the TV soap 'Coronation Street'?

8. Rowing's Henley Royal Regatta takes place on the first weekend of which month?

9. 02920 is the telephone dialing code for which British city?

10. The Republic of Kiribati is an island nation situated in which ocean?

11. Starring Kevin Costner, the 2000 political drama 'Thirteen Days' was about which 20th-century historical event?

12. Who was the last US president to have been born in the state of Texas?

13. The Andrew Lloyd Webber musical 'Stephen Ward' centres on which famous political scandal from the early 1960s?

14. Dyce Airport is in which British city?

Answers – page 169

15. What nationality is the singer Rihanna?

16. In 2011, Marine Le Pen succeeded her father as the leader of which French political party?

17. The winter sport biathlon combines which two disciplines?

18. Barbara Bach was the second wife of which Beatle?

19. Which of the following was the title of a 1969 number one for The Move?
a) Blackberry Way
b) Gooseberry Way
c) Raspberry Way

20. Complete the title of a 2014 Grammy-winning album by Alicia Keys – 'Girl on ...'
a) Fire
b) Girl
c) A Wire

MEDIUM

Answers to Quiz 81: Family Ties

1. Brotherhood of Man
2. How I Met Your Mother
3. Father Ted
4. The Man From U.N.C.L.E.
5. Motherwell
6. Mother Teresa
7. Sister Sledge
8. Grandad
9. Brother Beyond
10. David Walliams
11. O Brother, Where Art Thou?
12. Granny Smith
13. Mother's Day
14. Cain
15. Father of the Bride
16. Pawnbroker
17. James Brown
18. Family Guy
19. Mothers of Invention
20. Sister Wendy

Quiz 83: India

1. What is the capital city of India?

2. What is India's largest city by population?

3. What is the currency of India?

4. In which year did India gain independence from Britain?

5. October 2 is a public holiday in India to celebrate the birth of which person?

6. India is made up how many different time zones?

7. True or false – India has the largest road network in the world?

8. Which four colours appear on the flag of India?

9. The Taj Mahal is situated in which Indian city?

10. India won gold medals at six consecutive Olympic Games between 1928 and 1956 in which team sport?

11. Who was the first prime minister of independent India?

12. Which country covers a larger area – India or the USA?

13. What is the official flower of India?

14. The 2010 Commonwealth Games were held in which city?

15. Which Indian batsman is the leading run-scorer in the history of Test and One Day International cricket?

16. Sharing its name with a famous sitcom character from the 1970s, what is the national bird of India?

17. India shares borders with which six countries?

18. Bengaluru is the official name of which Indian city?

MEDIUM

19. Approximately what proportion of the world's population lives in India?
    a) one-quarter
    b) one-sixth
    c) one-eigthth

20. In which year did India win the Cricket World Cup for the first time?
    a) 1983
    b) 1987
    c) 1992

MEDIUM

Answers to Quiz 82: Pot Luck

1. Albatross
2. Lily Allen
3. Mexico
4. Howards' Way
5. Bill Clinton
6. Hillary Clinton (US secretaries of state)
7. Hayley Cropper
8. July
9. Cardiff
10. Pacific
11. The Cuban Missile Crisis
12. Lyndon Johnson
13. The Profumo Affair
14. Aberdeen
15. Barbadian
16. National Front
17. Skiing and rifle shooting
18. Ringo Starr
19. Blackberry Way
20. Girl on Fire

Quiz 84: Pot Luck

1. Which film was released first? 'Four Weddings and a Funeral' or 'The Full Monty'?

2. Appearing on the soundtrack to the 1998 film 'Godzilla', 'Deeper Undergound' was the only UK number-one single for which band?

3. Who was England's first protestant Archbishop of Canterbury?

4. How many balls are used in a game of billiards?

5. Which former president of Yugoslavia was found dead in his cell during his 2006 war-crimes trial?

6. The composer Mozart was born in which city?

7. Which Central American country was known until 1973 as British Honduras?

8. True or false – hip-hop star Kanye West has a daughter called North?

9. Carvings of which four US presidents feature on Mount Rushmore?

10. Which film and stage musical was based on the lives of the students at New York City's High School of Performing Arts?

11. On a tournament dartboard, what colour is the outer bullseye?

12. The Cathedral of Santa Maria del Fiore is in which Italian city?

13. German composer Richard Wagner died in which Italian city?

14. What are Prince George of Cambridge's two middle names?

15. Prior to adopting the name Windsor, what was the surname of the British Royal Family?

16. Slavica Radic is the former wife of which British business magnate?

17. With six UK number-one singles, who was the most successful solo artist of the 1980s?

18. Who was the first, and up to 2014, only US president to have been born in the state of California?

19. Which Caribbean island featured in the title of a 1975 number one for Typically Tropical?
    a) Antigua
    b) Barbados
    c) Jamaica

20. At what time of year is a simnel cake traditionally eaten?
    a) Christmas
    b) Easter
    c) Halloween

Answers to Quiz 83: India

1. Delhi
2. Mumbai
3. Rupee
4. 1947
5. Mahatma Gandhi
6. One
7. False
8. Orange, white, green and blue
9. Agra
10. Hockey
11. Jawaharlal Nehru
12. USA
13. Lotus
14. Delhi
15. Sachin Tendulkar
16. Peacock
17. Pakistan, Nepal, China, Bhutan, Myanmar (Burma) and Bangladesh
18. Bangalore
19. One-sixth
20. 1983

MEDIUM

Quiz 85: China

1. What was the former name of the Chinese capital Beijing?

2. How many stars appear on the Chinese flag?

3. China is governed by the CPC. What do the initials CPC stand for?

4. What is the largest city in China by population?

5. In Chinese culture, what colour traditionally symbolizes happiness?

6. What is the longest river in China?

7. Who was the president of the People's Republic of China from 2003 to 2013?

8. In which sport is Yao Ming a world-class performer?

9. Which Chinese artist and activist was the subject of the 2012 documentary 'Never Sorry'?

10. Hong Kong is one of two Chinese special administrative regions. What former Portuguese colony is the other?

11. Who was the first US president to visit Communist China?

12. American space travellers are astronauts. Russian space travellers are cosmonauts. What name is given to Chinese space travellers?

13. Who was the first leader of the People's Republic of China?

14. What is the name of China's army?

15. Who topped the charts in 1987 with the song 'China in Your Hand'?

16. Which dynasty ruled China between 1368 and 1644?

17. China shares borders with 14 countries. Name them.

18. Ding Junhui and Liang Wenbo are notable performers in which sport?

19. What was the name of the peasant rebellion that attempted to drive foreigners out of China in the late 19th and early 20th century?
    a) Boxer Rebellion
    b) Judo Rebellion
    c) Karate Rebellion

20. China is made up of how many time zones?
    a) one
    b) three
    c) five

Answers to Quiz 84: Pot Luck

1. Four Weddings and a Funeral
2. Jamiroquai
3. Thomas Cranmer
4. Three
5. Slobodan Milosevic
6. Salzburg
7. Belize
8. True
9. George Washington, Thomas Jefferson, Theodore Roosevelt and Abraham Lincoln
10. Fame
11. Green
12. Florence
13. Venice
14. Alexander Louis
15. Saxe-Coburg-Gotha
16. Bernie Ecclestone
17. Madonna
18. Richard Nixon
19. Barbados
20. Easter

Quiz 86: Pot Luck

1. The alcoholic drink mead is made by fermenting what?

2. Often used in Chinese cuisine, what is bean curd more commonly known as?

3. The Super Eagles is the nickname of the national football team of which African country?

4. Who was the last British monarch to have been born outside Britain?

5. What name connects a play by Edmond Rostand, a market town in the Dordogne region of France and a 1980s TV series?

6. Which film awards are known as the 'SAGs'?

7. Who spent longer as the British prime minister – Sir Winston Churchill or Harold Wilson?

8. The Hoover Dam is on the border of which two western American states?

9. 'The Rain in Spain' is a song from which stage musical?

10. Which Olympic sport is sometimes referred to as 'horse ballet'?

11. Schönbrunn Palace is in which European capital?

12. How many tiles in total are used in a complete game of Scrabble?

13. Since 1937, the American presidential inauguration ceremony has taken place in which month?

14. Which famous figure, born in 1564, was the father of twins called Hamnet and Judith?

15. What is the name of the 2000-mile long footpath that stretches between the US states of Georgia in the south and Maine in the north?

16. Which British prime minister was in office longer – James Callaghan or Sir Anthony Eden?

17. What type of document can be amended by a codicil?

18. Which Mediterranean island is divided by a 'Green Line'?

19. How old was William Shakespeare when he died?
    a) 42
    b) 52
    c) 62

20. Stephen Roche was the first rider from which country to win cycling's Tour de France?
    a) America
    b) Australia
    c) Ireland

MEDIUM

Answers to Quiz 85: China

1. Peking
2. Five
3. Communist Party of China
4. Shanghai
5. Red
6. Yangtze
7. Hu Jintao
8. Basketball
9. Ai Weiwei
10. Macao
11. Richard Nixon
12. Taikonauts
13. Mao Zedong
14. The People's Liberation Army
15. T'Pau
16. Ming dynasty
17. North Korea, Mongolia, Russia, Kazakhstan, Kyrgyzstan, Tajikistan, Afghanistan, Pakistan, India, Nepal, Bhutan, Myanmar, Laos and Vietnam
18. Snooker
19. Boxer Rebellion
20. One

Quiz 87: Film Directors

Identify the film director who made the following films:

1. 'Shadow of a Doubt', 'I Confess', 'The Birds'

2. 'Jackie Brown', 'Grindhouse', 'Django Unchained'

3. 'Trainspotting', 'The Beach', 'A Life Less Ordinary'

4. 'Gangs of New York', 'Shutter Island', 'Hugo'

5. 'Full Metal Jacket', 'Eyes Wide Shut', 'The Shining'

6. 'Saving Private Ryan', 'Empire of the Sun', 'War Horse'

7. 'Apocalypse Now', 'Peggy Sue Got Married', 'Dracula'

8. 'True Lies', 'Titanic', 'Avatar'

9. 'The Prestige', 'Memento', 'Inception'

10. 'It Happened One Night', 'Arsenic and Old Lace', 'It's a Wonderful Life'

11. 'Deconstructing Harry', 'Bullets Over Broadway', 'Manhattan'

12. 'Romancing the Stone', 'Back to the Future', 'Forrest Gump'

13. 'Wall Street', 'Natural Born Killers', 'Nixon'

14. 'MASH', 'Nashville', 'Gosford Park'

15. 'Rushmore', 'Moonrise Kingdom', 'The Royal Tenenbaums'

16. 'Alien', 'Blade Runner', 'Thelma & Louise'

17. 'Boogie Nights', 'Punch Drunk Love', 'Magnolia'

18. 'Fight Club', 'The Curious Case of Benjamin Button', 'The Social Network'

19. 'Election', 'About Schmidt', 'The Descendants'

20. 'Aguirre – The Wrath of God', 'Cobra Verde', 'Grizzly Man'

MEDIUM

Answers to Quiz 86: Pot Luck

1. Honey
2. Tofu
3. Nigeria
4. George II
5. Bergerac
6. Screen Actors Guild Awards
7. Sir Winston Churchill
8. Nevada and Arizona
9. My Fair Lady
10. Dressage
11. Vienna
12. 100
13. January
14. William Shakespeare
15. Appalachian Trail
16. James Callaghan
17. A will
18. Cyprus
19. 52
20. Ireland

Quiz 88: Pot Luck

1. What name is shared by a breed of dog and an England wicketkeeper who played 54 Test matches in the late 1980s and 1990s?

2. In pre-decimal British currency, what was the lowest value coin?

3. According to the 2011 census, what is the most widely spoken language in England after English?

4. Excluding the Queen, who was the first woman to feature on a UK banknote?

5. A bar mitzvah is a coming-of-age ceremony for Jewish boys. What is the equivalent ceremony for Jewish girls?

6. As the crow flies, which city is closer to London – Los Angeles or New Delhi?

7. What name is given to a triangle which has no equal sides or angles?

8. Paramaribo is the capital city of which South American country?

9. Which alcoholic drink is the main ingredient in a daiquiri?

10. The city of Daegu, which hosted the 2011 World Athletics Championships, is in which country?

11. True or false – as the crow flies, London is closer to Bonn in Germany than it is to Edinburgh?

12. 'Heippa' is goodbye in which European language?

13. True or false – former British prime minister Tony Blair is a godfather to one of Rupert Murdoch's children?

14. A standard London 'Monopoly' board contains how many 'Chance' squares?

15. An iconic symbol of American independence, the Liberty Bell is located in which US city?

16. The TV comedy 'Everybody Hates Chris' was based on the childhood of which American actor and comedian?

17. Who is the only British prime minister not to have spoken English as his first language?

18. The revolutionary leader Ernesto 'Che' Guevara was born in which country?

19. Spending some 20 years and 314 days in office, who is Britain's longest-serving prime minister?
a) Gladstone   b) Disraeli   c) Walpole

20. Whom did Andy Murray beat in the 2013 Wimbledon final?
a) Novak Djokovic   b) Roger Federer   c) Rafael Nadal

MEDIUM

Answers to Quiz 87: Film Directors

1. Alfred Hitchcock
2. Quentin Tarantino
3. Danny Boyle
4. Martin Scorsese
5. Stanley Kubrick
6. Steven Spielberg
7. Francis Ford Coppola
8. James Cameron
9. Christopher Nolan
10. Frank Capra
11. Woody Allen
12. Robert Zemeckis
13. Oliver Stone
14. Robert Altman
15. Wes Anderson
16. Ridley Scott
17. Paul Thomas Anderson
18. David Fincher
19. Alexander Payne
20. Werner Herzog

Quiz 89: It's Chris

1. Which actor played the ninth incarnation of the TV time lord Dr Who?

2. With six golds and one silver, who is Britain's most decorated Olympian?

3. 'God Is Not Great – How Religion Poisons Everything' was a best-selling book by which British author and journalist who died of cancer in 2011?

4. Who was the longest-serving host of BBC Radio One's breakfast show?

5. Chris Collins is the real name of which British comedian and broadcaster?

6. Who played Captain Kirk in the 2009 film 'Star Trek' and 2013's 'Star Trek Into Darkness'?

7. Who won Britain's only gold medal at the 2007 World Athletics Championships?

8. Which actor played Count Dooku in the 'Star Wars' film franchise?

9. Which actor is best known for playing 'Doc' in the 'Back to the Future' films?

10. Which American tennis player won singles titles at Wimbledon in 1974, 1976 and 1981?

11. The TV production company Ginger Productions was founded by which broadcaster?

12. 'If you seek his monument, look around you' reads whose epitaph at St Paul's Cathedral?

13. Which British actor won a Best Supporting Actor Oscar in 2010 for his performance in 'The Fighter'?

14. 'Tamburlaine' and 'Dr Faustus' are works by which 16th-century English dramatist?

15. German Chancellor Angela Merkel is the leader of which political party, which has the initials CDU?

16. The 2005 film 'Batman Begins' was directed by which filmmaker?

17. Red Sin, By Night and Unforgettable are brands of perfume created by which American pop star?

18. Which flame-haired actress is best known for playing Joan Harris in TV drama 'Mad Men'?

19. Chris Martin, Chris Harris and Chris Cairns played international cricket for which country?
    a) Australia
    b) New Zealand
    c) South Africa

20. In which sport is Britain's Chris Harris a notable name?
    a) snooker
    b) speedway
    c) swimming

MEDIUM

Answers to Quiz 88: Pot Luck

1. Jack Russell
2. Farthing
3. Polish
4. Florence Nightingale
5. Bat mitzvah
6. New Delhi
7. Scalene
8. Suriname
9. Rum
10. South Korea
11. True
12. Finnish
13. True
14. Three
15. Philadelphia
16. Chris Rock
17. David Lloyd George
18. Argentina
19. Walpole
20. Novak Djokovic

Quiz 90: Pot Luck

1. Which actor played Superman in the 2013 film 'Man of Steel'?

2. Who played Matron in the 1972 film comedy 'Carry On Matron'?

3. 'Nonnatus House' is featured in which popular BBC TV drama?

4. 'Siema' is the word for hello in which European language?

5. Benedick, Beatrice, Leonato, Don John and Don Pedro are characters in which Shakespeare play?

6. Which popular condiment is made by the American firm McIlhenny Co.?

7. What did the J in the name J Edgar Hoover stand for?

8. A tetrahedron is a shape that has how many faces?

9. The motor manufacturer Fiat is based in which Italian city?

10. True or false – broadcaster Jeremy Vine is the son of the late TV sports presenter David Vine?

11. By what name was the American outlaw Harry Alonzo Longabaugh more commonly known?

12. Which animal features on the badge of the motor manufacturer Lamborghini?

13. Who was the original host of TV quiz show 'Fifteen to One'?

14. Who was the host of the updated version of the show which aired in 2014?

15. And which Australian comedian hosted the celebrity versions of the updated show?

16. How old was Adrian Mole when he penned his first diary?

17. What is the only capital city of a European Union country whose name starts and ends with the same letter?

18. What is the most common christian name for a US president?

19. The sci-fi classic 'Dune' was written by which author?
    a) Isaac Asimov
    b) Frank Herbert
    c) John Wyndham

20. Transylvania, home of the fictional Count Dracula, is in which country?
    a) Bulgaria
    b) Czech Republic
    c) Romania

MEDIUM

Answers to Quiz 89: It's Chris

1. Christopher Eccleston
2. Sir Chris Hoy
3. Christopher Hitchens
4. Chris Moyles
5. Frank Skinner
6. Chris Pine
7. Christine Ohuruogu
8. Christopher Lee
9. Christopher Lloyd
10. Chris Evert
11. Chris Evans
12. Sir Christopher Wren
13. Christian Bale
14. Christopher Marlowe
15. Christian Democratic Union
16. Christopher Nolan
17. Christina Aguilera
18. Christina Hendricks
19. New Zealand
20. Speedway

Quiz 91: Sport part 1

1. A speedway race is run over how many laps of the track?

2. Which football term is known in Germany as an 'elfmeter'?

3. Which golfer won the Open Championship in 2002 then had to wait a decade for his second triumph in 2012?

4. Who stepped down as coach of the England cricket team in January 2014 after the team's 5–0 thrashing in Australia?

5. Who is the only world snooker champion from the Irish Republic?

6. Who was the youngest winner of golf's Open Championship in the 20th century? (He won in 1979.)

7. All British racehorses share an official birthday. On which date?

8. In darts, what is the lowest score that cannot be finished in three darts?

9. The Eastbourne Eagles and Kings Lynn Stars are teams in which sport?

10. Which five disciplines are featured in a modern pentathlon competition?

11. In Australian rules football, how many points are awarded for scoring a goal?

12. Who was the first, and so far only, snooker player to have won the BBC Sports Personality of the Year Award?

13. The Cesarewitch is a handicap race run at which English racecourse?

14. The ITU is the governing body of which Olympic sport?

15. Which was the first Summer Olympics to be opened by Queen Elizabeth II?

16. Which Portuguese football club lost its eighth successive European final after losing to Sevilla on penalties in the 2014 Europa League final?

17. Chemmy Alcott is a multiple British champion in which sport?

18. Which other European country was in England's group at the 2014 World Cup?

19. Golfer Lee Westwood is a huge fan of which football club?
    a) Birmingham City
    b) Nottingham Forest
    c) Wolverhampton Wanderers

20. The Airlie Birds is the nickname of which rugby league team?
    a) Hull
    b) Warrington
    c) Widnes

MEDIUM

Answers to Quiz 90: Pot Luck

1.	Henry Cavill	11.	The Sundance Kid
2.	Hattie Jacques	12.	Bull
3.	Call the Midwife	13.	William G Stewart
4.	Polish	14.	Sandi Toksvig
5.	Much Ado About Nothing	15.	Adam Hills
6.	Tabasco sauce	16.	$13\frac{3}{4}$
7.	John	17.	Warsaw
8.	Four	18.	James
9.	Turin	19.	Frank Herbert
10.	False	20.	Romania

Quiz 92: Pot Luck

1. Which major city is situated partly on the continent of Europe and partly on the continent of Asia?

2. How many stars appear on the flag of the European Union?

3. What is the square root of 441?

4. Which country is home to the world's largest Roman Catholic population?

5. Which actor plays Dominic Toretto in 'The Fast and the Furious' film franchise?

6. The UK National Lottery was introduced under which British prime minister?

7. The Emperor's Birthday is a national holiday in which Asian country?

8. Niccolò Paganini was a virtuoso on which musical instrument?

9. Which hymn, written by Henry Francis Lyte, is traditionally sung at the FA Cup final?

10. What was the name of the holiday camp in the TV sitcom 'Hi-De-Hi'?

11. The island state of Mauritius lies in which ocean?

12. The body of the Bank of England that decides the base interest rate is the MPC. What do the initials MPC stand for?

13. The Backs is an area of which British university city?

14. What colour are French post boxes?

15. Shin Bet is the domestic security service of which country?

16. The name of which wading bird also describes a style of frilly collar, popular in the 16th and 17th centuries?

17. Mt Teide, the highest point in Spain, is on which island?

18. In ballet, which word describes a leap from one foot to the other?

19. Which former Dr Who played Malekith in the 2013 film 'Thor: The Dark World'?
a) Christopher Eccleston
b) Matt Smith
c) David Tennant

20. What is the southernmost tip of South America?
a) Cape Cod
b) Cape Horn
c) Cape of Good Hope

MEDIUM

Answers to Quiz 91: Sport part 1

1. Four
2. A penalty kick
3. Ernie Els
4. Andy Flower
5. Ken Doherty
6. Seve Ballesteros
7. 1st January
8. 159
9. Speedway
10. Shooting, fencing, swimming, horse riding and running
11. Six
12. Steve Davis
13. Newmarket
14. Triathlon
15. Montreal (1976)
16. Benfica
17. Skiing
18. Italy
19. Nottingham Forest
20. Hull

Quiz 93: Brazil

1. What is the official language of Brazil?

2. In terms of population, what is the largest city in Brazil?

3. In which century did Brazil gain independence?

4. Completed in 1931, what is the name of the giant statue that overlooks the city of Rio de Janeiro?

5. True or false – Brazil is the world's leading producer of coffee?

6. Copacabana is a neighbourhood in which Brazilian city?

7. Brazil hosted football's World Cup for the first time in which year?

8. What is the national dance of Brazil?

9. Interlagos, the track which hosts the Brazilian Grand Prix, is in a district of which city?

10. In 2001/02, which Arsenal player became the first Brazilian to gain a Premier League winner's medal?

11. The famous Rio Carnival ends on which Christian feast day?

12. In which year did Brazil win football's World Cup for the first time?

13. What are the two countries in South America with which Brazil does not share a border?

14. Brazil is divided into how many different time zones?

15. Which popular politician was the President of Brazil from 2003 until 2011?

16. Who are the three Brazilians to have won Formula One's World Drivers' Championship?

17. What is the name of the Brazilian martial art that combines elements of dance, acrobatics and music?

18. Which best-selling Brazilian author's works include 'The Alchemist', 'The Pilgrimage' and 'The Winner Stands Alone'?

19. In addition to one federal district, Brazil is made up of how many states?
    a) 22
    b) 26
    c) 30

20. In terms of area, Brazil makes up approximately what percentage of the South American continent?
    a) 37%
    b) 47%
    c) 57%

MEDIUM

Answers to Quiz 92: Pot Luck

1. Istanbul
2. 12
3. 21
4. Brazil
5. Vin Diesel
6. John Major
7. Japan
8. Violin
9. Abide With Me
10. Maplins
11. Indian Ocean
12. Monetary Policy Committee
13. Cambridge
14. Yellow
15. Israel
16. Ruff
17. Tenerife
18. Jeté
19. Christopher Eccleston
20. Cape Horn

Quiz 94: Pot Luck

1. Mahela Jayawardene and Sanath Jayasuriya played international cricket for which country?

2. What note do orchestras traditionally tune up to?

3. @aplusk is the Twitter handle of which famous actor?

4. The Oireachtas is the legislature of which European country?

5. The American military complex known as the Pentagon is in which state?

6. According to the nursery rhyme, who found Lucy Locket's lost pocket?

7. At which racecourse is the Scottish Grand National run?

8. Which politician did Sir Winston Churchill describe as 'a modest man, who has much to be modest about'?

9. In 2014, the Irish Navy took delivery of a ship named after which Nobel Prize-winning playwright?

10. Which film comedy trilogy centres on the antics of characters called Phil Wenneck, Dr Stu Price and Alan Garner?

11. James Dougherty was the first husband of which Hollywood icon?

12. Which Christian holy day is known in France as 'Mercredi des Cendres'?

13. In 2014, who became the first footballer to score for seven different Premier League clubs?

14. Which Nobel Prize was awarded for the first time in 1969?

15. What was the first name of the composer Tchaikovsky?

16. 'Antigone', 'Oedipus Rex' and 'Oedipus at Colonus' are tragedies by which ancient Greek playwright?

17. The Alhambra and St George's Hall are theatres in which northern English city?

18. On a London 'Monopoly' board, what is the first railway station after Go?

19. Which of the following is the name of the organization made up of backbench members of the Conservative Party in the House of Commons?
a) 1921 Committee
b) 1922 Committee
c) 1923 Committee

20. Which of the following American states does not share a land border with Canada?
a) Montana
b) North Dakota
c) Wyoming

MEDIUM

Answers to Quiz 93: Brazil

1. Portuguese
2. Sao Paulo
3. 19th century
4. Christ the Redeemer
5. True
6. Rio de Janeiro
7. 1950
8. Samba
9. Sao Paulo
10. Edu
11. Ash Wednesday
12. 1958
13. Chile and Ecuador
14. Three
15. Luiz Inácio Lula da Silva
16. Emerson Fittipaldi, Nelson Piquet and Ayrton Senna
17. Capoeira
18. Paulo Coelho
19. 26
20. 47%

Quiz 95: Connections part 1

1. What was the name of cartoon character Popeye's girlfriend?

2. Slade Prison was the setting for which TV comedy?

3. 'What You See Is What You Get' was the title of which businessman's 2011 autobiography?

4. Which Canadian actor, who died in 1994, starred in 'Uncle Buck', 'Cool Runnings' and 'Planes, Trains and Automobiles'?

5. 'Sound Affects', 'The Gift' and 'Dig the New Breed' were albums by which band?

6. Which British actor played Charles Robinson in the James Bond films 'Die Another Day' and 'The World Is Not Enough'?

7. Who was the US Secretary of State from 2005 until 2009?

8. Which American musician was the leader of the band Tijuana Brass?

9. Who was the vocalist with the 1980s synth pop duo Soft Cell?

10. Which comic character made a keyboard-playing cameo appearance during the opening ceremony of the 2012 Olympic Games?

11. 'Buffalo Stance' and 'Manchild' were top-five singles for which Swedish-born singer?

12. Which actress plays Ororo Munroe / Storm in the 'X Men' film franchise?

13. Who was the host of the 2013 version of TV panel show 'Through the Keyhole'?

14. Anthony Kiedis is the lead singer with which American rock band?

Answers – page 195

15. Which actor plays Ryan Hardy in the contemporary crime drama 'The Following'?

16. Castlebar is the largest town in which Irish county?

17. Christopher Eccleston played DCI David Bilborough in which 1990s crime drama?

18. Which British figure skater won a gold medal at the 1976 Winter Olympics?

19. Which country finished third at football's 2008 European Championships?

20. What is the connection between the answers?

MEDIUM

Answers to Quiz 94: Pot Luck

1. Sri Lanka
2. A
3. Ashton Kutcher
4. Republic of Ireland
5. Virginia
6. Kitty Fisher
7. Ayr
8. Clement Attlee
9. Samuel Beckett
10. The Hangover
11. Marilyn Monroe
12. Ash Wednesday
13. Craig Bellamy
14. Economics
15. Pyotr
16. Sophocles
17. Bradford
18. King's Cross
19. 1922 Committee
20. Wyoming

Quiz 96: Pot Luck

1. What do the initials LBC stand for in LBC Radio?

2. 'The Boy in the Dress' is the title of a children's book by which actor and comedian?

3. @TheRealAC3 is the Twitter handle of which British sportsman?

4. Which planet of the solar system is named after the Greek god of the sky?

5. By what name is Charles Dickens' pickpocketing character Jack Dawkins better known?

6. Which musical won eight Oscars in 1972 but missed out on the Best Picture award?

7. What are the two books of the Old Testament that start with the letter P?

8. What is eight cubed?

9. What do the initials JK in the name JK Rowling stand for?

10. In relation to the art world, what do the initials YBA stand for?

11. Who was pop superstar Madonna's first husband?

12. In which month does the Queen celebrate her Official Birthday?

13. Which country was runner-up in the Rugby World Cup in 1991 and 2007?

14. Meaning 'for example', what do the initials e.g. stand for?

15. What was the first film directed by a black director to win the Oscar for Best Picture?

Answers – page 197

16. Which rank of the Royal Air Force is abbreviated as Flt Lt?

17. The National Indoor Arena is located in which English city?

18. Sir David Brailsford is a successful coach in which sport?

19. What nationality is the former Wimbledon champion
    Marion Bartoli?
    a) French
    b) Italian
    c) Spanish

20. In March 2014, Graeme Smith announced his retirement
    from Test cricket. Which country did he play for?
    a) Australia
    b) New Zealand
    c) South Africa

MEDIUM

Answers to Quiz 95: Connections part 1

1. Olive Oyl
2. Porridge
3. Alan Sugar
4. John Candy
5. The Jam
6. Colin Salmon
7. Condoleezza Rice
8. Herb Alpert
9. Marc Almond
10. Mr Bean
11. Neneh Cherry
12. Halle Berry
13. Keith Lemon
14. Red Hot Chili Peppers
15. Kevin Bacon
16. Mayo
17. Cracker
18. John Curry
19. Turkey
20. They all contain a food

Quiz 97: Politics

1. US President John F Kennedy was assassinated while visiting which city?

2. Which controversial trade union leader died in March 2014 at the age of just 52?

3. Northfield, Perry Barr and Selly Oak are parliamentary constituencies in which English city?

4. Which high profile British politician's first tweet was, 'About to start meeting in constituency office with Dun Drainage and Environment Agency about waterways and drainage'?

5. Who was the Labour Party candidate in the 2012 London mayoral election?

6. What is the name of the Israeli parliament?

7. The headquarters of the International Monetary Fund are in which city?

8. Which American President said, 'The only thing we have to fear is fear itself'?

9. Who was Britain's longest-serving 20th-century prime minister?

10. In 2013, Tony Abbott became the prime minister of which country?

11. Which former politician wrote three volumes of prison diaries subtitled 'Hell', 'Purgatory' and 'Heaven'?

12. Fine Gael and Fianna Fáil are political parties in which country?

13. Who was the British prime minister during the so-called 'winter of discontent'?

14. Milhous was the middle name of which American president?

15. Which politician did Tony Banks describe as having 'the sensitivity of a sex-starved boa constrictor'?

16. Whom did George Osborne succeed as Chancellor of the Exchequer?

17. Which political party was founded in 1981 by the so-called 'Gang of Four'?

18. In 1799, income tax was introduced by which British prime minister?

19. Lev Davidovich Bronstein was the real name of which Russian revolutionary leader?
    a) Lenin
    b) Stalin
    c) Trotsky

20. Which Conservative politician was an airline pilot before entering politics?
    a) Geoffrey Howe
    b) Nigel Lawson
    c) Norman Tebbit

MEDIUM

Answers to Quiz 96: Pot Luck

1. London Broadcasting Company
2. David Walliams
3. Ashley Cole
4. Uranus
5. The Artful Dodger
6. Cabaret
7. Psalms and Proverbs
8. 512
9. Joanne Kathleen
10. Young British Artists
11. Sean Penn
12. June
13. England
14. Exempli gratia
15. 12 Years a Slave
16. Flight Lieutenant
17. Birmingham
18. Cycling
19. French
20. South Africa

Quiz 98: Pot Luck

1. The TV drama 'Endeavour' is a prequel to which detective series?

2. In 2013, who became the fourth English bowler to take 300 Test wickets?

3. Which 1985 sporting event provided BBC2 with its largest ever viewing figures of over 18 million?

4. True or false – broadcaster and writer Victoria Coren is also a double tournament winner on the European Poker Tour?

5. Berkshire, Lop, Saddleback and Landrace are breeds of which animal?

6. Who said, 'Every child is an artist. The problem is how to remain an artist once we grow up'?

7. Which player holds the record for the most Premier League winner's medals with 13?

8. Which Oscar-winning actor is older – Daniel Day-Lewis or Colin Firth?

9. Which poet wrote, 'No man is an island / Entire of itself / Every man is a piece of the continent / A part of the main'?

10. Who is older – Ade Edmondson or Lenny Henry?

11. Which former flagship of the Royal Navy was decommissioned in 2011 almost 30 years after its launch?

12. What connects the Caribbean island of Anguilla and Charlton Athletic Football Club?

13. The International Olympic Committee is based in which European city?

14. Who was the first Briton to win golf's US Masters?

15. Which of Henry VIII's wives is buried next to him?

16. Which popular board game celebrated its 75th anniversary in 2010?

17. Which Beatle spent nine days in a Japanese jail before being deported in 1980?

18. Which Hollywood film-maker directed 'The 10 Commandments' not once but twice?

19. In which field of film-making is Hans Zimmer a notable name?
    a) cinematography
    b) costumes
    c) soundtrack composing

20. Which of the following is a noted radio broadcaster?
    a) Nick Ferrari
    b) Nick Mercedes
    c) Nick Porsche

MEDIUM

Answers to Quiz 97: Politics

1. Dallas
2. Bob Crow
3. Birmingham
4. Ed Miliband
5. Ken Livingstone
6. The Knesset
7. Washington DC
8. Franklin D Roosevelt
9. Margaret Thatcher
10. Australia
11. Jeffrey Archer
12. Republic of Ireland
13. James Callaghan
14. Richard Nixon
15. Margaret Thatcher
16. Alistair Darling
17. The Social Democratic Party
18. William Pitt the Younger
19. Trotsky
20. Norman Tebbit

Quiz 99: Sport part 2

1. What nationality is the major-winning golfer Adam Scott?

2. What is the only national football team that wears a checkerboard home shirt?

3. Which course has hosted golf's Open Championship the most times?

4. In which country was Olympic champion Mo Farah born?

5. Who was the first cyclist to win the Tour de France in five consecutive years?

6. In which sport do teams compete for the Ove Fundin Trophy?

7. Which England spin bowler called time on his international career midway through the disastrous Ashes tour of 2013/14?

8. Boothferry Park is the former home of which English football club?

9. Which number lies between 14 and 12 on a standard dartboard?

10. What colours are the two rings on the bottom row of the Olympic flag?

11. Which was the first country to lose in the Cricket World Cup final not once but twice?

12. In 2014, the Manchester Thunder defeated the Surrey Storm to become the British champions in which sport?

13. In rugby league, what number shirt is worn by the hooker?

14. The Welsh Grand National horse race is run at which racecourse?

15. Renaldo Nehemiah was the first man to break 13 seconds in which athletics event?

Answers – page 203

16. Which Scottish football team plays its home games at Firhill Stadium?

17. 'The Cobra' is the nickname of which British boxing champion?

18. The Parks is the home cricket ground of which English university?

19. The Pirates is the nickname of which English football club?
    a) Bristol City
    b) Bristol Rovers
    c) Plymouth Argyle

20. Sir Viv Richards holds the record for the fastest century in Test cricket history. How many balls did it take him?
    a) 56   b) 60   c) 64

Answers to Quiz 98: Pot Luck

1. Inspector Morse
2. James Anderson
3. The World Snooker Championship final between Dennis Taylor and Steve Davis
4. True
5. Pig
6. Pablo Picasso
7. Ryan Giggs
8. Daniel Day-Lewis
9. John Donne
10. Ade Edmondson
11. HMS Ark Royal
12. The Valley (Anguilla's capital and Charlton's home ground)
13. Lausanne
14. Sandy Lyle
15. Jane Seymour
16. Monopoly
17. Paul McCartney
18. Cecil B DeMille
19. Soundtrack composing
20. Nick Ferrari

Quiz 100: Pot Luck

1. What does the first 'A' in the acronym BAFTA stand for?

2. And what does the second 'A' stand for?

3. In the Christmas pantomime Cinderella, what is the name of the title character's father?

4. A ream is made up of how many sheets of paper?

5. In 1995, who became the first British rock star to receive a knighthood?

6. The Proms is an annual series of classical music concerts. What is 'Prom' short for?

7. Susan Delfino, Lynette Scavo, Bree Van de Kamp and Gabrielle Solis were the central characters in which long-running US TV drama?

8. Which female newsreader was the original host of the TV motoring show 'Top Gear'?

9. Which portly children's-book character is known in America as Sir Topham Hatt?

10. American architect Alfred Mosher Butts was the inventor of which popular board game?

11. Missy Franklin is a multiple Olympic gold medal-winner in which sport?

12. The Oscar-winning film 'Argo' was largely set in which Middle Eastern country?

13. Actor Michael Keaton's real name is the same as that of another Hollywood star. What is it?

14. The original version of the board game 'Monopoly' was based on which city?

15. Julian Wilson, who died in April 2014, was a long-time commentator on which sport?

16. Which actor won his first Oscar in 1980 for his performance in 'Kramer vs Kramer'?

17. Complete the phrase attributed to the artist Matisse: 'Creativity takes ...'?

18. True or false – the euro is the currency in parts of South America?

19. Which of the following is not a denomination of euro banknote?
    a) €25
    b) €50
    c) €200

20. 'Reem' is a word associated with which reality TV star?
    a) Joey Essex
    b) Joey Sussex
    c) Joey Wessex

MEDIUM

Answers to Quiz 99: Sport part 2

1. Australian
2. Croatia
3. St Andrews
4. Somalia
5. Miguel Indurain
6. Speedway
7. Graeme Swann
8. Hull City
9. 9
10. Green and yellow
11. England
12. Netball
13. 9
14. Chepstow
15. 110m hurdles
16. Partick Thistle
17. Carl Froch
18. Oxford University
19. Bristol Rovers
20. 56

Quiz 101: Connections part 2

1. Who captained Australia to a 5–0 Ashes whitewash over England in 2013/14?

2. What is the French word for the colour pink?

3. Which actor played Detective Sergeant Roger Murtaugh in the 'Lethal Weapon' film series?

4. Suranne Jones and Lesley Sharp star in which Manchester-set police drama?

5. What was the theme song to the 1982 boxing movie 'Rocky III'?

6. Which former Manchester United footballer was the manager of Northern Ireland from 2000 to 2003?

7. What is the real name of the model and tabloid favourite Jordan?

8. Who was nominated for a Best Actor Oscar in 2013 for his performance in 'Silver Linings Playbook'?

9. The golden eagle is the logo of which Scottish knitwear label?

10. Which Scottish actor and broadcaster is known for his brightly coloured turbans?

11. 'It may be paradise but it's no vacation' was the tagline to which 2009 romantic comedy starring Vince Vaughn?

12. Which 1992 film, directed by Robert Altman, stars Tim Robbins as a Hollywood movie executive who murders a budding screenwriter whom he thought was blackmailing him?

13. Which comedian, who died in 2013, was best known for his 'faulty microphone' routine?

14. What was the title of the best-selling 2004 novel by Khaled Hosseini that was turned into a successful film in 2007?

Answers – page 207

15. Which veteran actor co-starred alongside Dame Judi Dench in the long-running BBC sitcom 'As Time Goes By'?

16. De Pfeffel is part of the full name of which high-profile British politician?

17. Which American scientist was awarded a Nobel Prize in 1962, along with Francis Crick and Maurice Wilkins, for his work on the discovery of DNA?

18. Which journalist and broadcaster was the Director of Communications and Strategy for Prime Minister Tony Blair between 1997 and 2003?

19. Which actress played detective Mary Beth Lacey in the 1980s police drama 'Cagney and Lacey'?

20. What is the connection between the answers?

MEDIUM

Answers to Quiz 100: Pot Luck

1. Academy
2. Arts
3. Baron Hardup
4. 500
5. Sir Cliff Richard
6. Promenade
7. Desperate Housewives
8. Angela Rippon
9. The Fat Controller (from 'The Railway Series' featuring Thomas the Tank Engine)
10. Scrabble
11. Swimming
12. Iran
13. Michael Douglas
14. Atlantic City
15. Horse racing
16. Dustin Hoffman
17. Courage
18. True (in French Guiana)
19. €25
20. Joey Essex

Quiz 102: Pot Luck

1. Which European country's flag is made up of three horizontal bands: blue at the top, black in the middle, white at the bottom?

2. The European Court of Justice is based in which country?

3. Who is the only Canadian to have won the World Snooker Championship?

4. The title of which Verdi opera translates into English as 'The Fallen Woman'?

5. True or false – former prime minister Gordon Brown's real first name is James?

6. In 2013, Queen Beatrix stepped down as the monarch of which European country?

7. Which ground-breaking musical was subtitled 'The American Tribal Love-Rock Musical'?

8. According to the nursery rhyme, on which day of the week did Solomon Grundy take ill?

9. Who was enthroned as Archbishop of Canterbury in March 2013?

10. German Kirsten Mehr is the wife of which British politician?

11. The mobile phone operating system iOS was developed by which giant technology company?

12. What is nine cubed?

13. Which Oscar-winning film was based on an 1853 memoir written by Solomon Northup?

14. 'I'll go home and I'll think of some way to get him back. After all, tomorrow is another day' is the last line from which classic film?

15. Which modern-day motor-racing driver was named after a multiple Olympic gold medal-winning athlete?

16. Inky, Pinky, Blinky and Clyde are characters in which classic video game?

17. 'Trying is the first step towards failure' according to which animated TV character?

18. What is the name of the dot found above the letters 'i' and 'j'?

19. What is politician George Osborne's real first name?
    a) Gary
    b) Gideon
    c) Giles

20. Which of the following is a successful Broadway musical?
    a) Peetown
    b) Urinetown
    c) Weetown

MEDIUM

Answers to Quiz 101: Connections part 2

1. Michael Clarke
2. Rose
3. Danny Glover
4. Scott and Bailey
5. Eye of the Tiger
6. Sammy McIlroy
7. Katie Price
8. Bradley Cooper
9. Lyle and Scott
10. Hardeep Singh Kohli
11. Couples Retreat
12. The Player
13. Norman Collier
14. The Kite Runner
15. Geoffrey Palmer
16. Boris Johnson
17. James Watson
18. Alastair Campbell
19. Tyne Daly
20. They all contain the name of the winner of one of golf's major tournaments

Quiz 103: Movies

1. What are the two sequels to have won the Oscar for Best Picture?

2. The Oscar-winning film 'Slumdog Millionaire' is set in which city?

3. Which British actress received her first Oscar nomination for her performance in the 1997 film 'Mrs Brown'?

4. Which European city plays host to the Raindance Film Festival?

5. The cult classic 'Trainspotting' was set in which city?

6. 'A Boy's Life' was the working title of which multiple-Oscar-winning 1982 film?

7. 'Infamy! Infamy! They've all got it in for me!' is a line from which 'Carry On' film?

8. What nationality is the controversial director Lars von Trier?

9. Which movie superhero has an artificial computer called 'JARVIS'?

10. 'Malcolm X', 'Do The Right Thing' and 'Inside Man' were all films made by which director?

11. Which 1980 film comedy was released in France as 'Is There a Pilot on This Plane?' and in Brazil as 'Tighten Up Your Seatbelt, The Pilot's Gone'?

12. Who is the only member of the cast from 'The Lord of the Rings' trilogy to have met author JRR Tolkien?

13. Which Oscar-winning actor died during the filming of the 2008 film 'The Imaginarium of Dr Parnassus'?

14. Which soul musician won his only Oscar for his theme song to the 1971 film 'Shaft'?

Answers – page 211

15. What 1995 movie was the first full-length animated feature film from the Pixar studio?

16. Which film was released first – 'Jaws' or 'Star Wars'?

17. Which leading man made his debut behind the camera on the 2002 film 'Confessions of a Dangerous Mind'?

18. What was the first feature film to be directed by Quentin Tarantino?

19. The Oscar-winning film 'A Man for All Seasons' is set during the reign of which English king?
    a) Henry V
    b) Henry VIII
    c) George III

20. What was the first film in the 'Carry On' series?
    a) Camping
    b) Sergeant
    c) Up the Khyber

MEDIUM

Answers to Quiz 102: Pot Luck

1. Estonia
2. Luxembourg
3. Cliff Thorburn
4. La Traviata
5. True
6. The Netherlands
7. Hair
8. Thursday
9. Justin Welby
10. Nigel Farage
11. Apple
12. 729
13. 12 Years a Slave
14. Gone with the Wind
15. Lewis Hamilton
16. Pac-Man
17. Homer Simpson
18. Tittle
19. Gideon
20. Urinetown

Quiz 104: Pot Luck

1. Which pantomime character has a brother called Wishy Washy?

2. Disneyland Park is in which American state?

3. True or false – movie legend Orson Welles once appeared in an episode of detective drama 'Magnum, PI'?

4. Which African capital takes its name from the Greek for 'three cities'?

5. Gordon Brown served as the Chancellor of the Exchequer for how many years?

6. 'Love Never Dies' is the sequel to which hit musical?

7. Who was Time magazine's Man of the Year in 1938?

8. Which gold medal-winning British athlete competed at six successive Olympic Games between 1976 and 1996?

9. George, Jane, Judy, Elroy and a dog called Astro were members of which cartoon family?

10. The bearded 2014 Eurovision Song Contest winner Conchita Wurst represented which country?

11. 'Another Way to Die' by Alicia Keys and Jack White was the theme song to which James Bond film?

12. The OSS was for forerunner of which American organization?

13. Which is the only Grand Slam tennis tournament that uses tie-breaks in the fifth set of matches?

14. Which member of the Royal Family has children called Louise and James?

15. The Diamond League is a series of events in which sport?

16. The style of acting known as 'method acting' was developed by which Russian actor and theatre director?

17. What was the first name of the title character in the classic novel 'The Great Gatsby'?

18. The European Court of Human Rights is based in which city?

19. Which sporting figure's collection of 5000 bottles of vintage wine was sold at auction in 2014?
    a) Sir Alex Ferguson
    b) David Gower
    c) Nigel Mansell

20. What is the currency of Egypt?
    a) dollar
    b) franc
    c) pound

MEDIUM

Answers to Quiz 103: Movies

1. The Godfather Part II' and 'The Lord of the Rings: Return of the King'
2. Mumbai
3. Dame Judi Dench
4. London
5. Edinburgh
6. ET – The Extra Terrestrial
7. Carry On Cleo
8. Danish
9. Iron Man
10. Spike Lee
11. Airplane
12. Christopher Lee
13. Heath Ledger
14. Isaac Hayes
15. Toy Story
16. Jaws
17. George Clooney
18. Reservoir Dogs
19. Henry VIII
20. Sergeant

Quiz 105: Connections part 3

MEDIUM

1. The 2013 film 'Blue Jasmine' was directed by which veteran film maker?

2. Which actress played Sandy Olsson in the film 'Grease'?

3. Bloomsday is a festival that celebrates the works of which Irish author?

4. In TV soap 'EastEnders' which actress plays Sharon Watts?

5. Which rank outsider knocked out Mike Tyson to win the world heavyweight boxing championship in 1990?

6. Who is the lead singer with the rock band Blondie?

7. Which actor, best known for his role in a sci-fi comedy, played Lloyd Mullaney in the TV soap 'Coronation Street'?

8. The 1959 hit 'It Doesn't Matter Anymore' was the only UK number one for which rock and roll star?

9. Which British philosopher was awarded the Nobel Prize for Literature in 1950?

10. 'Ozymandias', 'Ode to the West Wind' and 'To a Skylark' are works by which romantic poet?

11. 'Wonderful World Beautiful People' and 'Wide World' were hits for which reggae singer?

12. Which two-time Mercury-Prize-winning singer and musician was awarded an MBE in June 2013?

13. The 1997 hit 'Professional Widow' was the only UK number-one single by which female American singer?

14. Which female vocalist sang alongside Westlife on their 2000 number one hit 'Against All Odds'?

15. Which British singer recorded the number-one albums 'Faith' and 'Listen Without Prejudice Volume 1'?

16. Which British comedian and panel-show regular was the winner of Heat magazine's 'Weird Crush of the Year Award' in 2013?

17. Bernard Schwartz was the real name of which Hollywood star, who died in 2010?

18. 'Alfie' is the nickname of which former rugby star who won 100 caps for Wales between 1995 and 2007?

19. Who is the central character in the cult American sitcom 'Curb Your Enthusiasm'?

20. What is the connection between the answers?

MEDIUM

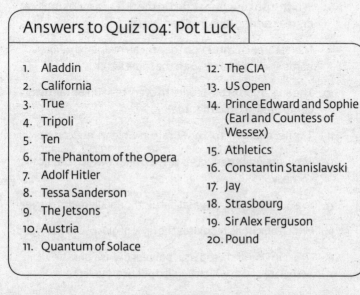

Answers to Quiz 104: Pot Luck

1. Aladdin
2. California
3. True
4. Tripoli
5. Ten
6. The Phantom of the Opera
7. Adolf Hitler
8. Tessa Sanderson
9. The Jetsons
10. Austria
11. Quantum of Solace
12. The CIA
13. US Open
14. Prince Edward and Sophie (Earl and Countess of Wessex)
15. Athletics
16. Constantin Stanislavski
17. Jay
18. Strasbourg
19. Sir Alex Ferguson
20. Pound

Quiz 106: Pot Luck

1. Actor Roger Lloyd-Pack, who died in January 2014, played Owen Newitt in which long-running TV comedy?

2. Which Roman emperor, author of 'Meditations', was known as 'the philosopher emperor'?

3. Which sport is featured on the Saturday morning TV show 'The Morning Line'?

4. Who was the original host of the TV panel show 'Never Mind the Buzzcocks'?

5. In the espionage drama 'Homeland', what is Brody's first name?

6. Which breed of dog features in the name of a Canadian province?

7. Which musician was forced to quit playing the cello in 2014 because of a slipped disc?

8. Which Irish county featured in the title of a 1960s medical drama starring Richard Chamberlain?

9. Name three countries on the African mainland whose name starts and ends with the same letter.

10. The allocation of postcodes to every town in Britain was completed in which decade?

11. The headquarters of the FBI are in which American city?

12. 'Well, nobody's perfect!' is the last line of which classic 1959 comedy?

13. In a non-leap year, on what date is the middle day of the year?

14. Which hormone regulates the level of glucose in the blood?

15. 'Trust in God and keep your powder dry' is a phrase associated with which English political leader?

Answers – page 217

16. 'You wouldn't let it lie!' is a catchphrase associated with which comedy duo?

17. The giant Westfalenstadion is home to which European football club?

18. The equator passes through which three South American countries?

19. In which year did South Africa host its first multi-racial elections?
    a) 1992   b) 1993   c) 1994

20. Cameroon's Roger Milla is the oldest player to take part in a World Cup match. How old was he when he made his final appearance?
    a) 40   b) 41   c) 42

Answers to Quiz 105: Connections part 3

1. Woody Allen
2. Olivia Newton-John
3. James Joyce
4. Letitia Dean
5. James 'Buster' Douglas
6. Debbie Harry
7. Craig Charles
8. Buddy Holly
9. Bertrand Russell
10. Percy Bysshe Shelley
11. Jimmy Cliff
12. PJ Harvey
13. Tori Amos
14. Mariah Carey
15. George Michael
16. Russell Howard
17. Tony Curtis
18. Gareth Thomas
19. Larry David
20. They all feature a person whose surname is also a first name

MEDIUM

Quiz 107: Science

MEDIUM

1. What is the name of the pigment that determines skin and eye colour?

2. Which Polish astronomer was the first person to show that the earth travelled round the sun?

3. On a flat-screen television, what do the initials LCD stand for?

4. What oath is taken by doctors to swear that they will practise medicine in an honest fashion?

5. Which element of the periodic table derives its chemical symbol from the Latin 'ferrum'?

6. Which gas is released by plants during photosynthesis?

7. The first successful heart transplant was carried out in which country?

8. What are the names of the tiny blood vessels that connect arteries to veins?

9. What is the name of a line drawn on a map to indicate places that have the same atmospheric pressure?

10. In the human body, what is the name of the tissue that connects a bone to another bone?

11. Which element of the periodic table has the chemical symbol W and the atomic number 74?

12. In degrees Fahrenheit, at what temperature does water freeze?

13. What was the name of the space shuttle that disintegrated during re-entry into the Earth's atmosphere in February 2003?

14. Launched in 1957, what was the name of the world's first artificial satellite?

15. By what name is the temperature −273.5°C better known?

16. The hallux is the scientific name for which part of the human body?

17. In chemistry, which word describes the process by which one substance is incorporated into another?

18. Oxygen is one of two elements of the periodic table to start with the letter O. What is the other?

19. The speed of sound is approximately how many miles per hour?
a) 661 mph
b) 761 mph
c) 861 mph

20. A human skeleton is made up of how many bones?
a) 206
b) 226
c) 246

Answers to Quiz 106: Pot Luck

1. The Vicar of Dibley
2. Marcus Aurelius
3. Horse racing
4. Mark Lamarr
5. Nicholas
6. Labrador
7. Julian Lloyd Webber
8. (Dr) Kildare
9. Algeria, Angola, Central African Republic
10. 1970s
11. Washington DC
12. Some Like It Hot
13. 2nd July
14. Insulin
15. Oliver Cromwell
16. Vic Reeves and Bob Mortimer
17. Borussia Dortmund
18. Brazil, Colombia and Ecuador
19. 1994
20. 42

MEDIUM

Quiz 108: Pot Luck

1. Ratified in 1951, the Twenty-second Amendment to the United States Constitution limited what?

2. Miriam González Durántez is the wife of which British politician?

3. Who was the first Canadian to win the World Darts Championship?

4. The 2020 Summer Olympics will be held in which city?

5. A 'Monopoly' board contains how many spaces?

6. Which British actor was Hollywood star Uma Thurman's first husband?

7. Circuit Gilles Villeneuve is a Formula One venue in which city?

8. Nunavut and Yukon are territories of which Commonwealth country?

9. Which classic film was loosely based on the life of a sportsman called Chuck Wepner?

10. True or false – the father of England rugby player Billy Twelvetrees is a tree surgeon?

11. In 2006, Evo Morales was elected president of which South American country?

12. In England, Scotland and Wales, the red grouse shooting season starts on the 12th of which month?

13. With a maximum length of 300 yards by 200 yards, which sport has the largest field of play?

14. Which Welsh holiday resort lies between two headlands called the Great Orme and Little Orme?

15. By what name was the Ethiopian leader Tafari Makonnen more commonly known?

16. In which sport do teams compete for the Bledisloe Cup?

17. Esteban is the Spanish equivalent of which English name?

18. According to the nursery rhyme, the man in the moon came tumbling down and asked his way to which English city?

19. How old was reggae musician Bob Marley when he died?
    a) 26
    b) 36
    c) 46

20. The names of how many American states end with the letter A?
    a) 17
    b) 19
    c) 21

MEDIUM

Answers to Quiz 107: Science

1. Melanin
2. Nicolaus Copernicus
3. Liquid crystal display
4. Hippocratic oath
5. Iron
6. Oxygen
7. South Africa
8. Capillaries
9. Isobar
10. Ligament
11. Tungsten
12. 32°F
13. Columbia
14. Sputnik 1
15. Absolute zero
16. Big toe
17. Absorption
18. Osmium
19. 761 mph
20. 206

Quiz 109: Steves

1. 'The Crocodile Hunter' was the nickname of which Australian wildlife broadcaster who died while snorkelling off the Great Barrier Reef in 2006?

2. Which sportsman is the owner of a Southport restaurant called 'Warehouse Kitchen+Bar'?

3. Which Briton won gold medals in five successive Olympic Games from 1984 to 2000?

4. 'Tugga' was the nickname of which cricketer, who won 168 Test caps for Australia between 1985 and 2004?

5. Michael Scott, the central character in the American version of 'The Office', is played by which actor?

6. Who is the youngest player to win the World Professional Snooker Championship?

7. Which British actor played porn king Paul Raymond in the 2013 film 'The Look of Love'?

8. 'The Bronzed Adonis' is the nickname of which former world darts champion?

9. Which singer was the biggest-selling singles artist of the 1980s?

10. 'EastEnders' hard man Phil Mitchell is played by which actor?

11. Which British comic actor played Darren Lamb in 'Extras', himself in 'Life's Too Short', and Stuart Pritchard in 'Hello Ladies'?

12. 'Songs in the Key of Life', 'Innervisions' and 'Hotter Than July' were top-ten albums for which legendary musician and singer?

13. Richard Bachmann is a pen name used by which best-selling author?

14. 'Ocean's 11', 'Magic Mike' and 'Behind the Candelabra' were all directed by which American film maker?

15. The 1980 thriller 'The Hunter' was the last film in which Hollywood icon appeared?

16. Which member of Bruce Springsteen's E Street Band played Silvio Dante in the long-running TV drama 'The Sopranos'?

17. Which actor plays crime lord Enoch 'Nucky' Thompson in the prohibition-era drama 'Boardwalk Empire'?

18. On which date is the Christian feast of St Stephen's Day celebrated?

19. Steve Wosniak was a co-founder of which giant technology company?
    a) Apple   b) Facebook   c) Microsoft

20. There was a king of England called Stephen in which century?
    a) 11th century   b) 12th century   c) 13th century

Answers to Quiz 108: Pot Luck

1. The terms a president could serve
2. Nick Clegg
3. John Part
4. Tokyo
5. 40
6. Gary Oldman
7. Montreal
8. Canada
9. Rocky
10. True
11. Bolivia
12. August
13. Polo
14. Llandudno
15. Haile Selassie
16. Rugby union
17. Stephen
18. Norwich
19. 36
20. 21

MEDIUM

Quiz 110: Pot Luck

1. Sir Roger Moore played 007 in how many James Bond films?

2. FIDE is the global governing body for which game?

3. Prior to David Cameron, who was the last British prime minister to head a coalition government?

4. Lynn Benfield is the long-suffering assistant to which famous sitcom character?

5. 'Modern Warfare', 'World at War', 'Black Ops' and 'Ghosts' are series in which video-game franchise?

6. President Barack Obama spent much of his early life in which Asian country?

7. Which play opened in London first – 'Les Miserables' or 'The Phantom of the Opera'?

8. The Treaty that formally ended the First World War was signed at which palace?

9. Which racing driver was killed in a crash the day before Ayrton Senna tragically died at the same circuit?

10. The man who co-founded Microsoft with Bill Gates has the same name as a much-travelled footballer, best known for spells at West Ham and Spurs in the 1980s. What is his name?

11. Gatcombe Park is the private country home of which member of the royal family?

12. In which month is the play 'Romeo and Juliet' set?

13. Which word describes the process where a chemical matter changes directly from a solid to a gas without becoming a liquid?

14. Fawley is the surname of the title character in which novel by Thomas Hardy?

15. Tony David was the first player from which country to win the BDO World Darts Championship?

16. Is London closer to Casablanca or Moscow?

17. Toby Jones and Philip Seymour Hoffman have both played which author in film biopics?

18. Which city in Northern Ireland is home to not one but two cathedrals called St Patrick's?

19. What is the name of the central character in the Franz Kafka novel 'The Trial'?
    a) Joseph K
    b) Joseph L
    c) Joseph M

20. In the 1990 film 'The Hunt for Red October' what was 'Red October'?
    a) a boat
    b) a plane
    c) a submarine

Answers to Quiz 109: Steves

1. Steve Irwin
2. Steven Gerrard
3. Sir Steve Redgrave
4. Steve Waugh
5. Steve Carell
6. Stephen Hendry
7. Steve Coogan
8. Steve Beaton
9. Shakin' Stevens
10. Steve McFadden
11. Stephen Merchant
12. Stevie Wonder
13. Stephen King
14. Steven Soderbergh
15. Steve McQueen
16. Steve Van Zandt
17. Steve Buscemi
18. 26th December
19. Apple
20. 12th century

MEDIUM

Quiz 111: Places

1. Hoylake, the venue for the 2014 edition of golf's Open Championship, is just outside which British city?

2. What is the second-largest city in Belgium?

3. What are the nine countries that share a border with Germany?

4. The MacGillycuddy's Reeks mountain range is in which country?

5. Odense is the third largest city in which European country?

6. Excluding Paris, what is the largest French-speaking city in the world?

7. Iwo Jima, the scene of a major World War Two battle is in which country?

8. Dnipropetrovsk, Kharkiv and Donetsk are cities in which European country?

9. Containing the grave of President John F Kennedy and the Tomb of the Unknown Soldier, Arlington National Cemetery is in which American state?

10. Which European country is bordered by Ukraine, Moldova, Hungary, Serbia, Bulgaria and the Black Sea?

11. NHK is the national broadcaster of which Asian country?

12. The San Siro stadium is located in which Italian city?

13. Ottawa, the capital city of Canada, is in which province?

14. Which town in Lincolnshire is also the name of an Irish county?

15. The towns of Cleveland and Cincinnati are in which American state?

16. Mezzogiorno is a region of which country?

17. The seaport of Mombasa is in which African country?

18. In terms of population, what is the largest city in Latin America?

19. The 2014 Giro d'Italia cycle race started where?
    a) Belfast
    b) Cardiff
    c) Edinburgh

20. What name is shared by mountain ranges in Australia and Jamaica?
    a) Blue Mountains
    b) Green Mountains
    c) Red Mountains

MEDIUM

Answers to Quiz 110: Pot Luck

1. Seven
2. Chess
3. Sir Winston Churchill
4. Alan Partridge
5. Call of Duty
6. Indonesia
7. Les Miserables
8. Versailles
9. Roland Ratzenberger
10. Paul Allen
11. Princess Anne
12. July
13. Sublimation
14. Jude the Obscure
15. Australia
16. Casablanca
17. Truman Capote
18. Armagh
19. Joseph K
20. Submarine

Quiz 112: Pot Luck

1. The classic film Casablanca is set during which conflict?

2. Which Anglo-Australian actress played the Princess of Wales in the 2013 film 'Diana'?

3. Which Christmas pantomime is based on a story from the 'One Thousand and One Nights'?

4. Which video-game franchise is set in the fictional American locations of Liberty City, Vice City and San Andreas?

5. Which international sporting venue is located in St John's Wood in north London?

6. Levenshulme, Withington and Whalley Range are areas of which English city?

7. In the films 'The Love Bug' and 'Herbie Goes Bananas', what type of car was Herbie?

8. In the cartoon 'The Flintstones', what was the name of Barney Rubble's wife?

9. The Sierra Nevada mountain range is in which European country?

10. Tintagel, the reputed birthplace of King Arthur, is in which English county?

11. A Japanese haiku poem contains how many lines?

12. Which bridge in London links St Paul's Cathedral with Tate Modern?

13. What nationality is the best-selling author Jo Nesbø?

14. In which year was the London Congestion Charge introduced?

15. Holly Golightly is the central character in which 1958 novel?

16. In the TV comedy 'The Simpsons', who is the father of boys called Rod and Todd?

17. Singer Jim Morrison, writer and wit Oscar Wilde, and dancer Isadora Duncan are all buried in which European city?

18. What is calcium oxide more commonly known as?

19. In humans, the stomach secretes which acid?
    a) hydrochloric acid
    b) nitric acid
    c) sulphuric acid

20. The town of Sheerness is on which island?
    a) Isle of Man
    b) Isle of Sheppey
    c) Isle of Wight

MEDIUM

Answers to Quiz 111: Places

1. Liverpool
2. Antwerp
3. Austria, Belgium, Czech Republic, Denmark, France, Luxembourg, Netherlands, Poland and Switzerland
4. Ireland
5. Denmark
6. Montreal
7. Japan
8. Ukraine
9. Virginia
10. Romania
11. Japan
12. Milan
13. Ontario
14. Louth
15. Ohio
16. Italy
17. Kenya
18. Mexico City
19. Belfast
20. Blue Mountains

Quiz 113: Russia

1. Which three colours feature on the flag of Russia?

2. Who began his second tenure as Russian president in May 2012?

3. In which year did Moscow first host the Summer Olympics?

4. The name of which Russian landmark translates into English as 'fortress'?

5. The Trans-Siberian Railway stretches from Moscow to which Pacific port?

6. Which Russian mountain range forms a natural boundary between Europe and Asia?

7. Who was the first president of Russia following the dissolution of the Soviet Union in 1991?

8. In which year will Russia host football's World Cup for the first time?

9. In 2004, who became the first Russian to win the Ladies' Singles at Wimbledon?

10. What is the name of the grand cathedral in Red Square, Moscow?

11. Which dynasty ruled Russia before the Communist Revolution of 1917?

12. The Hermitage Museum is in which Russian city?

13. Anatoly Karpov was a world champion in which game?

14. Which former England football manager was in charge of the Russian team at the 2014 World Cup?

15. Which Russian-born actor starred in the classic movie 'The Magnificent Seven'?

16. Which exclave of Russia is surrounded by Poland, Lithuania and the Baltic Sea?

17. One Russian rouble is divided into 100 what?

18. Who was the president of Russia between May 2008 and May 2012?

19. The classic novel 'Anna Karenina' was written by which Russian author?
a) Bulgakov
b) Dostoevsky
c) Tolstoy

20. With which of these countries does Russia not share a land border?
a) Mongolia
b) North Korea
c) South Korea

MEDIUM

Answers to Quiz 112: Pot Luck

1. World War Two
2. Naomi Watts
3. Aladdin
4. Grand Theft Auto
5. Lord's cricket ground
6. Manchester
7. Volkswagen Beetle
8. Betty
9. Spain
10. Cornwall
11. Three
12. Millennium Bridge
13. Norwegian
14. 2003
15. Breakfast at Tiffany's
16. Ned Flanders
17. Paris
18. Quicklime
19. Hydrochloric acid
20. Isle of Sheppey

Quiz 114: Pot Luck

1. The calcaneus is the medical name for which bone?

2. Which branch of the armed forces has an officer training college at Cranwell in Lincolnshire?

3. What are the three African countries whose names contain four letters?

4. In the TV sitcom 'Rising Damp', what was Rigsby's first name?

5. Who was the only footballer to make Time Magazine's list of the '100 Most Influential People in the World' in 2014?

6. True or false – Winston Churchill had a spell as Chancellor of the Exchequer?

7. The casino game craps is played using how many dice?

8. Which American soldier-turned-politician was the first Supreme Commander of NATO?

9. Espoo and Tampere are cities in which Nordic country?

10. Billy Bowden, Nigel Llong and Ian Gould are international match officials in which sport?

11. True or false – 'Deal or No Deal' presenter Noel Edmonds once hosted the Brit Awards?

12. What is 23 squared?

13. If a snooker player pots 15 reds, 15 pinks and all the colours what will be the total of the break?

14. What is the most common surname in America?

15. In which decade was the Tour de France cycle race staged for the first time?

16. In 2008, Canadian Autumn Kelly married which member of the British royal family?

17. The site of a bloody First World War battle, the Somme is in which country?

18. The music to the hit musical 'Chess' was written by members of which best-selling pop band?

19. Cricketer Sir Ian Botham also played football professionally for which club?
a) Hull City
b) Lincoln City
c) Scunthorpe United

20. What is the name of the pub in the long-running US comedy 'How I Met Your Mother'?
a) McGinteys
b) MacLaren's
c) Molloy's

MEDIUM

Answers to Quiz 113: Russia

1. White, blue and red
2. Vladimir Putin
3. 1980
4. The Kremlin
5. Vladivostok
6. The Urals
7. Boris Yeltsin
8. 2018
9. Maria Sharapova
10. St Basil's
11. Romanov
12. St Petersburg
13. Chess
14. Fabio Capello
15. Yul Brynner
16. Kaliningrad Oblast
17. Kopecks
18. Dmitry Medvedev
19. Tolstoy
20. South Korea

Quiz 115: History

1. The Siege of Mafeking was an action in which conflict?

2. The ill-fated archbishop Thomas Becket was murdered in 1170 in which cathedral?

3. In which year did Hitler become German Chancellor?

4. Which king was the intended target of the 'Gunpowder Plot'?

5. Which country underwent a 'Great Leap Forward' between 1958 and 1961?

6. Eboracum was the Roman name for which English city?

7. The Charge of the Light Brigade took place during a battle in which war?

8. Nicolae Ceauşescu was the long-time leader of which former Communist country?

9. In which century was London's Tower Bridge opened?

10. Who was the King of Prussia and Emperor of Germany during the First World War?

11. David Ben-Gurion was the first prime minister of which country?

12. In which decade of the 19th century was Queen Victoria crowned?

13. The Battle of Passchendaele was fought in which country?

14. Winston Churchill was born in which stately home?

15. Which general commanded the American forces in The Battle of the Little Bighorn?

Answers – page 235

16. What nationality was the 15th-century explorer Bartolomeu Dias?

17. Trafalgar, scene of a famous 19th-century naval battle, lies off the coast of which country?

18. Which famous battle was fought on Sunday 18 June 1815?

19. Henry II was the first English king from which royal dynasty?
    a) Plantagenet
    b) Stuart
    c) Hanover

20. What was the nickname of King Edward I?
    a) Longshanks
    b) Shortshanks
    c) Wideshanks

MEDIUM

Answers to Quiz 114: Pot Luck

1. Heel
2. The RAF
3. Chad, Mali, Togo
4. Rupert
5. Cristiano Ronaldo
6. True
7. Two
8. Dwight Eisenhower
9. Finland
10. Cricket
11. True
12. 529
13. 132
14. Smith
15. 1900s
16. Peter Phillips
17. France
18. Abba
19. Scunthorpe United
20. MacLarens

Quiz 116: Pot Luck

1. The J Edgar Hoover Building is the headquarters of which American organization?

2. The Royal Exchange Theatre is located in which northern English city?

3. What are classified using a scale that ranges from 9H for hardest and 9B for softest?

4. Jon Pall Sigmarsson, Magnus Ver Magnusson and Mariusz Pudzianowski are former winners of which sporting event?

5. In which month does the Glastonbury Festival usually take place?

6. What was the first Caribbean country to host the Commonwealth Games?

7. In which classic Ealing comedy does Sir Alec Guinness play eight members of the aristocratic D'Ascoyne family?

8. Which author, best known for writing children's books, penned the screenplay to the James Bond film 'You Only Live Twice'?

9. What was the name of the puppet sidekick of TV presenters Andy Crane and Andi Peters?

10. True or false – chat-show host Jonathan Ross is the brother of former 'Crimewatch' presenter Nick Ross?

11. Which English city is home to a rugby league team nicknamed the Red Devils?

12. Oaxaca cheese comes from which country?

13. Susie Dent and Rachel Riley are regulars on which TV game show?

14. 'Some are born great, some achieve greatness, and some have greatness thrust upon them' is a line from which Shakespeare play?

Answers – page 237

15. Jamie Redknapp and Andrew Flintoff are the regular team captains on which sporting TV panel show?

16. In which month is All Souls' Day commemorated?

17. The Sargasso Sea is a region of which ocean?

18. What is the currency of the United Arab Emirates?

19. What is the name of the coach used by the British monarch for the State Opening of Parliament?
a) Irish state coach
b) Scottish state coach
c) Welsh state coach

20. A full set of dominoes contains how many dots?
a) 168
b) 186
c) 206

MEDIUM

Answers to Quiz 115: History

1. The Boer War
2. Canterbury
3. 1933
4. King James I (James VI of Scotland)
5. China
6. York
7. Crimean War
8. Romania
9. 19th century
10. Kaiser Wilhelm
11. Israel
12. 1830s
13. Belgium
14. Blenheim Palace
15. General Custer
16. Portuguese
17. Spain
18. Battle of Waterloo
19. Plantagenet
20. Longshanks

Quiz 117: By George

1. Who won his first acting Oscar for his performance in the 2004 espionage thriller 'Syriana'?

2. Georgetown is the capital city of which Commonwealth country?

3. Which actor played Mr Sulu in the original 'Star Trek' TV series?

4. Which pop star was born Georgios Kyriacos Panayiotou in June 1963?

5. Which actor played Hannibal in the 1980s TV series 'The A Team'?

6. Which author wrote that 'The reasonable man adapts himself to the world; the unreasonable one persists in trying to adapt the world to himself. Therefore all progress depends on the unreasonable man'?

7. Which flamboyant thrower was the runner-up in the World Darts Championship final in 1980 and 1984?

8. With which musical instrument is George Formby most commonly associated?

9. Which British diplomat-turned-KGB spy escaped from Wormwood Scrubs prison and fled to the Soviet Union in 1966?

10. Which Australian actress, whose credits include 'The Good Wife' and 'Grey's Anatomy', first found fame playing Angel Parrish in 'Home and Away'?

11. Eddie George was the governor of which financial institution from 1993 until 2003?

12. Which Northumberland-born engineer was the principal inventor of the railway locomotive?

13. Best known for playing Sir Humphrey in 'Yes, Minister', Nigel Hawthorne also received one Oscar nomination. For which film?

14. Which British boxer controversially lost a world super-middleweight title fight against Carl Froch in November 2013?

15. Who was nominated for his first Best Director Oscar in 1974 for the film 'American Graffiti'?

16. In 2014, The National Gallery spent £15.5m on a work entitled 'Men of the Docks'. Which American artist painted it?

17. Which 19th-century architect, known for the Gothic Revival style, designed the Albert Memorial and the St Pancras Hotel?

18. 'Adam Bede' was the first novel by which 19th-century novelist?

19. George North plays international rugby for which country?
a) Ireland   b) New Zealand   c) Wales

20. George Costanza was a character in which cult US comedy?
a) Family Guy   b) Seinfeld   c) South Park

MEDIUM

Answers to Quiz 116: Pot Luck

1. The FBI
2. Manchester
3. Pencils
4. World's Strongest Man
5. June
6. Jamaica
7. Kind Hearts and Coronets
8. Roald Dahl
9. Edd the Duck
10. False
11. Salford
12. Mexico
13. Countdown
14. Twelfth Night
15. A League of Their Own
16. November
17. Atlantic
18. Dirham
19. Irish state coach
20. 168

Quiz 118: Pot Luck

1. After 15 years and 30 series, which TV quiz show drew to a close in February 2014?

2. Which was the first American city to host the Summer Olympics?

3. Former MP Edwina Currie had a four-year affair with which British prime minister?

4. The Knight Riders is the nickname of an Indian Premier League cricket team based in which city?

5. In a UK plug, what colour is the neutral wire?

6. Which long-running West End play is based on a novel by John Buchan?

7. What was the name of the character played by Gregory Peck in the classic 1962 film 'To Kill a Mockingbird'?

8. True or false – the UK jury awarded the Abba song 'Waterloo' 'nul points' at the 1974 Eurovision Song Contest?

9. Which three colours appear on the flag of Trinidad and Tobago?

10. What nationality is the Formula One driver Felipe Massa?

11. Is the goal larger in a game of field hockey or ice hockey?

12. The DFB is football's governing body in which European country?

13. John Walton, Michael van Gerwen and Martin Adams have all been world champions in which sport?

14. In the Bible, Jesus was baptized in which river?

15. Which element of the periodic table has the chemical symbol K and the atomic number 19?

Answers – page 241

16. The football team Sampdoria is based in which Italian city?

17. Stephen Patrick are the Christian names of which controversial singer, usually referred to only by his surname?

18. Which country made its One Day International cricket debut in 1991?

19. Ascorbic acid is a form of which vitamin?
    a) vitamin A
    b) vitamin B
    c) vitamin C

20. Which British monarch was known as 'the mad king'?
    a) George I
    b) George II
    c) George III

MEDIUM

Answers to Quiz 117: By George

1. George Clooney
2. Guyana
3. George Takei
4. George Michael
5. George Peppard
6. George Bernard Shaw
7. Bobby George
8. Ukulele
9. George Blake
10. Melissa George
11. The Bank of England
12. George Stephenson
13. The Madness of King George
14. George Groves
15. George Lucas
16. George Bellows
17. Sir George Gilbert Scott
18. George Eliot
19. Wales
20. Seinfeld

Quiz 119: Play It Again, Sam

1. Samantha Sheffield is the maiden name of the wife of which British politician?

2. Which filmmaker directed the 2012 James Bond film 'Skyfall'?

3. Sam Malone was the central character in which long-running TV comedy?

4. Fat Sam Staccetto is a crime boss in which movie musical?

5. Which Scottish golfer sank the winning putt to win the 1985 Ryder Cup for the European team?

6. Who was 13th on the list of highest-paid football managers in the world in 2013?

7. Which singer had a number-two hit single in 1986 with 'Wonderful World' despite having been dead for over 20 years?

8. The 1955 song 'Love Me Or Leave Me' was the only UK top-ten hit for which American entertainer?

9. Which Hollywood star acted as a camera stand-in for Bill Cosby during the filming of the TV comedy 'The Cosby Show'?

10. 'Krapp's Last Tape' and 'Endgame' are works by which Dublin-born playwright?

11. The Arsenal and Manchester City footballer Samir Nasri plays international football for which country?

12. Which Antipodean actor played Inspector Chester Campbell in the BBC crime drama 'Peaky Blinders'?

13. Which Nottingham-born actress was nominated for Oscars in 2000 for 'Sweet and Lowdown' and in 2004 for 'In America'?

14. Sam Beckett was the central character in which time-travelling drama?

15. A character called Sam Weller appeared in which novel by Charles Dickens?

16. What is the American serial killer David Berkowitz more commonly known as?

17. Which Welshman captained the British and Irish Lions in the first two Tests of the 2013 series against Australia?

18. In which sport do teams compete for the Sam Maguire Cup?

19. Technology company Samsung was founded in which country?
    a) China   b) Japan   c) South Korea

20. Marlon Samuels plays international cricket for which country?
    a) Australia   b) South Africa   c) West Indies

MEDIUM

Answers to Quiz 118: Pot Luck

1. Who Wants to Be a Millionaire?
2. St Louis
3. John Major
4. Kolkata
5. Blue
6. The Thirty-Nine Steps
7. Atticus Finch
8. True
9. Red, white and black
10. Brazilian
11. Field hockey
12. Germany
13. Darts
14. River Jordan
15. Potassium
16. Genoa
17. Morrissey
18. South Africa
19. Vitamin C
20. George III

Quiz 120: Pot Luck

1. Edo is the former name of which Asian capital city?

2. 'Yes we can' is a campaign slogan associated with which American politician?

3. Gerry Dorsey is the real name of which veteran crooner?

4. Lion-O, Tygra and Cheetara were characters in which TV cartoon?

5. Which famous fictional diarist was 'Mad About the Boy' according to the title of a 2013 novel?

6. Scandinavian popsters A-ha performed the theme song to which James Bond film?

7. Which incumbent did Bill Clinton beat in the 1992 US Presidential election?

8. How many violins usually feature in a string quartet?

9. On a UK plug, what colour is the live wire?

10. What is the only capital city that features in the title of a Shakespeare play?

11. Who were the original captains on the TV panel show 'Give Us a Clue'?

12. Who is the patron saint of hopeless cases?

13. The flag of the African state Chad is the same as that of which European Union member country?

14. 'This Is Us', the fastest-selling DVD/Blu-ray title in UK history, is a fly-on-the-wall documetary featuring which band?

15. In Greek mythology, who was the father of Zeus?

16. What spirit is the main ingredient in a negroni cocktail?

17. Prior to Andy Murray, who was the last British player to win the Men's Singles at Wimbledon?

18. In May 2013, which Hollywood star underwent a double mastectomy operation because of a history of breast cancer in her family?

19. Which 'Fast Show' actor was the host of the TV quiz show 'The Link'?
    a) Charlie Higson
    b) Paul Whitehouse
    c) Mark Williams

20. What does the 'B' in the name of the union the GMB stand for?
    a) barristers
    b) boilermakers
    c) builders

MEDIUM

Answers to Quiz 119: Play It Again, Sam

1. David Cameron
2. Sam Mendes
3. Cheers
4. Bugsy Malone
5. Sam Torrance
6. Sam Allardyce
7. Sam Cooke
8. Sammy Davis Jr
9. Samuel L Jackson
10. Samuel Beckett
11. France
12. Sam Neill
13. Samantha Morton
14. Quantum Leap
15. The Pickwick Papers
16. Son of Sam
17. Sam Warburton
18. Gaelic football
19. South Korea
20. West Indies

Quiz 121: Music

1. Who is the only female solo artist to feature in the UK top ten best-selling albums of all time?

2. Lily Allen's 2013 hit 'Somewhere Only We Know' was originally recorded by which British band?

3. Which song by The Beatles includes the line, 'All the lonely people, where do they all belong'?

4. Which all-girl R&B act from the late 1990s had 'Bills Bills Bills' to pay?

5. Singer Van Morrison was born in which UK city?

6. Which band's first UK number one was the 1985 chart topper 'There Must Be an Angel (Playing With My Heart)'?

7. Which British singer's 2010 greatest-hits collection was called 'In and Out of Consciousness'?

8. In which decade did the UK singles chart first appear?

9. Which synth pop band have had 43 top-forty singles without ever reaching number one?

10. Which 1955 rock and roll classic was the UK's first million-selling single?

11. Which pop diva was 'Dirrty' in 2002?

12. 'Sie Liebt Dich' was a German-language version of which song by The Beatles?

13. Which band 'Crashed the Wedding' in 2003?

14. Which alliteratively-titled song was Elvis Presley's maiden UK chart hit?

15. Which woman's name provided Blondie with a 1999 number-one single?

16. Which crooner topped the first-ever UK album chart in 1955 with 'Songs for Swinging Lovers'?

17. One Direction were one of only two acts to have two albums amongst the top 40 best-selling albums of 2013. Which Canadian was the other?

18. Which ancient Roman town provided British rockers Bastille with the title of a 2013 hit single?

19. Complete the title of the hit single by One Republic – 'Counting ...'?
    a) Cash   b) Sheep   c) Stars

20. 'La La La' was a massive 2013 hit for which Watford-based producer?
    a) Cheeky Boy   b) Naughty Boy   c) Sneaky Boy

MEDIUM

Answers to Quiz 120: Pot Luck

1. Tokyo
2. Barack Obama
3. Engelbert Humperdinck
4. Thundercats
5. Bridget Jones
6. The Living Daylights
7. George H W Bush
8. Two
9. Brown
10. Athens (Timon of Athens)
11. Lionel Blair and Una Stubbs
12. St Jude
13. Romania
14. One Direction
15. Cronus
16. Gin
17. Fred Perry
18. Angelina Jolie
19. Mark Williams
20. Boilermakers

Quiz 122: Pot Luck

1. Which sport is played by a team called Catalan Dragons?

2. In 1969, PH Newey became the first winner of which prestigious literary award?

3. Thomas John Woodward is the real name of which pop legend?

4. In 1974, which group were 'Lonely This Christmas'?

5. Fill in the missing name – Tom Baker, ____, Sylvester McCoy, Colin Baker

6. In cricket, how many ways are there for a batsman to be dismissed?

7. 'The buck stops here' is a phrase associated with which American president?

8. In the cartoon 'Wacky Races', who drove a car called the Turbo Terrific?

9. True or false – comedian Dom Joly once stood in a parliamentary election representing a party called the Teddy Bear Alliance?

10. Fill in the blank – ME, XP, ____, 7

11. Which West End musical is based on the Puccini opera 'Madame Butterfly'?

12. New Road is the home ground of which English county cricket team?

13. The IWF is the global governing body for which Olympic sport?

14. According to the Bible story, how many people made it on to Noah's ark?

Answers – page 249

15. The character Roy of the Rovers first appeared in which comic?

16. The headquarters of the DVLA are in which British city?

17. Which soul singer performed the theme song to the James Bond film 'Licence to Kill'?

18. The Simpson Desert is in which Commonwealth country?

19. Are gorillas
    a) carnivores?
    b) herbivores?
    c) omnivores?

20. Who was the drummer with rock band Queen?
    a) Graham Taylor
    b) Phil Taylor
    c) Roger Taylor

MEDIUM

Answers to Quiz 121: Music

1. Adele
2. Keane
3. Eleanor Rigby
4. Destiny's Child
5. Belfast
6. Eurythmics
7. Robbie Williams
8. 1950s
9. Depeche Mode
10. Rock Around the Clock
11. Christina Aguilera
12. She Loves You
13. Busted
14. Heartbreak Hotel
15. Maria
16. Frank Sinatra
17. Michael Bublé
18. Pompeii
19. Stars
20. Naughty Boy

Quiz 123: North, South, East and West

1. What is Australia's largest state?

2. What is the name of the United States Military Academy in New York?

3. Erich Honecker was the leader of which country from 1971 until 1989?

4. 'Yeezus' was a 2013 album by which American hip-hop star?

5. Fargo is the largest city in which American state?

6. Published posthumously in 1817, 'Northanger Abbey' is a novel by which author?

7. Which team won the first ever Cricket World Cup?

8. Which actor won his first Oscar as a director in 1993 for the western 'Unforgiven'?

9. What nationality is the singer Psy, who enjoyed a global hit with 'Gangnam Style'?

10. Charleston is the capital city of which American state?

11. Which American state is nicknamed the 'Tar Heel State'?

12. Juba is the capital and largest city in which African country?

13. Morden is the southern terminus of which line on the London Underground?

14. What was the title of the Pet Shop Boys' debut single, which topped the charts in 1986?

15. The Doonhamers is the nickname of which Scottish football club?

16. Roots Hall is the home ground of which English football club?

17. Dili is the capital and largest city of which Asian sovereign state, which became independent in 2002?

18. Which actor played Detective Jimmy McNulty in the cult TV drama 'The Wire'?

19. What was the newspaper proprietor Alfred Harmsworth also known as?
a) Viscount Eastcliffe
b) Viscount Northcliffe
c) Viscount Westcliffe

20. 'North Country Boy' was a top-five hit in 1997 for which band?
a) The Charlatans
b) Oasis
c) Pulp

Answers to Quiz 122: Pot Luck

1. Rugby league
2. The Booker Prize
3. Tom Jones
4. Mud
5. Peter Davison (Dr Who actors)
6. Ten
7. Harry S Truman
8. Peter Perfect
9. True
10. Vista (Windows operating systems)
11. Miss Saigon
12. Worcestershire
13. Weightlifting
14. 8
15. Tiger
16. Swansea
17. Gladys Knight
18. Australia
19. Herbivores
20. Roger Taylor

Quiz 124: Pot Luck

1. In which decade was the Glastonbury Festival held for the first time?

2. The theme to a long-running radio panel show, what is Frédéric Chopin's piano waltz in D flat major, Opus 64, Number 1, more commonly known as?

3. Which country has the larger sheep population – the UK or the USA?

4. The story of David and Goliath appears in which book of the Old Testament?

5. Who is the only US president to have been honoured with a star on the Hollywood Walk of Fame?

6. 'Beware the Ides of March' is a line from which Shakespeare play?

7. Which English county hosted the opening stage of the 2014 Tour de France?

8. The church of St Saviour in the Marshes is the setting for which popular TV comedy?

9. In June 2013, Jose Mourinho succeeded which Spaniard as manager of Chelsea?

10. 'Le renard' is the French name for which animal?

11. Which celebrity chef is the founder of the restaurant '15'?

12. 'Always On My Mind' was a Christmas number-one single in 1987 for which band?

13. Which of the senses is also known as olfactory perception?

14. Which planet is named after the Roman god of agriculture?

15. Which film director said, 'Life is full of misery, loneliness, and suffering – and it's all over much too soon'?

16. What is the only country that is crossed by both the equator and the Tropic of Capricorn?

17. What type of creature is a Bombay duck?

18. 'At Speed' was the title of a 2013 book by which British world champion cyclist?

19. Where does the Northern Ireland football team play its home matches?
    a) Stuart Park
    b) Tudor Park
    c) Windsor Park

20. The first example of which labour-saving device was called 'Lazy Bones'?
    a) iron
    b) TV remote control
    c) vacuum cleaner

MEDIUM

Answers to Quiz 123: North, South, East and West

1. Western Australia	11. North Carolina
2. West Point	12. South Sudan
3. East Germany	13. Northern line
4. Kanye West	14. West End Girls
5. North Dakota	15. Queen of the South
6. Jane Austen	16. Southend United
7. West Indies	17. East Timor
8. Clint Eastwood	18. Dominic West
9. South Korean	19. Viscount Northcliffe
10. West Virginia	20. The Charlatans

Quiz 125: Television

1. 'Endeavour' and 'Evolve' were names of the teams in which 2013 reality TV series?

2. Miss Hoolie, PC Plum and an inventor called Archie are characters in which children's TV show?

3. 'Insomnia Cafe' was the working title for which long-running American sitcom?

4. What is the name of the 'idiot' in the TV travel series 'An Idiot Abroad'?

5. Which former EastEnder plays Sandy Roscoe in the TV soap 'Hollyoaks'?

6. The hit comedy 'The Big Bang Theory' is set in which American state?

7. 'Florizel Street' was the working title of which British drama?

8. Which christian name was shared by the TV detectives Rockford, Taggart and Bergerac?

9. The Mysterons were the arch-enemy of which puppet character?

10. 16 Elwood Avenue, Torquay was the address of which classic sitcom establishment?

11. In what type of establishment was the sitcom 'Only When I Laugh' set?

12. Hastings is the unlikely setting for which wartime TV detective drama?

13. Fred Scuttle was a character created by which TV comedian?

14. Tour guide Brendan Sheerin appears on which travel-based reality TV show?

15. The 'CSI' TV franchise has had series set in which three American cities?

16. Ronnie Corbett played Timothy Lumsden in which sitcom?

17. Which quiz show, still running today, was first broadcast on 5 January 1970?

18. A random number generator called 'Cecil' is a feature of which TV show?

19. John Altman played which soap bad boy?
    a) Nick Cotton
    b) Terry Duckworth
    c) Barry Grant

20. Alicia Florrick is the central character in which legal and political drama?
    a) The Good Daughter
    b) The Good Sister
    c) The Good Wife

MEDIUM

Answers to Quiz 124: Pot Luck

1. 1970s
2. The Minute Waltz
3. The UK
4. Samuel
5. Ronald Reagan
6. Julius Caesar
7. Yorkshire
8. Rev
9. Rafael Benitez
10. Fox
11. Jamie Oliver
12. The Pet Shop Boys
13. Smell
14. Saturn
15. Woody Allen
16. Brazil
17. Fish
18. Mark Cavendish
19. Windsor Park
20. TV remote control

Quiz 126: Pot Luck

1. Which animal is known in French as 'le canard'?

2. True or false – only male bees can sting?

3. America bought Alaska from which country?

4. Soldier Field and Wrigley Field are sporting venues in which American city?

5. Cut-Throat Jake was the arch-nemesis of which fictional sailor?

6. Lhasa Apso is a breed of which animal?

7. Which breed of dog takes its name from the German for 'snout'?

8. In cricket's Indian Premier League, the team nicknamed the Royal Challengers is based in which city?

9. The phrase 'round up the usual suspects' first appeared in which classic 1942 film?

10. Robert Norman Davis is the real name of which English comedian, actor and game-show host?

11. What nationality was the singer Jacques Brel?

12. HIGNFY are the initials of which TV panel show?

13. True or false – comedian Jimmy Carr graduated from Cambridge University with a 2:1 degree in political science?

14. 'If music be the food of love, play on' is a line from which Shakespeare play?

15. By what name are the musical brothers Charlie and Craig Reid collectively known?

16. A pentadecagon is a shape with how many sides?

17. Which mythological creature was half man and half bull?

18. Who were the original team captains on the TV quiz show 'A Question of Sport' (one was a rugby player, the other a boxer)?

19. In 2011, Donald Tusk was re-elected as the prime minister of which country?
    a) Belgium
    b) Norway
    c) Poland

20. What was the name of the first permanent English settlement in America?
    a) Henrytown
    b) Jamestown
    c) Williamstown

Answers to Quiz 125: Television

1. The Apprentice
2. Balamory
3. Friends
4. Karl Pilkington
5. Gillian Taylforth
6. California
7. Coronation Street
8. Jim
9. Captain Scarlet
10. Fawlty Towers
11. A hospital
12. Foyle's War
13. Benny Hill
14. Coach Trip
15. Las Vegas, Miami and New York
16. Sorry!
17. A Question of Sport
18. Countdown
19. Nick Cotton
20. The Good Wife

Quiz 127: Fill In the Blank – Movies

Fill in the missing word from the titles of these Oscar-winning films:

1. The Hurt ____ (2009)

2. Million Dollar ____ (2004)

3. A Beautiful ____ (2001)

4. ____ in Love (1998)

5. The ____ Emperor (1987)

6. Terms of ____ (1983)

7. ____ People (1980)

8. The ____ Hunter (1978)

9. A Man for All ____ (1966)

10. All About ____ (1950)

11. All the ____ Men (1949)

12. Gentleman's ____ (1947)

13. The Best ____ of Our Lives (1946)

14. The Lost ____ (1945)

15. ____ My Way (1944)

16. Mrs ____ (1942)

17. How Green Was My ____ (1941)

18. The Life of Emile ____ (1936)

19. The ____ Ziegfeld (1935)

20. It ____ One Night (1934)

Answers to Quiz 126: Pot Luck

1. The duck
2. False
3. Russia
4. Chicago
5. Captain Pugwash
6. Dog
7. Schnauzer
8. Bangalore
9. Casablanca
10. Jasper Carrott
11. Belgian
12. Have I Got News for You
13. True
14. Twelfth Night
15. The Proclaimers
16. 15
17. Minotaur
18. Cliff Morgan and Henry Cooper
19. Poland
20. Jamestown

Quiz 128: Pot Luck

1. The Mound Stand, the Tavern Stand, and the Edrich and Compton Stands are features of which famous sporting venue?

2. The Gaelic name Seamus is the equivalent of what English name?

3. Which distance is longer, three feet or one metre?

4. Seismology is the scientific study of what?

5. What is 20% of 75?

6. Who sang the theme song to the James Bond film, 'The Man with the Golden Gun'?

7. Who won more Olympic gold medals – Sir Chris Hoy or Sir Steve Redgrave?

8. Frequently played at the end of wedding ceremonies, which composer wrote the 'Wedding March'?

9. What are the five African countries whose names start with the letter G?

10. What name is given to a gathering of a group of witches?

11. Which current Liberal Democrat politician represented Great Britain in the 200m sprint at the 1964 Olympics?

12. The most westerly point of mainland Europe is in which country?

13. Which current commentator is the only athlete to have been a permanent team captain on the TV quiz show 'A Question of Sport'?

14. Which sport is played at venues called the WACA, Sabina Park and the Wankhede Stadium?

15. Dar Es Salaam is the largest city in which East African country?

16. The town of Lourdes, visited by millions of pilgrims each year, is in which country?

17. Siam is the former name of which country?

18. AKL is the airport code for which southern hemisphere city?

19. Musician Bob Dylan was born and raised in which American state?
    a) Alaska
    b) California
    c) Minnesota

20. Which sport is played at an American venue called Valhalla?
    a) golf
    b) motor racing
    c) tennis

MEDIUM

Answers to Quiz 127: Fill In the Blank – Movies

1. The Hurt Locker
2. Million Dollar Baby
3. A Beautiful Mind
4. Shakespeare in Love
5. The Last Emperor
6. Terms of Endearment
7. Ordinary People
8. The Deer Hunter
9. A Man for All Seasons
10. All About Eve
11. All The King's Men
12. Gentleman's Agreement
13. The Best Years of Our Lives
14. The Lost Weekend
15. Going My Way
16. Mrs Miniver
17. How Green Was My Valley
18. The Life of Emile Zola
19. The Great Ziegfeld
20. It Happened One Night

Quiz 129: The Bible

1. In the Bible, Adam and Eve had three children. What were their names?

2. In the King James Bible, which book follows the four Gospels?

3. What did Judas Iscariot receive as a reward for betraying Jesus?

4. What was the name of the brother of Mary and Martha whom Jesus raised from the dead according to John's Gospel?

5. By what name is the series of precepts called the Decalogue better known?

6. The Old Testament was written in which language?

7. Which book of the Bible recalls the story of the Jews' escape from Egypt?

8. If the books of the Old Testament were listed alphabetically, which book would come first?

9. And which book would come last?

10. In the Old Testament, what is the name of Moses' elder brother?

11. According to John's Gospel, Jesus turned water into wine at a feast in which village?

12. What are the two books of the Old Testament that are named after women?

13. Who was chosen to replace Judas Iscariot as one of the 12 apostles after Judas betrayed Jesus?

14. What was the name of the mother of John the Baptist?

15. The name of which biblical queen is often used to describe a scheming, evil woman?

16. According to the Book of Genesis, which two notorious cities were destroyed by burning sulphur?

17. What is the fifth book of the Old Testament?

18. What is the name of the wooden chest believed to contain the stone tablets on which the Ten Commandments were written?

19. Which of the four Gospels is not described as a 'synoptic' Gospel?
    a) John
    b) Luke
    c) Matthew

20. Which of the 12 apostles was a tax collector?
    a) Matthew
    b) Peter
    c) Thomas

Answers to Quiz 128: Pot Luck

1. Lord's cricket ground
2. James
3. One metre
4. Earthquakes
5. 15
6. Lulu
7. Sir Chris Hoy
8. Mendelssohn
9. Gabon, Gambia, Ghana, Guinea and Guinea-Bissau
10. A coven
11. Menzies Campbell
12. Portugal
13. Brendan Foster
14. Cricket
15. Tanzania
16. France
17. Thailand
18. Auckland
19. Minnesota
20. Golf

Quiz 130: Pot Luck

1. Hattie McDaniel, the first African-American to win an Oscar, did so in which classic 1939 film?

2. On which radio panel show must contestants talk for sixty seconds on a given subject 'without repetition, hesitation or deviation'?

3. What were the first two countries to co-host football's World Cup?

4. Which classic 1990 science-fiction film, remade in 2012, was based on a short story called 'We Can Remember It for You Wholesale'?

5. True or false – horse long jump was once an event at the Olympic Games?

6. Who is older – Robert Downey Jr or Ben Stiller?

7. 'Ooh you are awful ... but I like you' was a catchphrase of which comedian?

8. True or false – US politician Sarah Palin is a second cousin of Monty Python star Michael Palin?

9. Janette and Ian Tough are the real names of which Scottish comedy duo?

10. Herat, Kandahar and Jalalabad are cities in which Asian country?

11. In the legal profession, what do the initials QC stand for?

12. The flag of Lithuania features which three colours?

13. Which award-winning British film-maker directed the films 'Kes', 'Looking for Eric' and 'The Wind That Shakes the Barley'?

14. Which England football captain started his professional career at West Bromwich Albion and enjoyed success at Manchester United before ending his playing career at Middlesbrough?

15. Luxembourg shares borders with which three countries?

16. Which ventriloquist created the characters Orville the Duck and Cuddles the Monkey?

17. The Footlights is a dramatic club run by students at which English university?

18. According to the 1999 film, what is the first rule of 'Fight Club'?

19. The winners of tournaments at the World Series of Poker are awarded what type of jewellery?
    a) bracelet   b) medal   c) ring

20. In which country was the actress Amy Adams born?
    a) France   b) Italy   c) Russia

MEDIUM

Answers to Quiz 129: The Bible

1. Cain, Abel and Seth
2. Acts of the Apostles
3. 30 pieces of silver
4. Lazarus
5. The Ten Commandments
6. Hebrew
7. Exodus
8. Amos
9. Zephaniah
10. Aaron
11. Cana
12. Ruth and Esther
13. Matthias
14. Elizabeth
15. Jezebel
16. Sodom and Gomorrah
17. Deuteronomy
18. Ark of the Covenant
19. John
20. Matthew

Quiz 131: Political Nicknames

Identify the political figure associated with the following nicknames:

1. The Iron Lady

2. Dubya

3. Two Jags

4. Teflon Tony

5. Flashman

6. 14 Pints

7. Chat Show Charlie

8. Tarzan

9. The Clunking Fist

10. The Prince of Darkness

11. Mad Nad

12. The Beast of Bolsover

13. The Grey Man

14. The Bicycling Baronet

15. The Quiet Man

MEDIUM

16. Beaker

17. The Chingford Skinhead

18. The Comeback Kid

19. Two Brains

20. Gorbals Mick

Answers to Quiz 130: Pot Luck

1. Gone with the Wind
2. Just a Minute
3. South Korea and Japan
4. Total Recall
5. True
6. Robert Downey Jr
7. Dick Emery
8. False
9. The Krankies
10. Afghanistan
11. Queen's Counsel
12. Red, yellow and green
13. Ken Loach
14. Bryan Robson
15. Belgium, France and Germany
16. Keith Harris
17. Cambridge
18. You do not talk about Fight Club
19. Bracelet
20. Italy

MEDIUM

Quiz 132: Pot Luck

1. The 1819 Peterloo Massacre occurred in which English city?

2. Who is older – Boris Johnson or Nigel Farage?

3. What order of Roman Catholic monks is also the name of a type of monkey?

4. Who said, 'What is a cynic? A man who knows the price of everything and the value of nothing'?

5. 'Mama Grizzly' is the nickname of which controversial US politician?

6. Ganymede is the largest moon of which planet of the Solar System?

7. The classic film 'The Shawshank Redemption' was based on a short story by which author?

8. Ian Hislop is the editor of which satirical magazine, first published in 1961?

9. What are the eight African countries whose names are made up of five letters?

10. Which US public figure has the Twitter handle @FLOTUS?

11. True or false – George Clooney appeared in the TV soap Dynasty?

12. Which former Soviet republic is also the name of a state in the USA?

13. Ewood Park is the home ground of which football team?

14. Montego Bay is the second largest city in which Commonwealth country?

15. The Braves, Falcons and Hawks are professional sports teams based in which American city?

16. Which element of the periodic table has the chemical symbol F and the atomic number 9?

17. Which actor received his first Best Actor Oscar nomination for his performance in the 1992 film 'Chaplin'?

18. What American federal holiday is observed each year on the third Monday in January?

19. The Church of Jesus Christ of Latter-day Saints is based in which American state?
a) California
b) New York
c) Utah

20. In 2012, 'Blue Peter' presenter Helen Skelton became the first person to reach the South Pole on what?
a) a bike
b) roller skates
c) a skateboard

MEDIUM

Answers to Quiz 131: Political Nicknames

1. Margaret Thatcher
2. George W Bush
3. John Prescott
4. Tony Blair
5. David Cameron
6. William Hague
7. Charles Kennedy
8. Michael Heseltine
9. Gordon Brown
10. Peter Mandelson
11. Nadine Dorries
12. Dennis Skinner
13. John Major
14. Sir George Young
15. Iain Duncan Smith
16. Danny Alexander
17. Norman Tebbit
18. Bill Clinton
19. David Willetts
20. Michael Martin

Quiz 133: Anagrams

Rearrange the letters to make the name of an English county:

1. Wire Rickshaw

2. Had Rum

3. Claw Lorn

4. Tree Moss

5. Her Mishap

6. I Arm Cub

7. Relish Wit

8. Off Sulk

9. Riches Eh

10. Hires Kerb

11. Hides Berry

12. Cleans Hair

13. Dasher Riffs To

14. Leeriest Riches

15. If Herds Bored

16. Lard Nut

17. Her Shop Sir

18. Blamed North Run

19. Chestier Rowers

20. Restore Whisky

MEDIUM

Answers to Quiz 132: Pot Luck

1. Manchester
2. Nigel Farage
3. Capuchin
4. Oscar Wilde
5. Sarah Palin
6. Jupiter
7. Stephen King
8. Private Eye
9. Benin, Egypt, Gabon, Ghana, Kenya, Libya, Niger and Sudan
10. First Lady of the United States (Michelle Obama)
11. False
12. Georgia
13. Blackburn Rovers
14. Jamaica
15. Atlanta
16. Fluorine
17. Robert Downey Jr
18. Martin Luther King Day
19. Utah
20. A bike

Quiz 134: Pot Luck

1. The port city of Agadir is in which African country?

2. Emiliano Zapata was a revolutionary figure in which country?

3. Which 20th-century British prime minister was nicknamed the 'Welsh Wizard'?

4. The island of Tristan da Cunha is in which ocean?

5. The Guardian newspaper was founded in which English city?

6. Which body of water was at one time known as the German Sea?

7. A tetradecagon is a shape with how many sides?

8. 'If you want to find Cherry Tree Lane all you have to do is ask a policeman at the crossroads' is the opening line of which classic children's novel?

9. 'On Liberty' is the most famous work by which 19th-century English philosopher?

10. WSJ are the initials of which American newspaper?

11. Cars in South Africa drive on which side of the road?

12. In which decade was the RAF founded?

13. RIBA is a professional organization for people with what occupation?

14. 'Claire' is the alter ego of which renowned British artist?

15. Titan is the largest moon of which planet of the Solar System?

Answers – page 139

16. Which British film-maker was named one of the '100 Most Influential People in the World' in 2014 according to Time magazine?

17. British Army unit the SAS is based in which city?

18. 'No plan like yours to study history wisely' is a mnemonic to remember what?

19. A deltiologist is a collector of what?
    a) coins
    b) key rings
    c) postcards

20. Which of the following is the name of a Somerset village?
    a) Curry Anvil
    b) Curry Hammer
    c) Curry Mallet

MEDIUM

Answers to Quiz 133: Anagrams

1. Warwickshire
2. Durham
3. Cornwall
4. Somerset
5. Hampshire
6. Cumbria
7. Wiltshire
8. Suffolk
9. Cheshire
10. Berkshire
11. Derbyshire
12. Lancashire
13. Staffordshire
14. Leicestershire
15. Bedfordshire
16. Rutland
17. Shropshire
18. Northumberland
19. Worcestershire
20. West Yorkshire

DIFFICULT QUIZZES

Quiz 135: Pot Luck

1. Ernest Hemingway's novel 'A Farewell to Arms' was set during which conflict?

2. Which Anglo-Australian actress and singer co-founded the drinks company Koala Blue Wines?

3. Which city will host the 2018 Commonwealth Games?

4. What is the musical note known in America as a sixteenth note more commonly known as in the UK?

5. 'March of the Volunteers' is the national anthem of which Asian country?

6. In 2011, Yingluck Shinawatra became the first female prime minister of which Asian country?

7. The 1960 film 'Saturday Night and Sunday Morning' is set in which English city?

8. Robin Williams played which American president in the 2013 film 'The Butler'?

9. In the 'Harry Potter' books and films, what type of animal is Hedwig?

10. The annual Latitude festival is held in which English county?

11. Portly politician Chris Christie is the governor of which American state?

12. Which American soldier was given a 35-year prison sentence in 2013 after leaking confidential documents to Wikileaks?

13. The London skyscraper nicknamed 'The Cheese Grater' was designed by which architect?

14. In November 2013, a space mission to Mars was launched by which Asian country?

DIFFICULT

15. Yasmina Siadatan and Michelle Dewberry are former winners of which TV show?

16. Dominika Cibulkova became the first woman from which country to reach a Grand Slam tennis final at the 2014 Australian Open?

17. In 2011, Helle Thorning-Schmidt became the first female prime minister of which country?

18. How old was Nelson Mandela when he died?

19. What was the artist Jackson Pollock's first name?
    a) John
    b) Paul
    c) George

20. +86 is the international dialling code for which Asian country?
    a) China
    b) India
    c) Japan

Answers to Quiz 200: Movies part 2

1. Crash
2. A Beautiful Mind
3. Graham Greene
4. Stephen
5. Mark Kermode
6. True
7. Hamlet
8. A César
9. Mexican
10. Live and Let Die
11. Tom Cruise
12. Arnold Schwarzenegger
13. Rome
14. C-3PO
15. Lupita Nyong'o
16. Venice
17. The Hurt Locker
18. Carry On Cruising
19. Movie 43
20. Indonesia

DIFFICULT

Quiz 136: Connections part 1

1. What is the name of the prize awarded to the best film at the Venice Film Festival?

2. Armando Perez is the real name of which rapper, who topped the UK charts in 2014 with 'Timber'?

3. Which Englishman, born in Leicestershire in 1624, was the founder of the religious movement known as the Society of Friends?

4. 'Desire' was U2's first UK number-one single. Which 1991 hit was their second?

5. What was the title of the only UK number one from Tight Fit?

6. What was the name of the popular TV comedy drama that starred Adam Faith as Ronald Bird?

7. In 2009, Susan Boyle had a top-ten UK hit single with a cover of which song by the Rolling Stones?

8. What is the name of the actress who played DS Mel Silver in 'Waking The Dead', Inspector Rachel Weston in 'The Bill', and nurse Tina Seabrook in 'Casualty'?

9. 'Suck It and See' was the title of a chart-topping 2011 album by which Yorkshire rockers?

10. Which long-running TV show was hosted by Phil Drabble and later Robin Page, Ben Fogle and Matt Baker?

11. What is the nickname of the rugby league Super League team based in Warrington?

12. Burgess Meredith and Danny DeVito have both played which big-screen baddie?

13. What was the title of Prince's first UK top-five single?

Answers – page 279

14. What was the name of the character played by Danny John-Jules in cult science-fiction comedy 'Red Dwarf'?

15. What was the only UK top-ten hit for the Bahamian band the Baha Men?

16. Ophidiphobia is the fear of what?

17. 'I Don't Like Mondays' was a number-one hit in 1979 for which band?

18. Which actor played Archie Mitchell in 'EastEnders' and Michael Shipman in 'Gavin and Stacey'?

19. What was the title of a 2000 film starring Piper Perabo, Adam Garcia and John Goodman?
    a) Badger Ugly
    b) Coyote Ugly
    c) Hyena Ugly

20. What is the connection between the answers?

Answers to Quiz 135: Pot Luck

1. The First World War	11. New Jersey
2. Olivia Newton-John	12. Bradley Manning
3. Gold Coast	13. Richard Rogers
4. A semiquaver	14. India
5. China	15. The Apprentice
6. Thailand	16. Slovakia
7. Nottingham	17. Denmark
8. Dwight Eisenhower	18. 95
9. Owl	19. Paul
10. Suffolk	20. China

DIFFICULT

Quiz 137: Pot Luck

1. Which was the first British city to be named European Capital of Culture?

2. Which economist said that 'the avoidance of taxes is the only intellectual pursuit that still carries any reward'?

3. What do the initials 'HW' stand for in the name of former US president George H W Bush?

4. In which country was the England cricketer Chris Jordan born?

5. In relation to a combat sport, what do the initials UFC stand for?

6. In the police drama 'DCI Banks', what is the title character's first name?

7. John Cusack, Sir Anthony Hopkins and Frank Langella have all played which US president on the big screen?

8. Drenthe, Flevoland and Friesland are provinces of which European country?

9. 'Fortune's Fool', 'A Provincial Lady' and 'A Month in the Country' are plays by which 19th-century Russian playwright?

10. Which director's films include 'Clerks', 'Jay and Silent Bob Strike Back' and 'Red State'?

11. What does the 'E' in the financial acronym EBITDA stand for?

12. A barman called Desmond Miles is the central character in which video-game franchise?

13. Baron Silas Greenback and his henchman Stiletto Mafiosa were characters in which children's animation?

14. 'Morning again in America' was a campaign slogan associated with which American president?

15. Sheldon, Yardley and Small Heath are areas of which English city?

16. Thousands of people were killed in late 2013 after Super Typhoon Haiyan devastated large parts of which Asian country?

17. The Quantock Hills are in which English county?

18. How old was Margaret Thatcher when she died?

19. Bjørn Dæhlie, the most successful Winter Olympian of all time, won eight gold medals in which sport?
a) bobsleigh
b) cross-country skiing
c) curling

20. How long is the University Boat Race course?
a) 3 miles 374 yards
b) 4 miles 374 yards
c) 5 miles 374 yards

Answers to Quiz 136: Connections part 1

1. Golden Lion
2. Pitbull
3. George Fox
4. The Fly
5. The Lion Sleeps Tonight
6. Budgie
7. Wild Horses
8. Claire Goose
9. Arctic Monkeys
10. One Man and His Dog
11. Wolves
12. The Penguin
13. When Doves Cry
14. The Cat
15. Who Let the Dogs Out?
16. Snakes
17. The Boomtown Rats
18. Larry Lamb
19. Coyote Ugly
20. They all contain an animal

DIFFICULT

Quiz 138: Fashion

1. Which politician gives his name to a hip-length tailored jacket with a round, mandarin collar?

2. Which hand-woven cloth is the UK's oldest registered trademark?

3. What nationality is the designer Issey Miyake?

4. The name of what item of underwear can also mean 'a flip-flop' in Australia?

5. Ralph Lauren and Calvin Klein were both born in which city?

6. A grabatologist is someone who likes to collect what item of clothing?

7. The 'New Look' was a style associated with which fashion designer?

8. Which fashion designer created the kit for the British team at the 2012 Olympic Games?

9. Which French fashion brand was the first to put a logo (an animal) on the outside, rather than the inside of its clothing?

10. Christian Louboutin is a notable designer of what?

11. The four major international fashion weeks are hosted in which cities?

12. Which American fashion designer directed the Oscar-nominated film 'A Single Man'?

13. Which high-street clothes shop was founded in 1969 by Americans Donald and Doris Fisher?

14. Which fashion designer was runner-up on the reality TV show 'I'm a Celebrity ... Get Me Out of Here' in 2013?

Answers – page 283

15. An equestrian knight containing the Latin word 'Prorsum' features on the logo of which British fashion brand?

16. Which designer created Catherine Middleton's wedding dress?

17. Espadrilles are worn on what part of the body?

18. What are the first names of the Italian design duo Dolce and Gabbana?

19. Model Alek Wek was born in which country?
    a) China
    b) India
    c) Sudan

20. Where on the body would a brassard be worn?
    a) on the arm
    b) on the feet
    c) on the head

Answers to Quiz 137: Pot Luck

1. Glasgow
2. John Maynard Keynes
3. Herbert Walker
4. Barbados
5. Ultimate Fighting Championship
6. Alan
7. Richard Nixon
8. The Netherlands
9. Ivan Turgenev
10. Kevin Smith
11. Earnings
12. Assassin's Creed
13. Danger Mouse
14. Ronald Reagan
15. Birmingham
16. The Philippines
17. Somerset
18. 87
19. Cross-country skiing
20. 4 miles 374 yards

DIFFICULT

Quiz 139: Pot Luck

1. Which Australian rock group produces fine wines called 'Back in Black Shiraz' and 'Hells Bells Sauvignon Blanc'?

2. 'Most men pursue pleasure with such breathless haste that they hurry past it' is a quote attributed to which Danish philosopher?

3. The capital of which former Soviet Republic was the European City of Culture in 2014?

4. René Redzepi is chef and co-owner of which Copenhagen restaurant, which was voted the world's best in 2011 and 2012?

5. What do the initials 'HG' stand for in the name HG Wells?

6. A men's lacrosse team is made up of how many players?

7. Which fictional dog took his name from a line in the Frank Sinatra song 'Strangers in the Night'?

8. Which British artist's work 'George Dyer Talking' was sold for £42.2m in February 2014?

9. Which English town was also the middle name of the American writer Hunter S Thompson?

10. A dim-witted construction worker named Emmett is the central character in which hit 2014 film animation?

11. Harris, home of the famous tweed, is part of which island group?

12. In feet, how high from the ground is a football goal's crossbar?

13. Journalist AA Gill won the 'Hatchet Job of the Year' in 2014 for his review of the autobiography of which singer?

14. In which decade was the first FA Cup final staged?

15. In which combat sport is Britain's Michael Bisping a notable name?

16. The breed of dog known as the Great Dane actually originated in which country?

17. Men's Olympic walking races take place over what two distances?

18. Australian athlete Sally Pearson won gold at the 2012 Olympics in which track event?

19. What is the name of the river that separates the Australian states of Victoria and New South Wales?
a) River Bruce
b) River Murray
c) River Sheila

20. Which British music festival takes place at a venue known as Little John's Farm?
a) Glastonbury
b) Reading
c) T in the Park

Answers to Quiz 138: Fashion

1. Jawaharlal Nehru
2. Harris Tweed
3. Japanese
4. Thong
5. New York
6. Ties
7. Christian Dior
8. Stella McCartney
9. Lacoste
10. Shoes
11. New York, London, Milan and Paris
12. Tom Ford
13. Gap
14. David Emanuel
15. Burberry
16. Sarah Burton
17. Feet
18. Domenico and Stefano
19. Sudan
20. On the arm

DIFFICULT

Quiz 140: Alliterative Answers part 1

1. Which American, who won Wimbledon in 1972, gave his name to an iconic pair of trainers produced by Adidas?

2. What is the name of the actress who plays Bianca in TV soap 'EastEnders'?

3. Most of which award-winning playwright's works were premiered at the Stephen Joseph Theatre, Scarborough?

4. Manny Bianco and Fran Katzenjammer were characters in which literary sitcom?

5. Which football manager steered Arsenal to the League title in 1989/90 and 1990/91?

6. 'Boom Boom' was the nickname of which Wimbledon winner?

7. Ant and Dec starred in which 2006 film comedy about a pair of British lads who faked a documentary about a UFO crash in New Mexico?

8. Which British actor impersonated opera singer Luciano Pavarotti on TV talent show 'Stars In Their Eyes'?

9. Which American musician and composer had a top-ten hit in 1983 with 'Rockit'?

10. What was the title of the 2012 film starring Elizabeth Olsen who tries to re-integrate into her family after fleeing a cult?

11. Which former 'Bond girl' partnered Anton Du Beke in the 2013 series of 'Strictly Come Dancing'?

12. The 1960 film 'The Magnificent Seven' was a western-style remake of which Japanese classic?

13. Which British actor, who died in 2011, received his only Oscar nomination for his performance in the 1993 film 'In the Name of the Father'?

Answers – page 287

14. Which footballer was sent off in the 2006 World Cup final after headbutting an opponent?

15. What is the name of the German spa town that lies alongside the Oos River in the Black Forest?

16. What is the name of the American reality TV show about an animal business run by Louisiana's Robertson family?

17. Who was the only English player to win the European Footballer of the Year award in the 1970s?

18. Which Hollywood star's film credits include 'Dodgeball', 'Swingers', 'The Internship' and 'The Wedding Crashers'?

19. Who was nominated for a Best Actress Oscar in 2014 for her performance in 'American Hustle'?

20. Which singer and actress played Aunty Entity in the 1985 apocalyptic thriller 'Mad Max: Beyond the Thunderdome'?

Answers to Quiz 139: Pot Luck

1. AC/DC
2. Søren Kierkegaard
3. Latvia (Riga)
4. Noma
5. Herbert George
6. Ten
7. Scooby Doo
8. Francis Bacon
9. Stockton
10. The Lego Movie
11. Outer Hebrides
12. Eight feet
13. Morrissey
14. 1870s
15. Mixed Martial Arts
16. Germany
17. 20km and 50km
18. 100m hurdles
19. River Murray
20. Reading

DIFFICULT

Quiz 141: Pot Luck

1. The aviation term 'dogfight' originated during which conflict?

2. RAMC are the initials of which corps of the British army?

3. 'Finlandia' is a piece of music by which classical composer?

4. Bob 'Bulldog' Briscoe, Gil Chesterton and Chopper Dave were characters in which long-running US sitcom?

5. Which Scottish actor played Cardinal Richelieu in the 2014 TV drama 'The Musketeers'?

6. What is the capital city of the Indian state of Tamil Nadu?

7. Which mountain range takes its name from the Sanskrit words for snow and abode?

8. Classical musician Boris Berezovsky is an accomplished performer on which instrument?

9. Which businessman and football-club chairman founded the retailer Sports Direct?

10. Manu Tuilagi plays international rugby union for which country?

11. In 2014, who succeeded Michael Bloomberg as the mayor of New York?

12. Who is the only footballer to have both captained and managed a World Cup-winning team?

13. Who said, 'Good resolutions are simply cheques that men draw on a bank where they have no account'?

14. Which British band were the most streamed artists during 2013?

15. Which cartoon character lived at 52 Festive Road?

16. In relation to education, what do the initials UCAS stand for?

17. Which comedian penned the 2013 children's book 'Demon Dentist'?

18. Which American author wrote, 'At 18 our convictions are hills from which we look; at 45 they are caves in which we hide'?

19. Which Conservative Party politician wrote the 2003 novel 'The Devil's Tune'?
    a) Edwina Currie
    b) Iain Duncan Smith
    c) Ann Widdecombe

20. Jazz musician Scott Hamilton is best known for playing which instrument?
    a) piano
    b) saxophone
    c) trumpet

Answers to Quiz 140: Alliterative Answers part 1

1. Stan Smith
2. Patsy Palmer
3. Sir Alan Ayckbourn
4. Black Books
5. George Graham
6. Boris Becker
7. Alien Autopsy
8. Brian Blessed
9. Herbie Hancock
10. Martha Marcy May Marlene
11. Fiona Fullerton
12. Seven Samurai
13. Pete Postlethwaite
14. Zinedine Zidane
15. Baden-Baden
16. Duck Dynasty
17. Kevin Keegan
18. Vince Vaughn
19. Amy Adams
20. Tina Turner

DIFFICULT

Quiz 142: Seconds Out

1. What is the second-largest city in South Africa?

2. Which world champion was the only British athlete to win a silver medal on the track at the 2012 Olympics?

3. Soviet airman Yuri Gagarin was the first man to travel into space. Who was the second?

4. What is the second-largest island in the Mediterranean Sea?

5. What is the second-largest country in South America by area?

6. Aarhus is the second-largest city in which European country?

7. What was the second film in the 'Carry On' series?

8. Which 59-year-old finished second in the 2009 Open Golf Championship?

9. What is the second-longest river in Europe?

10. Which country won the World Cup for the second time in 1950?

11. What is the second book in the Harry Potter series of novels?

12. Dehiwala-Mount Lavinia is the second city of which Commonwealth country?

13. Which Welsh rugby player finished second in the voting for the 2013 Sports Personality of the Year Award?

14. Which country was runner-up in the World Cup in 1974, 1978 and 2010?

15. Mindanao is the second-largest island of which Asian country?

16. Sir Roger Bannister was the first man to run a four-minute mile. Which Australian runner was the second?

17. Which was the first country to lose in the World Cup final not once but twice?

18. What is the second most expensive property on a London 'Monopoly' board?

19. Who was the second president of the USA?
    a) John Adams
    b) Benjamin Franklin
    c) Thomas Jefferson

20. In terms of population, Mumbai is India's largest city. What is the second largest?
    a) Bangalore
    b) Chennai
    c) Delhi

Answers to Quiz 141: Pot Luck

1. World War One
2. Royal Army Medical Corps
3. Sibelius
4. Frasier
5. Peter Capaldi
6. Chennai
7. The Himalayas
8. Piano
9. Mike Ashley
10. England
11. Bill de Blasio
12. Franz Beckenbauer
13. Oscar Wilde
14. Arctic Monkeys
15. Mr Benn
16. Universities and Colleges Admission Service
17. David Walliams
18. F Scott Fitzgerald
19. Iain Duncan Smith
20. Saxophone

DIFFICULT

Quiz 143: Pot Luck

1. Which US Army general, who later had a missile named after him, commanded the American Expeditionary Forces in Europe during the First World War?

2. Which journalist, critic, TV presenter and poet was shortlisted for a prize at the 2014 Costa Book Awards for a translation of Dante's 'The Divine Comedy'?

3. Which stand-up comic stars in the comedy show 'Much A-Stew About Nothing'?

4. Who is older – Sir Tom Jones or Sir Cliff Richard?

5. In which decade did the first commercial airline flight take place?

6. Perugia is the capital city of which region of Italy?

7. In 2006, Gurbanguly Berdymukhammedov became the presdient of which former Soviet Republic?

8. Which record label, noted for its soul and R&B artists, was founded by Jim Stewart and his sister Estelle Axton in 1960?

9. Which African country is the largest producer of cocoa in the world?

10. What is the name of the BAFTA-winning actor who plays children's TV favourite Mr Tumble?

11. What is the only country in Central America that has English as an official language?

12. What does the 'K' in the name of American author Philip K Dick stand for?

13. What are the eight countries that end with the letter I?

14. Which veteran musician received his first Best Album Brit Award nomination in 2014 for 'The Next Day'?

15. 'The Golden Girl of the West' is an opera by which Italian composer?

16. What was the real first name of actor, writer, producer and director Orson Welles?

17. The 'Robocop' film franchise is set in which American city?

18. Which British trade union has the initials NAHT?

19. What is the name of the Manchester band that topped the charts with an eponymous 2013 album?
    a) The 1973   b) The 1974   c) The 1975

20. By what nickname is a British man called Stephen Gough known?
    a) The Naked Angler
    b) The Naked Gambler
    c) The Naked Rambler

Answers to Quiz 142: Seconds Out

1. Cape Town
2. Christine Ohuruogu
3. Alan Shepard
4. Sardinia
5. Argentina
6. Denmark
7. Carry On Nurse
8. Tom Watson
9. River Danube
10. Uruguay
11. Harry Potter and the Chamber of Secrets
12. Sri Lanka
13. Leigh Halfpenny
14. Holland
15. The Philippines
16. John Landy
17. Hungary
18. Park Lane
19. John Adams
20. Delhi

DIFFICULT

Quiz 144: Movies part 1

Which sports and games feature in the following films?

1. 'The Blind Side' (2009)

2. 'Stick It' (2006)

3. 'The Seventh Seal' (1957)

4. 'Lucky You' (2007)

5. 'Miracle' (2004)

6. 'Chasing Mavericks' (2012)

7. 'Secretariat' (2010)

8. 'Lagaan' (2001)

9. 'Backwards' (2012)

10. 'Hoosiers' (1986)

11. 'Fast Girls' (2012)

12. 'Murderball' (2005)

13. 'Million Dollar Baby' (2004)

14. 'Eight Men Out' (1988)

15. 'The Flying Scotsman' (2006)

16. 'The Cutting Edge' (1992)

17. 'The Greatest Game Ever Played' (2005)

18. 'Once in a Lifetime' (2006)

19. 'Balls of Fury' (2007)

20. 'Legendary' (2010)

Answers to Quiz 143: Pot Luck

1. John J Pershing
2. Clive James
3. Stewart Lee
4. Sir Tom Jones
5. 1910s
6. Umbria
7. Turkmenistan
8. Stax
9. Ivory Coast
10. Justin Fletcher
11. Belize
12. Kindred
13. Brunei, Burundi, Djibouti, Fiji, Haiti, Kiribati, Malawi, Mali
14. David Bowie
15. Puccini
16. George
17. Detroit
18. National Association of Head Teachers
19. The 1975
20. The Naked Rambler

DIFFICULT

Quiz 145: Pot Luck

1. Gene Simmons from rock band Kiss recorded an unlikely duet in 2013 with which veteran crooner?

2. The Jupiler League is the name of the top-flight football division in which country?

3. Ella Maria Lani Yelich-O'Connor is the real name of which New Zealand singer who topped the charts in 2013 with 'Royals'?

4. Which American golfer won the Open Championship for the first time in 2013?

5. Which brand of bread takes its name from the Latin words for 'strength of man'?

6. Which cartoonist, illustrator and children's writer, best known for his work with Roald Dahl, was appointed Britain's first Children's Laureate?

7. Eusuchian is a term used to describe things relating to what types of animals?

8. 'The Last of England' is a painting by which Pre-Raphaelite artist?

9. Which actor and comedian made his 'Coronation Street' debut in 2014, playing Michael Rogers?

10. Which comedian and social activist performed a stage show called '100 Acts of Minor Dissent'?

11. Which European country is the largest producer of cork in the world?

12. 'It's the economy, stupid' is a political slogan associated with which US president?

13. British classical musician Paul Lewis is a player of which musical instrument?

Answers – page 297

14. What is the only Belgian city to have hosted the Olympic Games?

15. 'Moon Landing' was a 2013 album by which English singer-songwriter?

16. Which religious organization is known for leaving Bibles in hotel rooms?

17. St Johnstone Football Club is based in which Scottish city?

18. Siôn Corn is Father Christmas in which language?

19. Which popular soft drink was originally known as 'Brad's Drink'?
    a) Coca Cola   b) Pepsi   c) Tango

20. What is the name of the Twitter app that enables users to make and publish short video clips?
    a) Fine   b) Vine   c) Wine

Answers to Quiz 144: Movies part 1

1. American football	11. Athletics
2. Gymnastics	12. Wheelchair rugby
3. Chess	13. Boxing
4. Poker	14. Baseball
5. Ice hockey	15. Cycling
6. Surfing	16. Ice skating
7. Horse racing	17. Golf
8. Cricket	18. Football
9. Rowing	19. Table tennis
10. Basketball	20. Wrestling

DIFFICULT

Quiz 146: History part 1

1. Which US president witnessed the signing of the United Nations Charter?

2. In which century was the Mormon church founded?

3. Which was the first European country to give women the vote?

4. The Russian revolutionary Trotsky was assassinated by a Soviet agent in 1940 while in which country?

5. Who was the British prime minister during the 1926 General Strike?

6. Eleanor of Aquitaine was the mother of which two English kings?

7. Who was the last Plantagenet king of England?

8. Former senior Nazis were indicted and tried as war criminals in a series of trials held in which German city?

9. In 1901, Edmund Barton became the first prime minister of which country?

10. In which year did the Queen Mother die?

11. What was the name of Hitler's chief architect and later minister for armaments and war production?

12. The Tamworth Manifesto was issued by which 19th-century British prime minister?

13. Who was the Republican candidate defeated by Bill Clinton in the 1996 US presidential election?

14. Which English king was nicknamed 'the Hammer of the Scots'?

15. During the Second World War, by what name was Operation Chastise better known?

16. Who was the last English monarch to die on the battlefield?

17. In which decade did the driving test become compulsory in the UK?

18. Thomas Jefferson was one of two US presidents who died on 4 July 1826. Who was the other?

19. The first BBC local radio station in mainland Britain launched in 1967 in which city?
a) Derby   b) Leicester   c) Nottingham

20. How many British soldiers died on the first day of the Battle of the Somme in 1916?
a) 10,000   b) 15,000   c) 20,000

Answers to Quiz 145: Pot Luck

1. Engelbert Humperdinck
2. Belgium
3. Lorde
4. Phil Mickelson
5. Hovis
6. Quentin Blake
7. Alligators and crocodiles
8. Ford Madox Brown
9. Les Dennis
10. Mark Thomas
11. Portugal
12. Bill Clinton
13. Piano
14. Antwerp
15. James Blunt
16. Gideons International
17. Perth
18. Welsh
19. Pepsi
20. Vine

DIFFICULT

Quiz 147: Pot Luck

1. Which former Israeli prime minister died in January 2014 after spending eight years in a coma?

2. Glanford Park is the home ground of which English football club?

3. In November 2013, Magnus Carlsen beat Viswanathan Anand to become world champion in which game?

4. Sports teams called the Rams, Cardinals and Blues are based in which American city?

5. Who was the world's first and only 'consulting detective'?

6. Designed by Spanish architect Santiago Calatrava, the Calatrava Bridge can be found in which Italian city?

7. Who was the lead singer with the influential 1980s electronic pop band Tubeway Army?

8. What nationality is the tennis star Stanislas Wawrinka?

9. Which Pakistani schoolgirl, who was shot by the Taliban, was nominated for the Nobel Peace Prize in 2013?

10. Who won an Oscar for Best Screenplay for 'Sense and Sensibility' and one for Best Actress for 'Howard's End'?

11. Which spirit is used to make the Brazilian cocktail caipirinha?

12. Which brand of beer is associated with the year 1664?

13. Which was the first American city to host the Winter Olympic Games?

14. Which pantomime is known in French as 'La belle au bois dormant'?

15. Which Radio 2 DJ provides the commentary for the TV game show 'Reflex'?

16. 'Per Mare, Per Terram' is the motto of which British military corps?

17. Who was the last male British athlete to hold the world record for the mile?

18. Which African currency is also the surname of an author who whose books include 'Atlas Shrugged' and 'The Fountainhead'?

19. Jayne Torvill and Christopher Dean won Olympic gold in 1984 skating in which city?
    a) Belgrade
    b) Sarajevo
    c) Split

20. In which sector does a charity called the Sutton Trust operate?
    a) education
    c) homelessness
    c) overseas aid

Answers to Quiz 146: History part 1

1. Harry S Truman	11. Albert Speer
2. 19th century	12. Robert Peel
3. Finland	13. Bob Dole
4. Mexico	14. Edward I
5. Stanley Baldwin	15. The Dambusters Raid
6. Richard I and King John	16. Richard III
7. Richard III	17. 1930s
8. Nuremberg	18. John Adams
9. Australia	19. Leicester
10. 2002	20. 20,000

DIFFICULT

Quiz 148: Colours

1. Which fictional detective featured in a story called 'The Adventure of the Blue Carbuncle'?

2. Tom Selleck stars as Police Commissioner Frank Reagan in which TV drama?

3. Who was appointed Britain's Children's Laureate from 2013 until 2015?

4. Which legendary country singer went on a 'Blue Smoke World Tour' in 2014?

5. 'From Hackney to Hollywood' is a musical that celebrates the career of which British songwriter?

6. Denzel Washington starred alongside Gene Hackman in which 1995 submarine drama directed by Tony Scott?

7. In late 2013, which former Radio 4 newsreader and continuity announcer became the first woman to read the classified football scores on BBC Radio 5?

8. RAF were the initials of which 1970s militant organization, also known as the Baader-Meinhof Group?

9. Cate Blanchett won the Best Actress Oscar in 2014 for her performance in which film?

10. Which author writes the series of books featuring a character called Robert Langdon?

11. Who starred opposite Patrick Swayze in the 1987 romantic drama 'Dirty Dancing'?

12. Which actress played battleaxe Ena Sharples in TV soap 'Coronation Street'?

13. Mr Crockett, the Garage Man, Mickey Murphy, the Baker and Windy Miller all lived in which fictional village?

14. Who wrote the international bestseller 'The Joy Luck Club'?

15. 'An Ordinary Copper' was the title of the theme tune to which police drama?

16. What was the title of the 2005 football hooligan film starring 'Lord of the Rings' actor Elijah Wood?

17. Which team won football's European Cup in 1991?

18. What is the opening track on the 1971 Rolling Stones album 'Sticky Fingers'?

19. What is the nickname for a member of the Royal Military Police?
    a) Blue Cap
    b) Green Cap
    c) Red Cap

20. According to the title of an acclaimed 2013 TV drama, what is 'The New Black'?
    a) Brown
    b) Orange
    c) Purple

Answers to Quiz 147: Pot Luck

1. Ariel Sharon
2. Scunthorpe United
3. Chess
4. St Louis
5. Sherlock Holmes
6. Venice
7. Gary Numan
8. Swiss
9. Malala Yousafzai
10. Emma Thompson
11. Rum
12. Kronenbourg
13. Lake Placid
14. Sleeping Beauty
15. Ken Bruce
16. Royal Marines
17. Steve Cram
18. Rand (Ayn Rand)
19. Sarajevo
20. Education

DIFFICULT

Quiz 149: Pot Luck

1. The first Winter Olympic Games were hosted in which country?

2. Which is the easternmost of New York City's five boroughs?

3. Which Italian architect designed the London skyscraper 'The Shard'?

4. In June 2013, Hassan Rouhani was elected president of which Middle Eastern country?

5. Which cinema legend did Tom Hanks play in the 2013 film 'Saving Mr Banks'?

6. Tumucumaque National Park, the world's largest tropical forest park, is located in which country?

7. What nationality is the world-record holder for the mile and 1500m, Hicham El Guerrouj?

8. The Latin phrase 'Utrinque Paratus' is the motto of the Parachute Regiment. What does it mean in English?

9. The loti is the currency of which landlocked African country?

10. A statue of Charles Dickens was unveiled in 2014 in which English city?

11. In February 2014, Facebook paid $19bn to acquire which instant-messaging subscription service for smartphones?

12. Which Asian capital city stands high above the Taedong River?

13. Which song by the Beach Boys was also the title of a 2012 movie about the Belfast punk scene?

14. Which African capital city lies at the confluence of the Blue and White Nile Rivers?

Answers – page 305

15. The Atatürk Olympic Stadium is in which city?

16. What was the former name of the Indian city of Karnataka?

17. In which decade was the singer Dame Shirley Bassey born?

18. The Olympic host city of Sochi lies on the coast of which sea?

19. The modern Russian alphabet consists of how many letters?
    a) 31
    b) 33
    c) 35

20. The first McDonalds restaurant in the UK opened in 1974 in which London suburb?
    a) Streatham
    b) Tooting
    c) Woolwich

Answers to Quiz 148: Colours

1. Sherlock Holmes
2. Blue Bloods
3. Malorie Blackman
4. Dolly Parton
5. Don Black
6. Crimson Tide
7. Charlotte Green
8. Red Army Faction
9. Blue Jasmine
10. Dan Brown
11. Jennifer Grey
12. Violet Carson
13. Camberwick Green
14. Amy Tan
15. Dixon of Dock Green
16. Green Street
17. Red Star Belgrade
18. Brown Sugar
19. Red Cap
20. Orange

DIFFICULT

Quiz 150: I'm All Right Jack

1. Who was the seventh president of the USA?

2. Which comedian starred in the TV sitcom 'Lead Balloon'?

3. What is the largest city in the US state of Florida?

4. What long-running children's programme aired on the BBC from 1965 until 1996?

5. Which soul singer, who died in 1984, had a posthumous Christmas number one in 1986?

6. Which 1987 number one was the only UK hit for house-music producer Steve 'Silk' Hurley?

7. Which triple Oscar-winning Hollywood actor co-wrote the 1968 film starring The Monkees, 'Head'?

8. Jackie Aprile was a character in which American crime drama?

9. The 1978 song 'Stay' was the only UK hit single for which American singer-songwriter?

10. Which Australian racing driver and later team owner won the Formula One Drivers' Championship in 1959, 1960 and 1966?

11. Which French cyclist, who won the Tour de France on five occasions, was nicknamed 'Monsieur Chrono'?

12. Which actor and comedian played JP in the university-set comedy drama 'Fresh Meat'?

13. The fictional character Tracy Beaker was created by which best-selling children's author?

14. 'The Singing Butler', 'A Voyage of Discovery' and 'After the Thrill Is Gone' are works by which Scottish painter?

15. Which author created the Lucky Santangelo and Madison Castelli series of books?

16. Which actor's two Oscars came for his performances in 'Save the Tiger' (1974) and 'Mister Roberts' (1955)?

17. Which Hawaiian musician recorded the 2013 top-ten album 'From Here to Now to You'?

18. Harrison Ford, Alec Baldwin, Ben Affleck and most recently Chris Pine have all played which movie character?

19. 'SuperStars' winner Brian Jacks was an Olympic medal-winner in which sport?
    a) athletics   b) judo   c) swimming

20. Curtis Jackson is the real name of which American hip-hop star?
    a) Dr Dre   b) Snoop Dogg   c) 50 Cent

Answers to Quiz 149: Pot Luck

1. France	11. WhatsApp
2. Queens	12. Pyongyang
3. Renzo Piano	13. Good Vibrations
4. Iran	14. Khartoum
5. Walt Disney	15. Istanbul
6. Brazil	16. Mysore
7. Moroccan	17. 1930s
8. Ready for Anything	18. The Black Sea
9. Lesotho	19. 33
10. Portsmouth	20. Woolwich

DIFFICULT

Quiz 151: Pot Luck

1. Who was the first player to score 30 goals in a Premier League season without scoring a penalty?

2. In 2008, which city became England's first European Capital of Culture?

3. Which of the Baldwin brothers plays Jack Donaghy in the US comedy '30 Rock'?

4. What does the internet acronym DNS stand for?

5. The World Economic Forum hosts an annual meeting in which Swiss resort?

6. 'Unstoppable' was the last film directed by which British film-maker, who died in August 2012?

7. 'Haircut Saloon' is an anagram of which US state?

8. In which European language is Father Christmas known as Télapó?

9. Which Olympic sport was originally known as 'mintonette'?

10. Which Mancunian band created their own beer called 'Charge'?

11. Tinker Dill, Eric Catchpole and Lady Jane Felsham were characters in which popular BBC drama, which ran from 1986 until 1994?

12. The wines Gusbourne Estate, Nyetimber and Ridgeview are produced in which country?

13. Which 2014 film from the Coen brothers features a cat called Ulysses?

14. The famous horseracing venue The Curragh is in which Irish county?

15. Which actor lost over four stone for his role in 'The Machinist' and put on three stone for the 2013 film 'American Hustle'?

16. 'Don Pasquale' is a comic opera by which Italian composer?

17. What did the 'B' in the name of film producer and director Cecil B DeMille stand for?

18. In an Olympic 400m hurdles race, each athlete jumps how many hurdles?

19. What was the middle name of the Nobel Prize-winning author Samuel Beckett?
    a) Barclay   b) Lloyd   c) Woolwich

20. In which country was the award-winning architect Zaha Hadid born?
    a) Iran   b) Iraq   c) Syria

Answers to Quiz 150: I'm All Right Jack

1. Andrew Jackson
2. Jack Dee
3. Jacksonville
4. Jackanory
5. Jackie Wilson
6. Jack Your Body
7. Jack Nicholson
8. The Sopranos
9. Jackson Browne
10. Jack Brabham
11. Jacques Anquetil
12. Jack Whitehall
13. Jacqueline Wilson
14. Jack Vettriano
15. Jackie Collins
16. Jack Lemmon
17. Jack Johnson
18. Jack Ryan
19. Judo
20. 50 Cent

DIFFICULT

Quiz 152: Chris Cross

1. In 2012, which West Indian cricketer became the first batsman to score a six off the first ball of a Test match?

2. Which footballer, who won 62 caps for England between 1985 and 1991, worked in a sausage factory before turning professional?

3. Which actor played Lukewarm in the classic prison comedy 'Porridge'?

4. The hit musical 'Cabaret' was based on works by which British author?

5. Which artist, who won the Turner Prize in 1998, used elephant dung in a number of his works?

6. Christopher Moltisanti was a character in which long-running TV drama?

7. Which Melbourne-born actor played the title character in the 2011 superhero film 'Thor'?

8. Who was the first British athlete to run 100m in under 10 seconds?

9. Who directed the films 'Home Alone', 'Mrs Doubtfire' and 'Harry Potter and the Sorcerer's Stone'?

10. Which actress won her only Oscar in 1965 playing an amoral model in the drama 'Darling'?

11. The Christie Hospital is located in which English city?

12. Which Austrian actor won Best Supporting Actor Oscars in 2010 and 2013, both times in films directed by Quentin Tarantino?

13. Who was the US Secretary of State from January 1993 until January 1997?

14. Which former England cricketer was jailed in 2009 after being found guilty of smuggling cocaine?

15. Who was the founder of the Island record label which helped popularize reggae around the world?

16. Which supermodel popularized navel piercings after appearing with one at a 1993 fashion show?

17. Which former MP and diarist's works include 'A Very British Coup' and 'A View from the Foothills'?

18. Which artist's only UK top-ten hit was 1990's 'Wicked Game'?

19. In which sport do teams compete for a trophy called the Christy Ring Cup?
    a) bowls   b) hurling   c) snooker

20. British Tour de France winner Chris Froome was born in which country?
    a) Australia   b) Kenya   c) South Africa

Answers to Quiz 151: Pot Luck

1. Andy Cole
2. Liverpool
3. Alec Baldwin
4. Domain Name System
5. Davos
6. Tony Scott
7. South Carolina
8. Hungarian
9. Volleyball
10. Elbow
11. Lovejoy
12. England
13. Inside Llewyn Davis
14. Kildare
15. Christian Bale
16. Donizetti
17. Blount
18. 10
19. Barclay
20. Iraq

DIFFICULT

Quiz 153: Pot Luck

1. What is the westernmost borough of New York?

2. In which classic 1987 family film does a character called Dread Pirate Roberts appear?

3. Which country hosted cricket's World T20 competition in 2014?

4. Evil Nurse Ratched presided over a psychiatric ward in which classic 1974 film?

5. Eleanor of Aquitaine was married to which English king?

6. 2013 marked the 50th anniversary of the Élysée Treaty signed by France and which other country?

7. Prior to Ed Miliband, who was the last leader of the Labour Party to attend a secondary school in England?

8. Which sport was invented by the Canadian-born educator James Naismith?

9. Which European football team plays its home games at the Vicente Calderón Stadium?

10. In addition to the UK, what are the three countries in Europe where cars are driven on the left-hand side of the road?

11. The 2013 film 'Enough Said' was the last to feature which actor, best known for playing a gangster?

12. What are the three common English words that end with the letters -cion?

13. There is a station on the Paris Metro named after which British monarch?

14. Which giant telecommunications company is based in Espoo, Finland?

DIFFICULT

15. In February 2014, Frenchman Renaud Lavillenie broke a world record that had been held for 21 years. In which athletics event?

16. The French cheese Rocamadour is made with the milk of which animal?

17. Who was named Time Magazine's Person of the 20th Century?

18. What team sport is played with a ball called a 'sliotar'?

19. The headquarters of which technology company are in Cupertino, California?
a) Apple   b) Facebook   c) Microsoft

20. Which European capital city provided Lou Reed with the title of a 1973 top ten album?
a) Berlin   b) Paris   c) Rome

Answers to Quiz 152: Chris Cross

1. Chris Gayle
2. Chris Waddle
3. Christopher Biggins
4. Christopher Isherwood
5. Chris Ofili
6. The Sopranos
7. Chris Hemsworth
8. Linford Christie
9. Chris Columbus
10. Julie Christie
11. Manchester
12. Christoph Waltz
13. Warren Christopher
14. Chris Lewis
15. Chris Blackwell
16. Christy Turlington
17. Chris Mullin
18. Chris Isaak
19. Hurling
20. Kenya

DIFFICULT

Quiz 154: Connections part 2

1. Which actress, who first found fame in teen drama 'Dawson's Creek', was nominated for an Oscar in 2012 for her performance in 'My Week with Marilyn'?

2. Which tennis player won a silver medal playing alongside Andy Murray in the mixed doubles at the 2012 London Olympics?

3. Which New Zealander was the first man to climb Mount Everest?

4. Which politician, who was MP for Blackburn for over 30 years, was nicknamed the 'Red Queen'?

5. In 2007, which politician became the first woman to serve as speaker of the US House of Representatives?

6. Which song by The Beatles was released as a double-A side alongside 'Yellow Submarine'?

7. America Ferrera played the title character in which fashion-industry TV drama that ran from 2006 to 2010?

8. In the TV cartoon 'Wacky Races', who drove a vehicle called the Convert-a-Car?

9. Coccinellidae is the scientific name for which family of beetles?

10. Which author was Britain's Children's Laureate between 2005 and 2007?

11. 'Summertime' and 'It Ain't Necessarily So' are songs from which George Gershwin opera?

12. Count Alexei Kirillovich Vronsky and Prince Stepan 'Stiva' Arkadyevich Oblonsky are characters in which classic Russian novel?

13. 'Transformer' was a critically acclaimed 1972 album by which singer and songwriter, who died in October 2013?

14. Which Gloucestershire and England cricketer scored more than 54,000 runs and took over 2800 wickets in a 44-year career that stretched from 1865 to 1908?

15. Who set the world record for the women's 100m of 10.49s at the 1988 Olympic Games?

16. Marion Cotillard won an Oscar in 2008 for her portrayal of which singer?

17. In 2005, which yachtswoman set a world record for the fastest solo nonstop voyage around the world?

18. Which actress won a Laurence Olivier Award in 2013 for her performance as The Queen in the play 'The Audience'?

19. Who played Miss Jones in the classic 1970s TV comedy 'Rising Damp'?

20. What is the connection between the answers?

Answers to Quiz 153: Pot Luck

1. Staten Island
2. The Princess Bride
3. Bangladesh
4. One Flew Over the Cuckoo's Nest
5. Henry II
6. Germany
7. Michael Foot
8. Basketball
9. Atletico Madrid
10. Cyprus, Republic of Ireland and Malta
11. James Gandolfini
12. Coercion, scion and suspicion
13. King George V
14. Nokia
15. Pole vault
16. Goat
17. Albert Einstein
18. Hurling
19. Apple
20. Berlin

DIFFICULT

Quiz 155: Pot Luck

1. What are the two Irish cities to have been the European Capital of Culture?

2. What do the initials ZIP stand for in relation to American postal addresses?

3. Which English county plays its home cricket matches at the Rose Bowl?

4. Kathy Bates won her only Oscar playing psychopathic killer Annie Wilkes in which horror film based on a Stephen King novel?

5. 'Los Conchonelos' is the nickname of which Spanish football team?

6. In measurement, how many yards make up one chain?

7. The name of which rugby union team was also the title of a 2013 Channel 4 comedy starring Kat Reagan and Sinead Keenan?

8. What does the letter 'A' in the acronym 'laser' stand for?

9. First published in 2012, 'Standing in Another Man's Grave' featured which Scottish detective?

10. Which novelist and playwright is the only Nobel Prize-winner to have played first-class cricket?

11. 'Homeland' star David Harewood, ELO guitarist Jeff Lynne and actress Julie Walters are all honoured on a 'Walk of Stars' in which British city?

12. Bill Pertwee, who died in May 2013, is best known for playing which character in 'Dad's Army'?

13. 'The Baby-Faced Assassin' was the nickname of which Premier League footballer, who is now a manager?

14. In squash, a coloured dot indicates the level of bounce and speed of the ball. What colour dot indicates the fastest ball?

15. In Spain, it is considered lucky to eat one of what with each chime at midnight on 31 December?

16. Which event was held first – football's European Championships or the Eurovision Song Contest?

17. Which former mental-health nurse won the 2013 Costa Book Prize for his debut novel 'The Shock of the Fall'?

18. The English words dollar, pistol and robot all derived from which language?

19. Which unit of area is equal to 1,210 square yards?
    a) lood   b) nood   c) rood

20. Dr Tom Parry Jones, who died in 2013, was the inventor of which road-safety tool?
    a) electronic breathalyser
    b) electronic parking sensor
    c) electronic countdown crossing

Answers to Quiz 154: Connections part 2

1. Michelle Williams
2. Laura Robson
3. Sir Edmund Hillary
4. Barbara Castle
5. Nancy Pelosi
6. Eleanor Rigby
7. Ugly Betty
8. Professor Pat Pending
9. Ladybird
10. Jacqueline Wilson
11. Porgy and Bess
12. Anna Karenina
13. Lou Reed
14. WG Grace
15. Florence Griffith Joyner
16. Edith Piaf
17. Dame Ellen MacArthur
18. Dame Helen Mirren
19. Frances De La Tour
20. They all contain the first name of a US First Lady

DIFFICULT

Quiz 156: Famous Dans

1. Who was the American vice-president from 1989 until 1993?

2. Daniel Passarella captained which team to victory in football's World Cup?

3. Who is the highest points scorer in the history of international rugby union?

4. Which actor's only Oscar nomination came in 1990 for his performance in 'Driving Miss Daisy'?

5. A judge on the first two series of TV talent show 'The Voice', Danny O'Donoghue is the lead singer with which band?

6. 'The Sins of the Mother', 'Winners' and 'Friends Forever' are novels by which prolific, best-selling American author?

7. Which actor played 'Tunnel King' Danny in the 1963 film 'The Great Escape'?

8. Between 1978 and 2002 Daniel arap Moi was the president of which African country?

9. What was the last novel written by 19th-century author George Eliot?

10. The 2012 bestseller 'Thinking, Fast and Slow' was written by which Israeli psychologist?

11. Which actor, best known for appearing in the comedy 'Red Dwarf', played policeman Dwayne Myers in crime drama 'Death in Paradise'?

12. The noted conductor Daniel Barenboim is also an accomplished player of which musical instrument?

13. Which Liberal Democrat politician was appointed Chief Secretary to the Treasury in May 2010?

14. The children's book 'Danny, the Champion of the World' was written by which author?

15. In 2007, Daniel Ortega was elected president of which Central American country?

16. Which England rugby union international was struck by a bus during a team night out in Leeds in 2013?

17. Birmingham-born Irishman Daniel Martin is a noted performer in which sport?

18. Which Polish-born American architect designed the Imperial War Museum North in Manchester and the Jewish Museum in Berlin?

19. Barcelona footballer Dani Alves plays international matches for which country?
    a) Argentina   b) Brazil   c) Paraguay

20. Uruguayan Danny Bergara was the first foreign manager to lead an English club side at Wembley. Which team was he managing?
    a) Southend United   b) Stockport County   c) Stoke City

Answers to Quiz 155: Pot Luck

1. Dublin and Cork
2. Zone Improvement Plan
3. Hampshire
4. Misery
5. Atletico Madrid
6. 22
7. London Irish
8. Amplification
9. Rebus
10. Samuel Beckett
11. Birmingham
12. Hodges
13. Ole Gunnar Solskjaer
14. Blue
15. A grape
16. Eurovision Song Contest
17. Nathan Filer
18. Czech
19. Rood
20. Electronic breathalyser

DIFFICULT

Quiz 157: Pot Luck

1. What is the most northerly of New York City's five boroughs?

2. The ringgit is the currency of which Asian country?

3. Of what is glossophobia the fear?

4. In 2003 Shami Chakrabati became the director of which human-rights pressure group?

5. Which British model is the goddaughter of actress Joan Collins?

6. Tramway is an arts centre located in which Scottish city?

7. Which film, that won Best Picture at the 2005 Oscars, made its debut as an opera in 2014?

8. Nicola Benedetti is a noted performer of which musical instrument?

9. Acklam Russet, Charlestown Pippin and Flower of the Town are varieties of apple that originate from which English county?

10. Asmara is the capital city of which African country?

11. In which decade was the first party political broadcast televised?

12. A person suffering from coulrophobia fears what?

13. Which revolutionary leader was the unlikely founder of a short-lived Argentine rugby magazine called 'Tackle'?

14. Who was the first US president to deliver a State of the Union speech that was broadcast on television?

15. The open-air Minack Theatre is located in which English county?

16. In which decade were the Winter Olympics held for the first time?

17. The Spanish football club Espanyol is based in which city?

18. Quezon City is the largest city in which Asian country?

19. The first McDonalds restaurant in Europe opened its doors in 1971 in which country?
    a) France
    b) The Netherlands
    c) Norway

20. Ellis Park is a famous rugby ground located in which city?
    a) Auckland
    b) Johannesburg
    c) Sydney

Answers to Quiz 156: Famous Dans

1. Dan Quayle
2. Argentina
3. Dan Carter
4. Dan Aykroyd
5. The Script
6. Danielle Steel
7. Charles Bronson
8. Kenya
9. Daniel Deronda
10. Daniel Kahneman
11. Danny John-Jules
12. Piano
13. Danny Alexander
14. Roald Dahl
15. Nicaragua
16. Danny Cipriani
17. Cycling
18. Daniel Libeskind
19. Brazil
20. Stockport County

DIFFICULT

Quiz 158: Music part 1

1. Who in 2012 became the first artist to have a different album in the UK charts every year for 25 consecutive years?

2. What is the biggest-selling album in the UK to have been recorded by a solo artist?

3. 'Spirit' was a best selling album by which TV talent-show star?

4. Which legendary Chic guitarist appeared on Daft Punk's best-selling single 'Get Lucky'?

5. What nationality are the chart topping band 5 Seconds of Summer?

6. Which alliteratively-titled album by One Direction was the UK's fastest selling album of 2013?

7. 'I run for the bus, dear / While riding I think of us, dear' are lines from which classic Bacharach and David song?

8. What is Madonna's biggest-selling UK single?

9. What colour provided Taylor Swift with the title of a 2013 album?

10. Thomas Bangalter and Guy-Manuel de Homen-Christo are the two halves of which publicity-shy pop duo?

11. The 2009 release 'Reality Killed the Video Star' is the only album by which artist to not reach number one in the charts?

12. Mike Rosenberg is the real name of which British singer-songwriter who recorded the 2012 album 'All the Little Lights'?

13. The dance craze 'Macarena' was started by which Spanish duo, whose name translates into English as 'the ones from the river'?

14. Since the UK charts started, which artist has sold the most singles?

15. 'Good Morning, this ain't Vietnam / Still, people lose hands, legs, arms, for real' are lines from which song by Kanye West?

16. The 2010 single 'Dog Days Are Over' is the biggest-selling single which didn't break into the top 20. Which British band recorded it?

17. The name of which American state appeared in the title of the debut single by Roxy Music?

18. Which folk musician and activist, who died in January 2014 at the age of 94, was described as 'America's tuning fork'?

19. Which school subject did not feature in the title of a top-ten hit by Girls Aloud?
    a) Biology   b) Geography   c) History

20. Which of the following was the title of a 2013 album by Arctic Monkeys?
    a) AM   b) Noon   c) PM

Answers to Quiz 157: Pot Luck

1. The Bronx
2. Malaysia
3. Public speaking
4. Liberty
5. Cara Delevingne
6. Glasgow
7. Brokeback Mountain
8. Violin
9. Yorkshire
10. Eritrea
11. 1950s
12. Clowns
13. Che Guevara
14. Harry S Truman
15. Cornwall
16. 1920s
17. Barcelona
18. The Philippines
19. The Netherlands
20. Johannesburg

DIFFICULT

Quiz 159: Pot Luck

1. Published in 2014, 'Going Off Alarming' is the second volume of autobiography by which DJ and broadcaster?

2. What is the only landlocked European country that is surrounded by landlocked countries?

3. Which politician is associated with the phrase 'continuous effort – not strength or intelligence – is the key to unlocking our potential'?

4. In 2013, which New Zealand novelist became the youngest winner of the Booker Prize for 'The Luminaries'?

5. Matt Damon played which South African sportsman in the 2009 film 'Invictus'?

6. How many children did Queen Victoria have?

7. Which actor played Mr Spock in the 2009 film 'Star Trek' and 2013's 'Star Trek Into Darkness'?

8. Who are the two Germans to have won the Men's Singles at Wimbledon?

9. In which year did Madonna enjoy her first UK hit single?

10. In French, what creature is known as 'une abeille'?

11. In 2014, who became the first British producer to be inducted into the Broadway Theatre Hall of Fame?

12. Blenheim, scene of a famous 18th-century battle, is in which country?

13. In which branch of the arts is Thomas Adès a notable name?

14. The Salad Bowl is the nickname of the trophy awarded to the winner of which country's top-flight football league?

15. Which 2014 movie set the record for the most uses of the F-word in a single film with 506 in its 2hr 59m running time?

16. Mysophobia is the irrational fear of what?

17. Which of New York's five boroughs has the smallest population?

18. What is the only African capital city whose name starts with the letter O?

19. Which app was removed from the App Store after 'ruining its creator's life'?
    a) Flappy Bird
    b) Flippy Bird
    c) Floppy Bird

20. The Boris Paichadze National Stadium is located in which capital city?
    a) Kiev
    b) Riga
    c) Tbilisi

Answers to Quiz 158: Music part 1

1. Daniel O'Donnell
2. '21' by Adele
3. Leona Lewis
4. Nile Rodgers
5. Australian
6. Midnight Matters
7. I Say a Little Prayer
8. Into the Groove
9. Red
10. Daft Punk
11. Robbie Williams
12. Passenger
13. Los del Rio
14. Cliff Richard
15. Diamonds from Sierra Leone
16. Florence and the Machine
17. Virginia (Virginia Plain)
18. Pete Seeger
19. Geography
20. AM

DIFFICULT

Quiz 160: Fill in the Blank part 1

Fill in the word that is missing from the following Booker Prize-winning novels:

1. 'Bring Up The ____' – Hilary Mantel

2. 'The ____ of an Ending' – Julian Barnes

3. 'The Finkler ____' – Howard Jacobson

4. 'The White ____' – Aravind Adiga

5. 'The ____ of Beauty' – Alan Hollinghurst

6. '____ God Little' – DBC Pierre

7. 'The Inheritance of ____' – Kiran Desai

8. 'Life of ____' – Yann Martel

9. 'The True History of the ____ Gang' – Pater Carey

10. 'The ____ Assassin' – Margaret Atwood

11. 'The God of ____ Things' – Arundhati Roy

12. 'The ____ Road' – Pat Barker

13. 'The ____ Patient' – Michael Ondaatje

14. 'The ____ Road' – Ben Okri

15. 'The ____ of the Day' – Kazuo Ishiguro

16. 'Oscar and ____' – Peter Carey

17. 'Midnight's ____' – Salman Rushdie

18. 'Something to ____ For' – PH Newby

19. 'In a Free ____' – VS Naipul

20. '____ Hall' – Hilary Mantel

Answers to Quiz 159: Pot Luck

1. Danny Baker
2. Liechtenstein
3. Winston Churchill
4. Eleanor Catton
5. Francois Pienaar
6. Nine
7. Zachary Quinto
8. Boris Becker and Michael Stich
9. 1984
10. A bee
11. Sir Cameron Mackintosh
12. Germany
13. Classical music
14. Germany
15. The Wolf of Wall Street
16. Germs
17. Staten Island
18. Ouagadougou
19. Flappy Bird
20. Tbilisi

DIFFICULT

Quiz 161: Pot Luck

1. Which European capital was known as Titograd from 1946 to 1992?

2. Dustin Hoffman won his second Best Actor Oscar for his performance as Raymond Babbitt in which 1988 film?

3. Which British actress, who won her first Oscar in 2007, was awarded a BAFTA fellowship in 2014?

4. Which American actor, best known for appearing in a TV sitcom that ran from 1974 until 1984, wrote a series of children's books featuring Hank Zipzer?

5. What do the initials JJ in the name of film director JJ Abrams?

6. @Beathhigh is the Twitter handle of which best-selling British crime novelist?

7. In February 2014, Janet Yellen took office as the Chair of the Board of Governors at which major financial organization?

8. The Vistula is the longest river in which European country?

9. The ancient city of Persepolis was the former capital of which empire?

10. Hampden Park is the home ground of which Scottish football club?

11. Armie Hammer and Clayton Moore have both played which fictional character?

12. Plessey, the scene of a famous 18th-century battle, is in which country?

13. Which footballer caused controversy after making a gesture known as a 'quenelle' after scoring for West Bromwich Albion against West Ham in December 2013?

14. Which Central Asian mountain range is known as 'the roof of the world'?

15. Which king of England was born in Pembroke in west Wales in 1457?

16. The award-winning British singer Laura Mvula is from which English city?

17. From 1932 to 1990, the Russian city of Nizhny Novgorod was named after which author, who was born there in 1868?

18. Gelderland is the largest province of which European country?

19. What is the name of JK Rowling's crime-writing alter ego?
    a) Robert Friedman
    b) Robert Galbraith
    c) Robert Keynes

20. The Michael Edwards Studio is a theatre in which unlikely venue?
    a) Buckingham Palace
    b) The Cutty Sark
    c) HMS Belfast

Answers to Quiz 160: Fill in the Blank part 1

1.	Bodies	11.	Small
2.	Sense	12.	Ghost
3.	Question	13.	English
4.	Tiger	14.	Famished
5.	Line	15.	Remains
6.	Vernon	16.	Lucinda
7.	Loss	17.	Children
8.	Pi	18.	Answer
9.	Kelly	19.	State
10.	Blind	20.	Wolf

DIFFICULT

Quiz 162: Places part 1

1. The African country Eritrea was formerly a province of which state?

2. Donau is the German name for which river?

3. The Loop is the main commercial district of which American city?

4. Lolland, Falster and Bornholm are islands of which European country?

5. Which north African capital city takes its name from the Arabic for 'The Islands'?

6. Which city in western Germany is known in France as Aix-la-Chapelle?

7. Which English city lies at the confluence of the Rivers Ouse and Foss?

8. Between 1821 to 1920 which Irish port was named Kingstown?

9. Ararat, the supposed resting place of Noah's Ark, is in which modern-day country?

10. Which Australian city is situated on the estuary of the Derwent River?

11. Which American state was the birthplace of motoring pioneer Henry Ford and is also home to the largest mosque in the Western world?

12. Chequers, the official residence of the British prime minister is located in which historic English county?

13. Guipuzcoa is the smallest province of which European country?

14. Which central European capital city is also the name of a theatre in the city of Coventry?

Answers – page 331

15. The island state of Comoros lies in which ocean?

16. Which town in Croatia is known in Italy as Ragusa?

17. Dens Park and Tannadice Park are football grounds in which British city?

18. Baile Átha Cliath is the local name for which European capital city?

19. The Charles River flows through which American city?
    a) Boston
    b) Chicago
    c) Denver

20. Which Irish county derives its name from the Norse word for meadow?
    a) Kerry
    b) Kilkenny
    c) Wicklow

Answers to Quiz 161: Pot Luck

1. Podgorica
2. Rain Man
3. Helen Mirren
4. Henry Winkler
5. Jeffrey Jacob
6. Ian Rankin
7. The Federal Reserve
8. Poland
9. Persian Empire
10. Queen's Park
11. The Lone Ranger
12. India
13. Nicolas Anelka
14. Pamir Mountains
15. Henry VII
16. Birmingham
17. Gorky
18. The Netherlands
19. Robert Galbraith
20. The Cutty Sark

DIFFICULT

Quiz 163: Pot Luck

1. Which English king was beaten by Robert the Bruce in the Battle of Bannockburn?

2. Evergreen is the US Secret Service codename for which high-profile American politician?

3. The name of which European capital translates into English as 'white fortress'?

4. 'The News: A User's Manual' is a 2014 book by which contemporary philosopher?

5. 'Eyes Open' was a million-selling album in 2008 for which Northern Irish band?

6. Who were proclaimed king and queen of England following the 'Glorious Revolution'?

7. Who was the first British monarch to visit China?

8. What is the world's busiest single runway airport?

9. What does the 'D' in the financial acronym EBITDA stand for?

10. Which American thriller writer was the world's best-selling author between 2001 and 2013?

11. Which Oscar-winning film was a remake of the Hong Kong crime drama 'Infernal Affairs'?

12. Who was the eldest of the famous Mitford sisters?

13. The River Danube flows into which sea?

14. Who are the two actors to have won Best Actor Oscars in consecutive years?

15. Which American state was also the title of a 1982 album by Bruce Springsteen?

16. Beginning with the letter R, what is the first name of the fictional detective Inspector Alleyn?

17. In which year was Prince Charles born?

18. Since 1977, who are the two players to have won snooker's World Championship whose first name and surname start with the same letter?

19. Which author created the fictional detective partnership 'Rizzoli & Isles'?
a) Tess Gerritsen
b) Val Mcdermid
c) Karin Slaughter

20. Nullarbor Links, the world's longest golf course, is in which country?
a) Australia
b) Canada
c) South Africa

Answers to Quiz 162: Places part 1

1. Ethiopia
2. River Danube
3. Chicago
4. Denmark
5. Algiers
6. Aachen
7. York
8. Dún Laoghaire
9. Turkey
10. Hobart
11. Michigan
12. Buckinghamshire
13. Spain
14. Belgrade
15. Indian Ocean
16. Dubrovnik
17. Dundee
18. Dublin
19. Boston
20. Wicklow

DIFFICULT

Quiz 164: Numbers

1. What was the first word in Abraham Lincoln's famous 'Gettysburg Address'?

2. Which rapper played Jimi Hendrix in the 2013 film biopic 'All Is By My Side'?

3. In the Bible, what is the only miracle that appears in all four Gospels?

4. Which fictional detective featured in a story called 'The Adventure of the Six Napoleons'?

5. Which English monarch was known as The Nine Days' Queen?

6. Which band asked 'When Will I See You Again' in 1974?

7. What was the only UK number-one single by The Commodores?

8. Eric Stewart, Kevin Godley, Graham Gouldman and Lol Creme were the original members of which chart-topping band from the 1970s?

9. Which English band recorded the theme song to the TV drama 'The Sopranos'?

10. 'Labour of Love', 'Signing Off' and 'Present Arms' were hit albums in the 1980s for which band?

11. What was the debut novel by American writer Joseph Heller?

12. In which TV quiz show are contestants given the option to question or nominate?

13. By what name is the star cluster Pleiades also known?

14. Whose painting 'No.5 1948' was sold in 2006 for a price of around $140m?

15. In May 1911, Ray Harroun became the first winner of which annual sporting event?

16. Colonel Steve Zodiac and Dr Venus were the central characters in which puppet animation series?

17. Ted Rogers was the host of which TV game show?

18. 'I returned from the City about three o'clock on that May afternoon pretty well disgusted with life' is the opening line to which classic espionage novel?

19. The 2014 novel 'The Four Streets' is by which Conservative MP?
    a) Nadine Dorries
    b) Iain Duncan Smith
    c) Jacob Rees-Mogg

20. In 1958, French footballer Just Fontaine set the record for the most goals in a single World Cup tournament. How many goals did he score?
    a) 11   b) 12   c) 13

Answers to Quiz 163: Pot Luck

1. Edward II
2. Hillary Clinton
3. Belgrade
4. Alain de Botton
5. Snow Patrol
6. William III and Mary
7. Queen Elizabeth II
8. Gatwick Airport
9. Depreciation
10. James Patterson
11. The Departed
12. Nancy
13. Black Sea
14. Spencer Tracy and Tom Hanks
15. Nebraska
16. Roderick
17. 1948
18. Ray Reardon and Joe Johnson
19. Tess Gerritsen
20. Australia

DIFFICULT

333

Quiz 165: Pot Luck

1. 'Kittyhawk' and 'Redfern' are code names given by the US Secret Service to identify which member of the British royal family?

2. The 'Golden Heart' trilogy is a series of films directed by which controversial film maker?

3. H5N1, H7N9 and H10N8 are strains of which virus?

4. Which Hollywood actress is the daughter Tippi Hedren, who starred in the Alfred Hitchcock chiller 'The Birds'?

5. Which American artist's sculpture 'Balloon Dog (Orange)' sold for over $58m in November 2013?

6. In February 2014, Satya Nadella was appointed the CEO of which technology giant?

7. When is Queen Elizabeth II's birthday?

8. Which Manchester band was the subject of the 2007 film 'Control'?

9. Which event was held first – the Boat Race or the Grand National?

10. Which author, who died in June 2013, wrote the comic novels 'Wilt', 'Porterhouse Blue' and 'Blott on the Landscape'?

11. Which Disney cartoon character is known in Denmark as 'Anders And' and in Finland as 'Aku Ankka'?

12. Who played the title character in the Martin Scorsese's 1983 film 'The King of Comedy'?

13. Which country won the most gold medals at the 2014 Winter Olympics?

14. Which author writes novels that feature the quadriplegic forensic criminologist Lincoln Rhyme?

15. Meydan Racecourse is in which Asian country?

16. In measurement, how many chains make up one furlong?

17. 'La fourmi' is the French name for which insect?

18. Celtic is the US Secret Service code name for which modern-day American politician?

19. Which of the following is a play written by US playwright Tracy Letts?
a) Superior Cupcakes
b) Superior Donuts
c) Superior Eclairs

20. Where does an annual fire festival called 'Up-Helly-Aa' take place?
a) Isle of Man
b) Orkney
c) Shetland

Answers to Quiz 164: Numbers

1. Four
2. Andre 3000
3. The Feeding of the Five Thousand
4. Sherlock Holmes
5. Lady Jane Grey
6. The Three Degrees
7. Three Times a Lady
8. 10cc
9. Alabama 3
10. UB40
11. Catch-22
12. Fifteen to One
13. Seven Sisters (also Messier object 45)
14. Jackson Pollock
15. The Indianapolis 500
16. Fireball XL5
17. 3-2-1
18. The Thirty-Nine Steps
19. Nadine Dorries
20. 13

DIFFICULT

Quiz 166: Famous Eds

1. Which British university is based in the Lancashire town of Ormskirk?

2. 'The History of the Decline and Fall of the Roman Empire' was written by which 18th-century historian?

3. Which award-winning Irish novelist's works include 'Country Girls', 'August Is a Wicked Month' and 'Wild Decembers'?

4. Which British film-maker directed 'Shaun of the Dead', 'Hot Fuzz' and 'Scott Pilgrim Versus the World'?

5. 'A Bar at the Folies-Bergère' and 'Olympia' are works by which 19th-century French painter?

6. What is the name of Bart Simpson's female schoolteacher in the TV comedy 'The Simpsons'?

7. Regan is the middle name of which American comedian, actor and voice artist, who was born in 1951?

8. Which Australian was the runner-up in the World Snooker Championship in 1968, 1973 and 1975?

9. What was the name of the pool hustler played by Paul Newman in the 1961 film 'The Hustler' and the 1986 film 'The Color of Money'?

10. Emanuel Goldenberg was the real name of which Romanian-born actor, best known for playing criminals and gangsters?

11. Which prolific London-born character actor played Inspector Lestrade in the 2009 film 'Sherlock Holmes' and the 2011 sequel 'Sherlock Holmes: A Game of Shadows'?

12. Which famous lighthouse lies 14 miles off the coast of Plymouth in the English Channel?

13. Who was the founder of the religious denomination known as Christian Science?

14. Which tennis player won the Men's Singles at Wimbledon in 1988 and 1990?

15. The 1992 chart topper 'Would I Lie to You?' was the only top-ten single for which American duo?

16. Eddie Vedder is the lead singer with which American alternative rock band?

17. Which actress played Carmela, wife of mob boss Tony Soprano, in the acclaimed TV series 'The Sopranos'?

18. Which British actor played Marius Pontmercy in the 2012 film 'Les Miserables'?

19. Former Chelsea goalkeeper Eddie Niedzwiecki played international football for which country?
    a) Poland   b) Scotland   c) Wales

20. Eddie Hemmings is a regular TV commentator on which sport?
    a) boxing   b) rugby league   c) rugby union

Answers to Quiz 165: Pot Luck

1. Queen Elizabeth II
2. Lars Von Trier
3. Bird flu
4. Melanie Griffith
5. Jeff Koons
6. Microsoft
7. 21st April
8. Joy Division
9. The Boat Race (in 1829)
10. Tom Sharpe
11. Donald Duck
12. Robert De Niro
13. Russia
14. Jeffery Deaver
15. United Arab Emirates
16. Ten
17. Ant
18. Vice-President Joe Biden
19. Superior Donuts
20. Shetland

DIFFICULT

Quiz 167: Pot Luck

1. 'Yawara' is an alternative name for which Japanese martial art?

2. On a standard dartboard, what number sits between 2 and 10?

3. Where in Asia is Happy Valley Racecourse located?

4. Which former James Bond actor played the fictional British prime minister Adam Lang in the 2010 film 'The Ghost'?

5. 'New Thinking New Possibilities' is a slogan of which car manufacturer?

6. Which name connects a feature of The Wanderers sports ground in South Africa and a famous British shopping centre?

7. In which European language is Father Christmas known as Moş Crăciun?

8. 'Oh no, it wasn't the airplanes. It was beauty killed the beast' is the last line of which film classic?

9. 'Leisure' was the 1991 debut album album from which Britpop band?

10. What nationality was the artist Frida Kahlo?

11. Crime drama 'The Bridge' is set in which two countries?

12. What nationality was Alfred Nobel, after whom the famous prizes are awarded?

13. Which animal is known in French as 'l'écureil'?

14. Which comedy duo were awarded with a BAFTA fellowship in 2009?

15. 'The Crow Road' and 'The Wasp Factory' are novels by which Scottish author, who died in June 2013?

16. In relation to dieting, what do the initials IF stand for?

17. The music festival 'All Tomorrow's Parties' takes its name from a song by which rock band?

18. Which character from 'The Muppet Show' is also a name used to describe a style of journalism where the reporter becomes part of the story?

19. How long in metres is a single lap of an Olympic velodrome?
    a) 200m
    b) 250m
    c) 400m

20. What was the title of a 2009 film by the Coen brothers?
    a) A Serious Man
    b) A Sensuous Man
    c) A Strenuous Man

Answers to Quiz 166: Famous Eds

1. Edge Hill University
2. Edward Gibbon
3. Edna O'Brien
4. Edgar Wright
5. Édouard Manet
6. Edna Krabappel
7. Eddie Murphy
8. Eddie Charlton
9. Fast Eddie Felson
10. Edward G Robinson
11. Eddie Marsan
12. Eddystone Lighthouse
13. Mary Baker Eddy
14. Stefan Edberg
15. Charles and Eddie
16. Pearl Jam
17. Edie Falco
18. Eddie Redmayne
19. Wales
20. Rugby league

DIFFICULT

Quiz 168: Music part 2

1. Which harmonica player is the oldest person to have a UK top 40 single?

2. Which 2011 song by Maroon 5 and Christina Aguilera sold over 1.2m copies and was in the chart for over a year, but never reached number one?

3. Which song by The Beatles was named after a Salvation Army home where John Lennon played as a child?

4. What is the biggest-selling single in UK chart history to feature a girl's name in the title?

5. Which is the only band to have topped the UK singles chart with their first seven releases?

6. The biggest-selling soundtrack in UK chart history was from which 1987 film?

7. Which rapper and businessman's Twitter biography simply reads 'Genius'?

8. The names 'Susie', 'Claudette', 'Mary', 'Jenny', 'Cathy' and 'Lucille' are in the titles of UK hit singles by which siblings?

9. Sphere was the middle name of which legendary jazz pianist, who died in 1982?

10. The biggest-selling UK album by an Irish artist was recorded by which band?

11. 'Wonderwall' by Oasis was kept off the number one spot in the UK charts by which pair of actors' versions of 'I Believe' and 'Up on the Roof'?

12. Boyzone and Westlife were two of three Irish acts to have at least four UK number-one singles in the 1990s. Who was the third?

13. Which former Spice Girl topped the UK singles chart with 'Never Be the Same Again'?

Answers – page 343

14. Which female singer holds the record for the most UK number-two singles?

15. What was The Beatles' first US number-one single?

16. The Whitney Houston hit 'I Will Always Love You' was originally written and recorded by which country music legend?

17. Which 1995 hit was the first rap song to sell one million copies in the UK?

18. What is the biggest-selling single in UK chart history that wasn't a charity record?

19. The 'N Betweens was the original name of which veteran British rock band?
    a) Roxy Music   b) Slade   c) Status Quo

20. Which pop star wrote a 2001 children's book based on the story of Noah's Ark?
    a) Phil Collins   b) Sting   c) Paul Weller

Answers to Quiz 167: Pot Luck

1. Jujitsu	11. Denmark and Sweden
2. 15	12. Swedish
3. Hong Kong	13. The squirrel
4. Pierce Brosnan	14. French and Saunders
5. Hyundai	15. Iain Banks
6. The Bull Ring	16. Intermittent Fasting
7. Romanian	17. The Velvet Underground
8. King Kong	18. Gonzo
9. Blur	19. 250m
10. Mexican	20. A Serious Man

DIFFICULT

Quiz 169: Pot Luck

1. Which actor's Twitter bio reads 'I'm that actor in some of the movies you liked and some you didn't. Sometimes I'm in pretty good shape, other times I'm not. Hey, you gotta live, you know?'

2. What is the highest denomination Euro banknote?

3. 'Get Shorty', 'Out of Sight' and 'Rum Punch' are works by which American crime writer, who died in August 2013?

4. Israel Baline was the real name of which American composer and lyricist?

5. Discovered by astronomers in 2014, what type of celestial object is 2012 VP113?

6. What is the only song to have been a UK million-seller on three separate occasions and for three different artists?

7. In TV comedy 'The Simpsons', which character is the owner of a shop called 'The Leftorium'?

8. Which meat is traditionally used in the Italian dish 'osso bucco'?

9. Double Gloucester is combined with which other cheese to make Huntsman cheese?

10. Written by James Patterson, 'Along Came a Spider' was the first novel to feature which fictional detective?

11. Who was the British prime minister at the start of the American War of Independence?

12. In the classic screwball comedy 'Bringing Up Baby', what type of animal is baby?

13. Who are the five American presidents whose surname ends in a vowel?

14. The Hagia Sophia is a famous museum in which city?

15. A lawyer called Mr Jaggers appears in which novel by Charles Dickens?

16. In which year was the BBC founded?

17. The Konark Sun Temple is in which country?

18. The port sity of Valparaiso is in which South American country?

19. The 2014 film 'Starred Up' is set in which location?
    a) hospital
    b) prison
    c) school

20. Which godfather of house music died in 2014 at the age of 59?
    a) Frankie Fingers
    b) Frankie Knuckles
    c) Frankie Toes

Answers to Quiz 168: Music part 2

1. Larry Adler (on a 1994 duet with Kate Bush)
2. Moves Like Jagger
3. Strawberry Fields Forever
4. 'Mary's Boy Child' by Boney M
5. Westlife
6. Dirty Dancing
7. Jay-Z
8. The Everly Brothers
9. Thelonius Monk
10. The Corrs (Talk On Corners)
11. Robson and Jerome
12. B*Witched
13. Melanie C
14. Kylie Minogue
15. I Want to Hold Your Hand
16. Dolly Parton
17. 'Gangsta's Paradise' by Coolio
18. 'Mull of Kintyre' by Wings
19. Slade
20. Sting

DIFFICULT

Quiz 170: Television part 1

1. In crime drama 'Midsomer Murders', how are DCI John Barnaby and his predecessor Tom Barnaby related?

2. Birgitte Nyborg is the central character in which Scandinavian drama?

3. What is the first name of the title character in the police drama 'Luther'?

4. The father of which TV chat show host was a former professional footballer with Northampton Town and York City?

5. Moxie, Bomber, Neville and Oz were characters in which 1980s drama?

6. The crime drama 'Salamander' is set in which European country?

7. In the TV comedy 'Friends', what was the name of Ross's pet monkey?

8. Which of the 'chasers' from TV quiz show 'The Chase' is a qualified medical doctor?

9. The fictional country of Tazbekistan was the setting for which BBC comedy drama starring David Mitchell and Robert Webb as a pair of bumbling diplomats?

10. 'No Mean City' is the title of the theme song to which long-running police drama?

11. The name of which Manchester band is also the title of a detective drama starring Gillian Anderson?

12. First aired in 2003, what is Channel Four's longest-running British comedy show?

13. Greybridge Secondary is the setting for which TV comedy starring David Walliams and Catherine Tate?

14. Stephen Tompkinson played priest Father Clifford in which Irish-set drama?

DIFFICULT

Answers – page 347

15. Which member of the 'Dad's Army' cast narrated the children's TV animation 'Bod'?

16. Vod, Josie, Oregon and JP are the main characters in which university-set comedy drama?

17. The murder of a child called Danny Latimer was the central storyline in which 2013 crime drama?

18. The crime drama 'Hinterland' is set in which country?

19. In the classic comedy 'Are You Being Served?', what was Mr Humphries' first name?
    a) Churchill   b) Gladstone   c) Wilberforce

20. What is the name of the popular zombie drama starring Andrew Lincoln?
    a) The Walking Dead
    b) The Walking Living
    c) The Walking Wounded

Answers to Quiz 169: Pot Luck

1. Tom Hanks
2. €500
3. Elmore Leonard
4. Irving Berlin
5. A dwarf planet
6. Unchained Melody
7. Ned Flanders
8. Veal
9. Stilton
10. Alex Cross
11. Lord North
12. Leopard
13. Monroe, Fillmore, Pierce, Coolidge and Obama
14. Istanbul
15. Great Expectations
16. 1922
17. India
18. Chile
19. Prison
20. Frankie Knuckles

DIFFICULT

Quiz 171: Pot Luck

1. What is the most populous of New York's five boroughs?

2. Buxton and Cornish are the surnames of which comedy duo?

3. The last TV programme shown on the BBC before the start of the Second World War was a gala starring which cartoon character?

4. Which 1997 chart-topper is the only UK number-one single to be credited to 'Various Artists'?

5. Orchard Road is the main shopping street of which Asian city-state?

6. In which year was Channel 5 launched?

7. Which former Conservative cabinet minister was described by Labour leader Michael Foot as a 'semi-house-trained polecat'?

8. The fight known as 'the rumble in the jungle' took place in which city?

9. Who are the five American Presidents whose surname is made up of four letters?

10. Oliver Mellors is the title character in which controversial novel, first published in its complete form in the UK in 1960?

11. Which British newspaper was first published in 1785 as 'The Daily Universal Register'?

12. MINT is an acronym used to describe a group of countries with emerging economies. Which country is represented by the letter 'I'?

13. A red trident appears on the logo of which Italian motor manufacturer?

14. The Arabic alphabet is made up of how many letters?

15. Who was the eldest of the literary Bronte sisters?

16. What is the name of the graphic designer who created the London Underground map?

17. Who was the last British monarch to veto an Act of Parliament?

18. In Northern Irish politics, which party has the initials TUV?

19. King Bacchus is a feature of the Mardi Gras celebrations in which city carnival?
a) New Orleans
b) Port-of-Spain
c) Rio de Janeiro

20. The Spanish football club Osasuna is based in which city?
a) Malaga
b) Pamplona
c) Seville

Answers to Quiz 170: Television part 1

1. Cousins
2. Borgen
3. John
4. Alan Carr
5. Auf Wiedersehen, Pet
6. Belgium
7. Marcel
8. Paul Sinha
9. The Ambassadors
10. Taggart
11. The Fall
12. Peep Show
13. Big School
14. Ballykissangel
15. John Le Mesurier
16. Fresh Meat
17. Broadchurch
18. Wales
19. Wilberforce
20. The Walking Dead

DIFFICULT

Quiz 172: Science and Nature

1. The word 'science' derives from the Latin 'scientia'. What does 'scientia' mean?

2. C_2H_6O is the chemical formula for what?

3. The periodic table was devised in 1869 by which Russian chemist?

4. What was taken for the first time in 1895 by German physicist Wilhelm Röntgen?

5. What is the rarest of the four blood groups?

6. What does the 'S' in the acronym 'laser' stand for?

7. Which metallic element has the chemical symbol Sb and the atomic number 51?

8. Mycology is the name given to the scientific study of what?

9. In April 2013, a letter written by which Nobel Prize-winning scientist was sold at auction in New York for $5.3m (£3.45m)?

10. If the periodic table was listed alphabetically, which element would be first on the list?

11. And which element would be last?

12. CFCs are one of the causes of the hole in the Earth's ozone layer. What does CFC stand for?

13. What was the first name of Fahrenheit, after whom the temperature scale is named?

14. In which year did the Space Shuttle make its maiden flight?

15. US physicist Theodore Maiman was the inventor of which device, beloved of science-fiction heroes and Bond villains?

16. The European Organization for Nuclear Research is based in the suburbs of which city?

17. The biologist and author Richard Dawkins was born in which African country?

18. Riboflavin is the common name of which vitamin?

19. Which country sent a monkey into space in 2013 as part of a programme that eventually aims for manned missions?
    a) Iran
    b) North Korea
    c) Pakistan

20. In 2013, scientists at Bristol University managed to charge a mobile phone using what unlikely substance?
    a) blood
    b) lemonade
    c) urine

Answers to Quiz 171: Pot Luck

1. Brooklyn
2. Adam and Joe
3. Mickey Mouse
4. Perfect Day
5. Singapore
6. 1997
7. Norman Tebbit
8. Kinshasa
9. Polk, Taft, Ford, George H W Bush and George W Bush
10. Lady Chatterley's Lover
11. The Times
12. Indonesia
13. Maserati
14. 28
15. Charlotte
16. Harry Beck
17. Queen Anne
18. Traditional Unionist Voice
19. New Orleans
20. Pamplona

DIFFICULT

Quiz 173: Pot Luck

1. What is the largest of New York's five boroughs by area?

2. Best known for his operas, what was the first name of Italian composer Donizetti?

3. Lusophone is a name used to describe speakers of which language?

4. 'Nominates' is an anagram of which American state?

5. Which British author created the fictional American action hero Jack Reacher?

6. 'The Persistence of Memory' is a painting by which Spanish surrealist?

7. Who are the four teams to have won English football's top flight just once?

8. Who was the last American president whose christian name started with a vowel?

9. Which British prime minister was given the title the Earl of Beaconsfield?

10. Operation Mercury was a Nazi invasion of which Mediterranean island?

11. Featherstone Prison is in which English city?

12. What was the name of the Italian banker found hanging from scaffolding under Blackfriars Bridge in June 1982?

13. 'Independence forever' were the last words spoken in public by which American president?

14. What is the only novel by Charles Dickens to have a female narrator?

15. Prior to becoming president, Franklin D Roosevelt was the governor of which American state?

16. Ustinov and John Snow are colleges at which British university?

17. The headquarters of the UK Space Agency are in which English town?

18. Who were the first winners of English football's top flight?

19. Crockford's is a directory of people working in which profession?
    a) clergy
    b) law
    c) medicine

20. Al-Shabaab is the name of a militant Islamist organization. What does the name mean in English?
    a) The Glory
    b) The Power
    c) The Youth

Answers to Quiz 172: Science and Nature

1. Knowledge
2. Alcohol (ethanol)
3. Dmitry Mendeleev
4. An X-ray
5. AB
6. Stimulated
7. Antimony
8. Fungi
9. Francis Crick
10. Actinium
11. Zirconium
12. Chlorofluorocarbon
13. Gabriel
14. 1981
15. The laser
16. Geneva
17. Kenya
18. Vitamin B_2
19. Iran
20. Urine

DIFFICULT

Quiz 174: Return of the Mac

1. Which TV broadcaster went 'Beyond Breaking Point' to raise funds for Comic Relief in 2014?

2. Two American presidents were assassinated in the 20th century. John F Kennedy was one, who was the other?

3. Which Scottish actor provided the voice of Gnomeo in the 2011 film animation 'Gnomeo and Juliet'?

4. 'Jimmy Mack' was a UK hit single in 1967 for which Motown group?

5. The Oscars were hosted for the first time in 2013 by which actor?

6. What is the name of the British actor who played Emperor Palpatine in the 'Star Wars' film series?

7. Hazen is the middle name of which British comedian and broadcaster?

8. What was the name of the character played by Tony Osoba in classic TV comedy 'Porridge'?

9. Which Hollywood actor is a member of a rock band called The Pizza Underground?

10. Who was the first English footballer to win the UEFA Champions League with a non-English club?

11. Which author won the Booker Prize in 1998 for the novel 'Amsterdam'?

12. 'Pigeon' was the nickname of which fast bowler, who took 563 wickets for Australia between 1993 and 2007?

13. Which actress, who played Narcissa Malfoy in the final three 'Harry Potter' films is married to actor Damian Lewis?

14. Which fictional TV adventurer, beloved of Marge Simpson's sisters, is noted for his use of a Swiss Army knife?

Answers – page 355

15. What is the name of the character played by Beverley Callard in 'Coronation Street'?

16. Which actress won her only Oscar in 1984 for her performance in 'Terms of Endearment'?

17. Which Yorkshire writer and broadcaster is the poet-in-residence at Barnsley Football Club?

18. In the prohibition-era drama 'Boardwalk Empire', Margaret Thompson is played by which Scottish actress?

19. Liz McClarnon is a member of which pop group?
    a) All Saints   b) Atomic Kitten   b) Sugababes

20. The award-winning political memoir 'Power Trip: A Decade of Policy, Plots and Spin' was written by which former Downing Street spin doctor?
    a) Damian McBride   b) Declan McBride
    c) Dermot McBride

Answers to Quiz 173: Pot Luck

1. Queens
2. Gaetano
3. Portuguese
4. Minnesota
5. Lee Child
6. Salvador Dali
7. Ipswich Town, Nottingham Forest, Sheffield United and West Bromwich Albion
8. Ulysses S Grant
9. Benjamin Disraeli
10. Crete
11. Wolverhampton
12. Roberto Calvi
13. John Adams
14. Bleak House
15. New York
16. Durham
17. Swindon
18. Preston North End
19. Clergy
20. The Youth

DIFFICULT

Quiz 175: Pot Luck

1. The Himalayas mountain range crosses which six countries?

2. Which actor plays the amateur detective Father Brown in the modern-day BBC drama series?

3. Which honorific Indian title means 'great-souled'?

4. Umea, one of two cities designated European Capital of Culture in 2014, is in which Nordic country?

5. Dr Who's time-travelling craft the TARDIS is an acronym. What does the 'D' stand for?

6. Manchego cheese is made from the milk of which animal?

7. Which is the smallest of New York's five boroughs by area?

8. What are the six countries to have coasts on the Adriatic Sea?

9. 'Ordem e Progresso' is the national motto and appears on the flag of which country?

10. A mountain called Adam's Peak is located in which Asian country?

11. 'An Alpine Symphony, Op. 64' is a symphonic poem by which German composer?

12. If all of America's presidents were listed alphabetically, who would be first on the list?

13. 160lb is the maximum weight for a male boxer in which division?

14. Noted for its animated films, Studio Ghibli is a film production company based in which country?

15. Which national radio station broadcast for the first time on 28 March 1994?

16. What nationality was the painter Edvard Munch?

17. In the comedy 'Are You Being Served?', what was the first name of Captain Peacock?

18. A carpet appears on the flag of which central Asian republic?

19. What was the first name of the founder of the fashion house Givenchy?
    a) Henri
    b) Herbert
    c) Hubert

20. Complete the title of a 2013 bestseller by Deborah Rodriguez – 'The Little Coffee Shop of …'?
    a) Baghdad
    b) Damascus
    c) Kabul

Answers to Quiz 174: Return of the Mac

1. Davina McCall
2. William McKinley
3. James McAvoy
4. Martha Reeves and the Vandellas
5. Seth MacFarlane
6. Ian McDiarmid
7. Michael McIntyre
8. McLaren
9. Macaulay Culkin
10. Steve McManaman
11. Ian McEwan
12. Glenn McGrath
13. Helen McCrory
14. MacGyver
15. Liz McDonald
16. Shirley MacLaine
17. Ian McMillan
18. Kelly Macdonald
19. Atomic Kitten
20. Damian McBride

DIFFICULT

Quiz 176: History part 2

1. Which British statesman was the last vicerory of India?

2. Joan of Arc was burnt at the stake in which French town?

3. Which Archbishop of Canterbury crowned Queen Elizabeth II?

4. Prior to John Paul II, in which century was the last non-Italian pope in office?

5. Who was the first English monarch to abdicate?

6. Who was Time Magazine's Man of the Year in 1939?

7. What was the name of the ship on which Captain Cook first sailed to Australia and New Zealand?

8. In which decade were the comics 'The Beano' and 'The Dandy' first published?

9. The Pilgrimage of Grace was a popular uprising against which Tudor monarch?

10. Who was the shortest-serving British prime minister of the 20th century?

11. The 1356 Battle of Poitiers was a major battle in which war?

12. Who was South Africa's last white president?

13. Who was the last British prime minister to be educated at Cambridge University?

14. In which year did the prohibition of alcohol end in the USA?

15. Which 20th-century American president was the son of a former American ambassador to Great Britain?

16. In which year were women over 30 given the vote in the UK?

DIFFICULT

356

17. Who was the US president when Neil Armstrong became the first man to walk on the Moon?

18. Who were the four men to serve as British prime minister under King George VI?

19. Leptis Magna, a prominent city in the Phoenician and Roman era, is in which modern-day country?
    a) Libya
    b) Tunisia
    c) Turkey

20. In which year did the Suez Canal open?
    a) 1859
    b) 1869
    c) 1879

Answers to Quiz 175: Pot Luck

1. Bhutan, India, Nepal, China, Afghanistan and Pakistan
2. Mark Williams
3. Mahatma
4. Sweden
5. Dimension
6. Sheep
7. Manhattan
8. Italy, Croatia, Albania, Montenegro, Bosnia-Herzegovina, and Slovenia.
9. Brazil
10. Sri Lanka
11. Richard Strauss
12. John Adams
13. Middleweight
14. Japan
15. BBC Radio 5 Live
16. Norwegian
17. Stephen
18. Turkmenistan
19. Hubert
20. Kabul

DIFFICULT

Quiz 177: Pot Luck

1. Which fictional detective has been portrayed on screen by Rolf Lassgård, Krister Henriksson and Kenneth Branagh?

2. The soft drink Kia-Ora means 'be well' in which language?

3. What was the first name of the famous Regency-era dandy Beau Brummell?

4. Which central American country is known as the 'Land of Volcanoes'?

5. What is the currency of Saudi Arabia?

6. The oldest purpose-built mosque in Britain is situated in which Surrey town?

7. Which two letters signify a member of the parliament of the Republic of Ireland?

8. Which country won cricket's World T20 competition in 2014?

9. 'Holmia' is the Latin name for which European capital city?

10. In 2014, which 49-year-old became the oldest boxer to unify a weight division?

11. Which actor was Barbra Streisand's first husband?

12. What is the largest country in Central America?

13. What is measured using systolic and diastolic readings?

14. Which portly chef presented the TV show 'Proper Good Food' and the wrote the best-selling book of the same name?

15. In 2014, England's Lisa Ashton became a world champion in which sport?

16. Which bird provided author Donna Tartt with the title of a 2013 bestseller?

Answers – page 361

17. Which 19th-century British prime minister gave his name to a style of leather portmanteau bag?

18. In George Orwell's 'Animal Farm', what is the name of the owner of the farm?

19. Which of these teams did not take part in the first season of football's Premier League?
    a) Coventry City
    b) Newcastle United
    c) Oldham Athletic

20. The Forward Prize is awarded in which branch of the arts?
    a) classical music
    b) painting
    c) poetry

Answers to Quiz 176: History part 2

1. Louis, Lord Mountbatten	12. FW De Klerk
2. Rouen	13. Stanley Baldwin
3. Geoffrey Fisher	14. 1933
4. 16th century	15. John F Kennedy
5. Edward II	16. 1918
6. Josef Stalin	17. Richard Nixon
7. HMS Endeavour	18. Stanley Baldwin, Neville Chamberlain, Winston Churchill and Clement Attlee
8. 1930s	
9. Henry VIII	
10. Andrew Bonar Law	19. Libya
11. The Hundred Years' War	20. 1869

DIFFICULT

Quiz 178: Television part 2

1. Who was the first host of the UK version of 'The Price is Right'?

2. In 'The Simpsons', which actor provides the voice of Sideshow Bob?

3. Vince Pinner and Penny Warrender were the main characters in which sitcom?

4. Brenda Furlong, Dolly Bellfield and Philippa Moorcroft are characters in which TV sitcom?

5. In which year did BBC2 first appear on British TV screens?

6. Rick Spleen is the central character in which BBC sitcom, which first hit TV screens in 2006?

7. Who preceded David Dimbleby as the host of political debate show 'Question Time'?

8. What is the name of the sarcastic teenage character created by Catherine Tate who is famous for saying 'am I bovvered'?

9. 'The Liberty Bell March' by John Philip Sousa was the theme tune to which classic TV comedy?

10. The first ever UK National Lottery draw show was hosted by which broadcaster?

11. Which actor played 'Thermoman' in the TV comedy 'My Hero'?

12. Cornelius was the middle name of which annoying TV cartoon character?

13. Kevin Whateley played Dr Jack Kerruish in which medical drama?

14. What was the name of Alan Partridge's long-suffering first wife?

15. Patrick Troughton, Richard Green, Jonas Armstrong and Michael Praed have all played which character on TV?

16. Which politician made a guest appearance in the final episode of sitcom 'Gavin and Stacey'?

17. Which actor narrated the documentary series 'The World at War'?

18. Who were the original hosts of BBC favourite 'The One Show'?

19. In the sitcom 'Only Fools and Horses', what was Boycie's unusual middle name?
    a) Aubrey
    b) Bartleby
    c) Calliope

20. Who provided the voice for the TV animation 'King Rollo'?
    a) Ray Brooks
    b) Brian Cant
    c) Derek Griffiths

Answers to Quiz 177: Pot Luck

1. Kurt Wallander
2. Maori
3. George
4. El Salvador
5. Riyal
6. Woking
7. TD
8. Sri Lanka
9. Stockholm
10. Bernard Hopkins
11. Elliott Gould
12. Nicaragua
13. Blood pressure
14. Tom Kerridge
15. Darts
16. The Goldfinch
17. Gladstone
18. Mr Jones
19. Newcastle United
20. Poetry

DIFFICULT

Quiz 179: Pot Luck

1. New York state shares land borders with which five American states?

2. Ushuaia, the southernmost city in the world, is in which country?

3. Dame Judi Dench won a Best Supporting Actress Oscar in 1998 for an eight-minute appearance in which film?

4. What was the only UK number-one single for the Jimi Hendrix Experience?

5. What town in Kent gives its name to a species of the warbler bird?

6. Who were the two British male solo artists to have four UK number-one singles in the 1980s?

7. What were the three British bands that managed four UK number-one singles in the 1980s?

8. Which member of the royal family has the titles of Earl of Inverness and Baron Killyleagh?

9. Which popular North African food looks the same whether it is written in upper- or lower-case letters?

10. Rise, Pulse, Heat and Heat Rush are brands of perfumes created by which female singer?

11. The DCRI is the domestic security service in which European country?

12. Arctic, roseate and sandwich are species of which bird?

13. How many gallons are equal to one peck?

14. Which Oscar-winning Hollywood star married photographer Alexandra Hedison in April 2014?

15. Which medical condition was once known as 'the king's evil'?

16. The giant sportswear manufacturer Nike is based in which American state?

17. Baroness Jay of Paddington, the former Leader of the House of Lords, is the daughter of which 20th-century prime minister?

18. Petruchio and Christopher Sly are characters in which Shakespeare play?

19. In which branch of the arts is Savion Glover a notable name?
    a) poetry
    b) sculpture
    c) tap dancing

20. One square mile is equal to how many acres?
    a) 490
    b) 640
    c) 810

Answers to Quiz 178: Television part 2

1. Leslie Crowther
2. Kelsey Grammer
3. Just Good Friends
4. Dinnerladies
5. 1964
6. Lead Balloon
7. Peter Sissons
8. Lauren
9. Monty Python's Flying Circus
10. Noel Edmonds
11. Ardal O'Hanlon
12. Scrappy Doo
13. Peak Practice
14. Carol
15. Robin Hood
16. John Prescott
17. Sir Laurence Olivier
18. Adrian Chiles and Nadia Sawalha
19. Aubrey
20. Ray Brooks

DIFFICULT

Quiz 180: Books

1. Henry and Edward are the first names of which literary alter egos?

2. The first name of Mr Micawber from the Charles Dickens novel 'David Copperfield' is also the surname of a former England football captain. What is it?

3. 'An Officer and a Spy', 'The Fear Index' and 'Lustrum' are novels by which British thriller writer?

4. What do the initials PD stand for in the name PD James?

5. A creepy housekeeper called Mrs Danvers appears in which 1938 novel by Daphne Du Maurier?

6. Which member of the Bloomsbury Group wrote the novel 'To the Lighthouse'?

7. The Hugo Award is a prestigious literary prize in which genre?

8. 'Bring Me Home' was a 2014 best-seller for which British broadcaster and author?

9. 'Living History' was the title of a best-selling 2003 memoir by which American politician?

10. In the best-selling book 'It's All About Treo', what type of animal is Treo?

11. Which American author is often referred to as 'the man in the white suit'?

12. Which author created the fictional soldier 'Sharpe'?

13. In 1840, which novelist launched a weekly periodical called 'Master Humphrey's Clock'?

14. The word 'wicked' was used in print with the meaning 'excellent or remarkable' for the first time in the 1920 novel 'This Side of Paradise'. Which acclaimed author wrote it?

Answers – page 367

15. The TV series 'Tales of the Unexpected' was based on stories by which author, best known for his children's books?

16. 'How Not to Be a Football Millionaire' was the title of the autobiography of which Northern Irish footballer?

17. Which author wrote the series of books known as the Barsetshire Chronicles?

18. Which English county was also the title of a Pulitzer Prize-winning novel by Jeffrey Eugenides?

19. 'The Murder Bag' was the debut crime novel by which British author?
    a) Nick Hornby   b) Tony Parsons   c) Irvine Welsh

20. What nationality was the author Gabriel Garcia Marquez?
    a) Colombian   b) Mexican   c) Spanish

Answers to Quiz 179: Pot Luck

1. New Jersey, Pennsylvania, Connecticut, Massachusetts and Vermont
2. Argentina
3. Shakespeare in Love
4. Voodoo Chile
5. Dartford
6. David Bowie and Shakin' Stevens
7. The Jam, Pet Shop Boys and Wham!
8. Prince Andrew (Duke of York)
9. Couscous
10. Beyonce
11. France
12. Tern
13. Two
14. Jodie Foster
15. Scrofula
16. Oregon
17. James Callaghan
18. The Taming of the Shrew
19. Tap dancing
20. 640

DIFFICULT

Quiz 181: Pot Luck

1. The 'Irving G Thalberg Memorial Award' is presented periodically at which awards ceremony?

2. 'Nullius in verba', roughly translated as 'take nobody's word for it', is the motto of which scientific organization, founded in 1662?

3. In 'The Lord of the Rings', by what name is the character Peregrin Took more commonly known?

4. In 2014, Abdelaziz Bouteflika was elected president of which African country for the fourth time?

5. A Stopfordian is a name given to a person from which English town?

6. Prior to Luis Suarez, who was the last Liverpool player to score 30 goals in a top-flight season?

7. Which comedy duo are known in Germany and 'Dick und Doof' (Thick and Stupid)?

8. Which major American newspaper was bought by Amazon. com founder Jeff Bezos in Autumn 2013?

9. A body with the initials OPCW was the winner of the 2013 Nobel Peace Prize. What does OPCW stand for?

10. In December 2013, 92 people were injured after a ceiling collapsed at which London theatre?

11. As the crow flies, which city is closer to London – Chicago or Karachi?

12. In the English version of the board game 'Scrabble', which five letters have only one tile?

13. Which British actor was named as one of the '100 Most Influential People in the World' in 2014 according to Time Magazine?

14. Which British film-maker directed the films known as the 'Cornetto Trilogy?

15. Robben Island, site of a famous prison, lies off the coast of which South African city?

16. Which British politician was appointed a United Nations Special Envoy for Education in 2012?

17. Mark Corrigan and Jeremy Usborne are the central characters in which TV comedy?

18. Which British charity was founded in 1953 by the Reverend Chad Varah?

19. Something that is crural relates to which part of the body?
    a) arm   b) leg   c) skull

20. Which former prime minister said, after being hit by a stink bomb thrown by a schoolboy, 'With an arm like that he ought to be in the English cricket XI'?
    a) James Callaghan   b) John Major   c) Harold Wilson

Answers to Quiz 180: Books

1. Dr Jekyll and Mr Hyde
2. Wilkins
3. Robert Harris
4. Phyllis Dorothy
5. Rebecca
6. Virginia Woolf
7. Science fiction
8. Alan Titchmarsh
9. Hillary Clinton
10. Dog
11. Tom Wolfe
12. Bernard Cornwell
13. Charles Dickens
14. F Scott Fitzgerald
15. Roald Dahl
16. Keith Gillespie
17. Anthony Trollope
18. Middlesex
19. Tony Parsons
20. Colombian

DIFFICULT

Quiz 182: Sport

1. Which Swedish tennis player won seven grand slam titles between 1982 and 1988 but never won the singles title at Wimbledon?

2. Between 2001 and 2010, who were the three Englishmen to win snooker's World Championship?

3. In which decade was golf's Ryder Cup held for the first time?

4. According to 'The Sunday Times Rich List', who was Britain's richest sportsman in 2014?

5. Who was the first non-European to win the Tour de France?

6. In which sport do teams compete for the Wilkinson Sword and Iroquois Cup?

7. What was the only grand slam event that Boris Becker did not win?

8. In which year, and with which song, did the England football team first top the UK singles chart?

9. The Earthquake are an American soccer team based in which city?

10. In 2013, which Briton became the first driver to finish every race during his debut Formula One season?

11. The long-time Liverpool defender Martin Skrtel plays international football for which country?

12. The Irish Grand National horse race is run at which course?

13. Which multiple grand slam-winning tennis star also wrote a series of thrillers including 'Killer Instinct' and 'Match Point'?

14. The Cheshire Phoenix, Birmingham Knights, Newcastle Eagles and Plymouth Raiders play which sport?

15. Who was appointed coach of the England cricket team for the second time in April 2014?

16. Which multiple winner also holds the record for the most runner-up finishes in the Open golf championship?

17. In which city is an American basketball team nicknamed the Pelicans based?

18. In 2014, Fernando Amorebieta became the first player from which country to score a Premier League goal?

19. In 1989, which Australian cricketer set the record for downing the most cans of lager on a flight from Australia to England?
    a) David Boon   b) Allan Border   c) Merv Hughes

20. In which sport are the brothers John and Jim Harbaugh noted coaches?
    a) American football   b) basketball   c) ice hockey

Answers to Quiz 181: Pot Luck

1. The Oscars
2. The Royal Society
3. Pippin
4. Algeria
5. Stockport
6. Ian Rush
7. Laurel and Hardy
8. Washington Post
9. Organization for the Prohibition of Chemical Weapons
10. Apollo Theatre
11. Karachi
12. J, K, Q, X and Z
13. Benedict Cumberbatch
14. Edgar Wright
15. Cape Town
16. Gordon Brown
17. Peep Show
18. The Samaritans
19. Leg
20. Harold Wilson

DIFFICULT

Quiz 183: Pot Luck

1. Which political leader said, 'There are many causes that I am prepared to die for but no causes that I am prepared to kill for'?

2. Fictional secret agent Jack Ryan was created by which American novelist, who died in October 2013?

3. In terms of area, what is the largest country in Africa?

4. Vientiane is the capital city of which Asian country?

5. By what pseudonym is the British political blogger Paul Staines better known?

6. Durrës is the second-largest city in which European country?

7. What are netsuke?

8. The Battle of Brandywine was fought in which war?

9. The River Dodder, the River Poddle and the River Camac are tributaries of which river in the British Isles?

10. Created by Swede Markus Persson, what is the name of the computer game that allows players to create 3-D constructions out of textured cubes?

11. The United States Air Force Academy is based in which American state?

12. Which British actor directed the film musical 'Sunshine on Leith'?

13. Between 1954 and 1989 Alfredo Stroessner was the president of which South American country?

14. A napa is a variety of which vegetable?

15. Now open to the public, Arundells in Salisbury was the home of which former British prime minister?

16. Of what is carpology the the study?

17. Someone with emetophobia has an irrational fear of what?

18. Which city is closer to London – Nairobi or New Delhi?

19. The 2014 book 'This Boy – A Memoir of a Childhood' was written by which Labour politician?
    a) Alan Johnson
    b) Gordon Brown
    c) John Prescott

20. What is the name of the throne on which British monarchs are crowned?
    a) King Edward's Chair
    b) King Henry's Chair
    c) King William's Chair

Answers to Quiz 182: Sport

1. Mats Wilander
2. Ronnie O'Sullivan, Peter Ebdon and Shaun Murphy
3. 1920s
4. Lewis Hamilton
5. Greg LeMond
6. Lacrosse
7. French Open
8. 1970 with 'Back Home'
9. San Jose
10. Max Chilton
11. Slovakia
12. Fairyhouse
13. Martina Navratilova
14. Basketball
15. Peter Moores
16. Jack Nicklaus (seven)
17. New Orleans
18. Venezuela
19. David Boon
20. American football

DIFFICULT

Quiz 184: Football

1. The headquarters of football's governing body FIFA are in which city?

2. Who was sent off for a deliberate handball in the closing moments of a 2010 World Cup quarter-final?

3. Which Yorkshireman was the scorer of the Premier League's first goal?

4. 'Addicted' was the title of the autobiography of which former England captain?

5. England goalkeeper Joe Hart started his professional career with which club?

6. David Beckham had a brief spell with which Italian club?

7. In terms of population, what is the smallest country to qualify for the World Cup finals?

8. Which goalkeeper holds the record for the most consecutive Premier League appearances, with 310 between 2004 and 2012?

9. Whose goal for Scotland in the 1978 World Cup was immortalized in the cult movie 'Trainspotting'?

10. Which Spanish team plays its home matches at the Mestella Stadium?

11. What are the three clubs to have won all four divisions of English football?

12. St Jude's is the original name of which London club?

13. Who was the first manager to be relegated from the Premier League with three different clubs?

14. Which actor played Brian Clough's assistant, Peter Taylor, in the film 'The Damned United'?

15. Primrose is the middle name of which goalkeeper-turned-broadcaster?

16. Who is the only man to have lost in a World Cup final as both a player and a manager?

17. The names of the main characters in TV drama 'New Tricks' all have a connection with which Midlands club?

18. Which was the last Premier League club to field a starting XI made up entirely of English players?

19. How many steps led to the Royal Box at the old Wembley?
    a) 29   b) 39   c) 49

20. How many steps lead to the Royal Box in the refurbished Wembley?
    a) 87   b) 97   c) 107

Answers to Quiz 183: Pot Luck

1. Gandhi
2. Tom Clancy
3. Algeria
4. Laos
5. Guido Fawkes
6. Albania
7. Miniature Japanese pots
8. American War of Independence
9. River Liffey
10. Minecraft
11. Colorado
12. Dexter Fletcher
13. Paraguay
14. Cabbage
15. Edward Heath
16. Fruit and seeds
17. Vomiting
18. New Delhi
19. Alan Johnson
20. King Edward's Chair

DIFFICULT

Quiz 185: Pot Luck

1. Which Asian capital city is known locally as Krung Thep?

2. Which four colours feature on the flags of Kuwait, Jordan and the United Arab Emirates?

3. True or false – racing driver Stirling Moss never won the World Drivers' Championship?

4. First published in 1791, what is Britain's oldest Sunday newspaper?

5. What was the first name of the French sculptor Rodin?

6. What is the shortest of Shakespeare's plays?

7. Which city is closer to London as the crow flies – Johannesburg or Shanghai?

8. True or false – actor Benicio del Toro and film director Guillermo del Toro are brothers?

9. Directed by Welshman Gareth Evans, the 2011 action thriller 'The Raid: Redemption' and its 2014 sequel 'The Raid 2' were set in which Asian country?

10. Which Northern Irish town played host to the G8 summit in June 2013?

11. Who was the first Jamaican to have a UK number-one single?

12. In greyhound racing, which colour vest is worn by a dog running from trap one?

13. Who was Britain's shortest-serving prime minister, spending just 119 days in office in 1827?

14. The composer Richard Wagner was born in which German city?

15. Graz is the second-largest city in which country?

Answers – page 377

16. Who was the last man to win the Best Actor Oscar while still in his twenties?

17. 'The Little Sure Shot' was the nickname of which Wild West sharpshooter?

18. McLeod Cooper are the middle names of which footballer, who made his England debut in 2003?

19. Which of the following was not a founder member of the Football League?
    a) Arsenal   b) Blackburn Rovers   c) Derby County

20. 'Deeds not words' was the motto of which protest organization?
    a) The Black Panthers
    b) The Levellers
    c) The Suffragettes

Answers to Quiz 184: Football

1. Zurich
2. Luis Suarez
3. Brian Deane
4. Tony Adams
5. Shrewsbury Town
6. AC Milan
7. Trinidad and Tobago
8. Brad Friedel
9. Archie Gemmill
10. Valencia
11. Burnley, Preston North End and Wolverhampton Wanderers
12. Queens Park Rangers
13. Dave Bassett
14. Timothy Spall
15. Bob Wilson
16. Franz Beckenbauer
17. West Bromwich Albion
18. Aston Villa
19. 39
20. 107

DIFFICULT

Quiz 186: Anagrams part 1

Rearrange the letters to make the name of a winner of the BBC Sports Personality of the Year Award:

1. Snigger Bawdily

2. Fir Fondant Flew

3. Sir Flinched Riot

4. Farm Wide Habitat

5. Mail Jerk

6. Frosted Banner

7. Bedroom Diva

8. Obese Satanic

9. Subsonic Iron

10. Medal Typhoons

11. Televised Ad

12. Smell In Angle

13. Calm Zinc Log

14. Gulag Canopies

DIFFICULT

15. Jeez Coal Hag

16. Create Jaws Kit

17. Moms Piston

18. Neuters Josh

19. Haversack Mind

20. Drooping Ire

Answers to Quiz 185: Pot Luck

1. Bangkok
2. Red, white, black and green
3. True
4. The Observer
5. Auguste
6. The Comedy of Errors
7. Johannesburg
8. False
9. Indonesia
10. Enniskillen
11. Desmond Dekker
12. Red
13. George Canning
14. Leipzig
15. Austria
16. Adrien Brody
17. Annie Oakley
18. Glen Johnson
19. Arsenal
20. The Suffragettes

DIFFICULT

Quiz 187: Pot Luck

1. Which fictional detective is based in the Scandinavian city of Ystad?

2. Which French city was a European Capital of Culture in 2013?

3. In October 2012, Patrick Swaffer succeeded Sir Quentin Thomas as the president of which influential London-based film organization?

4. Which American president popularized the phrase 'It's amazing how much can be accomplished if no one cares who gets the credit'?

5. The prestigious Ivy League university Princeton is based in which American state?

6. A text message to his wife bearing the words 'noli timere' were the last words of which Irish poet, who died in 2013?

7. The Isle of Purbeck is a peninsula in which southern English county?

8. Which game features in a series of tournaments known as the WSOP?

9. Which three colours feature on the flag of Thailand?

10. In 2013, Thomas Bach succeeded Jacques Rogge as the president of which international organization?

11. Which Spanish football team takes its name from the Basque word for 'health'?

12. The port city of Busan is in which Asian country?

13. Which easy-listening singer described himself as 'the Justin Bieber of the '70s. Really. Ask your mother'?

14. Ketel One vodka is distilled in which western European country?

15. By what name was the South African city of Tshwane formerly known?

16. What type of food is markook?

17. The Express and Star is a local newspaper in which English midland city?

18. Which 16th-century English playwright was described by the poet Seamus Heaney as being 'a kind of cross between Oscar Wilde and Jack the Ripper'?

19. Which is the only county of Northern Ireland that does not have a shore on Lough Neagh?
    a) Antrim   b) Fermanagh   c) Tyrone

20. Building work on the Tower of London began during the reign of which English king?
    a) William the Conqueror   b) Henry II   c) Henry VIII

Answers to Quiz 186: Anagrams part 1

1. Bradley Wiggins
2. Andrew Flintoff
3. Linford Christie
4. Fatima Whitbread
5. Jim Laker
6. Brendan Foster
7. David Broome
8. Sebastian Coe
9. Robin Cousins
10. Daley Thompson
11. David Steele
12. Nigel Mansell
13. Liz McColgan
14. Paul Gascoigne
15. Joe Calzaghe
16. Jackie Stewart
17. Tom Simpson
18. John Surtees
19. Mark Cavendish
20. Gordon Pirie

DIFFICULT

Quiz 188: Art

1. In printing, which four colours are represented by CMYK?

2. What was the first name of the Russian painter Kandinsky?

3. Which world-famous landmark was designed by the French sculptor Frédéric Auguste Bartholdi?

4. Which French artist was renowned for his 'cut-outs'?

5. Which artistic technique was pioneered by the 19th-century French artist Georges Seurat?

6. In 2002, conceptual artist Sam Taylor-Wood created a video installation featuring which famous sportsman sleeping?

7. Jacopo Comin was the real name of which 16th-century Venetian painter?

8. Bought by the Professional Footballers' Association for £1.9m in 1999, 'Going to the Match' is a work by which English artist?

9. 'Strangeland' was the title of the 2006 autobiography by which British artist?

10. Which painter's 'Massacre of the Innocents' sold at auction in 2002 for £49.5m?

11. Which Swiss artist, who died in 1940, described his work as 'taking a line for a walk'?

12. True or false – Picasso followed a 'blue period' with a 'rose period'?

13. The famous painting 'The Rokeby Venus' was by which Spanish master?

14. Which Mumbai-born sculptor created the the Arcelor Mittal Orbit at London's Olympic Park?

15. By what name was the Renaissance master Alessandro di Mariano di Vanni Filipepi better known?

16. French artist Yves Klein was best known for his monochrome paintings in which colour?

17. Whose 1995 portrait 'Benefits Supervisor Sleeping' was sold at auction in 2008 for a record $33.6m?

18. Jheronimus van Aken was the real name of which Dutch painter, whose works include 'The Garden of Earthly Delights' and 'The Ship of Fools'?

19. In which country was the figurative painter Marc Chagall born?
a) France   b) Russia   c) USA

20. Which British artist is best known for her work with celebrity lookalikes?
a) Alison Jackson   b) Alison Johnson   c) Alison Jones

Answers to Quiz 187: Pot Luck

1. Wallander
2. Marseille
3. The British Board of Film Classification
4. Harry S Truman
5. New Jersey
6. Seamus Heaney
7. Dorset
8. Poker
9. Red, white and blue
10. The International Olympic Committee
11. Osasuna
12. South Korea
13. Barry Manilow
14. The Netherlands
15. Pretoria
16. Bread
17. Wolverhampton
18. Christopher Marlowe
19. Fermanagh
20. William the Conqueror

DIFFICULT

Quiz 189: Pot Luck

1. The Baseball Ground was the former home of which English football team?

2. 'The Whale', 'The Protecting Veil' and 'Song for Athene' are works by which British composer, who died in late 2013?

3. Which trade union was formed following the merger of Amicus and the Transport and General Workers' Union?

4. By what name was the architect Charles-Édouard Jeanneret-Gris better known?

5. Which was the first country to win the football World Cup more than once?

6. The blue agave plant is used to make which spirit?

7. 'A Mari Usque Ad Mare' (From Sea to Sea) is the motto of which Commonwealth country?

8. Which country has won football's Africa Cup of Nations the most times?

9. Which Italian city takes its name from the Greek for 'new town'?

10. 'It happened every year, was almost a ritual' is the opening line to which Scandinavian crime novel?

11. Stanhope is the surname of which eponymous TV detective?

12. Which animal replaced the iron as a token in the board game 'Monopoly' in 2013?

13. European football's governing body UEFA is based in which small Swiss city?

14. Kingsmead is a cricket stadium in which South African city?

15. While accepting an award at the 2001 Brits, Robbie Williams challenged which rock rival to a fight?

16. In the 'Star Wars' films, what is Princess Leia's surname?

17. How long did the Hundred Years' War last?

18. Which city is closer to London – Rio de Janeiro or Bangkok?

19. In 2013, Ryan Riess was crowned world champion in which game?
    a) backgammon
    b) chess
    c) poker

20. The Spanish football club Levante is based in which city?
    a) Madrid
    b) Seville
    c) Valencia

Answers to Quiz 188: Art

1. Cyan, magenta, yellow and black
2. Wassily
3. The Statue of Liberty
4. Matisse
5. Pointillism
6. David Beckham
7. Tintoretto
8. LS Lowry
9. Tracey Emin
10. Peter Paul Rubens
11. Paul Klee
12. True
13. Diego Velazquez
14. Anish Kapoor
15. Botticelli
16. Blue
17. Lucian Freud
18. Hieronymous Bosch
19. Russia
20. Alison Jackson

DIFFICULT

Quiz 190: Fill in the Blank part 2

Fill in the missing item in the following series:

1. Rafael Benitez, ____, Kenny Dalglish, Brendan Rodgers

2. George Washington, John Adams, Thomas Jefferson, ____

3. John Reid, ____, Alan Johnson, Theresa May

4. ____, Turin, Vancouver, Sochi

5. Howard Jacobson, Julian Barnes, ____, Eleanor Catton

6. Ballabriggs, Neptune Collonges, Auroras Encore, ____

7. Alaska, Texas, California, ____

8. ____, Henry McLeish, Jack McConnell, Alex Salmond

9. Afghanistan, Albania, Algeria, ____

10. ____, Walter Mondale, George H W Bush, Dan Quayle

11. Sergeant, Nurse, Teacher, ____

12. India, Pakistan, ____, West Indies

13. Raindrops on roses, whiskers on kittens, bright copper kettles, ____

14. Tom Hooper, Michel Hazanavicius, ____, Alfonso Cuaron

15. Jacques Delors, Jacques Santer, Romano Prodi, ____

16. Arthur Balfour, ____, Herbert Asquith, David Lloyd George

17. The Curse of the Black Pearl, Dead Man's Chest, ____, On Stranger Tides

18. Zephaniah, Haggai, Zechariah, ____

19. California, New York, Texas, ____

20. Nottinghamshire, Lancashire, Warwickshire, ____

Answers to Quiz 189: Pot Luck

1. Derby County
2. Sir John Tavener
3. Unite
4. Le Corbusier
5. Italy
6. Tequila
7. Canada
8. Egypt
9. Naples (Neapolis)
10. The Girl with the Dragon Tattoo
11. Vera
12. Cat
13. Nyon
14. Durban
15. Liam Gallagher
16. Organa
17. 116 years
18. Rio de Janeiro
19. Poker
20. Valencia

DIFFICULT

Quiz 191: Pot Luck

1. What colour is a €10 note?

2. Which actor, best known for playing Bodie in the action drama 'The Professionals', died in November 2013 at the age of 67?

3. Which European capital city lies on the banks of the Dnieper River?

4. If the provinces of Canada were listed alphabetically, which province would be first on the list?

5. The Fosse shopping park is on the outskirts of which English city?

6. The dormant volcano Mount Tambora is in which Asian country?

7. Which was the first country to host the World Athletics Championships more than once?

8. Which animated sequel was the top-grossing film at the UK and Ireland box office for 2013?

9. In which decade was American football's Super Bowl hosted for the first time?

10. In the Bible, who was the first person to speak to Jesus after the resurrection?

11. What type of event is known in France as a 'vide grenier'?

12. Which actor and comedian was the first winner of 'Celebrity Big Brother'?

13. The Formula One venue, Circuit of the Americas, is in which American city?

14. NH_3 is the chemical formula for which pungent, colourless gas?

15. Creator of the famous jeans company, Levi Strauss was born in which European country?

16. Rita Coolidge sang the theme song to which James Bond film?

17. A tiger features on the badge of which Asian motor manufacturer?

Answers – page 389

18. Which famous New York thoroughfare plays host to an annual Easter parade?

19. Which fruit is the main ingredient in the Japanese liqueur Midori?
    a) Melon   b) Pineapple   c) Strawberry

20. What was the name of Charles Saatchi's controversial 1997 exhibition at the Royal Academy that featured Tracey Emin's bed and Damien Hirst's 'Tiger Shark'?
    a) Scandal   b) Sensation   c) Tabloid

Answers to Quiz 190: Fill in the Blank part 2

1. Roy Hodgson (Liverpool FC managers)
2. James Madison (the first four US presidents)
3. Jacqui Smith (UK Home Secretaries)
4. Salt Lake City (Winter Olympics venues 2002 to 2014)
5. Hilary Mantel (Booker Prize winners (2010 to 2013)
6. Pineau De Re (Grand National winners 2011 to 2014)
7. Montana (largest US states by area)
8. Donald Dewar (First Ministers of Scotland)
9. Andorra (the first four members of the United Nations in alphabetical order)
10. Nelson Rockefeller (US Vice Presidents)
11. Constable (the first four Carry On films)
12. England (winners of the first four World T20 cricket competitions)
13. Warm woollen mittens (First four items from the song 'My Favourite Things')
14. Ang Lee (Best Director Oscar winners 2011 to 2014)
15. José Manuel Barroso (permanent presidents of the European Commission)
16. Sir Henry Campbell-Bannerman (British Prime Ministers 1902 to 1922)
17. At World's End ('Pirates of the Caribbean' films)
18. Malachi (the last four books of the Old Testament in the King James Bible)
19. Florida (largest US states by population)
20. Durham (winners of cricket's County Championship 2010 to 2013)

DIFFICULT

Quiz 192: Postcodes

Identify the town or city that has the following postcode prefixes (for example, M = Manchester):

1. AL

2. BR

3. CM

4. DL

5. DT

6. FY

7. HP

8. IG

9. KA

10. LD

11. NN

12. RH

13. SA

14. SG

Answers – page 391

15. SN

16. SR

17. SS

18. TF

19. TN

20. WS

Answers to Quiz 191: Pot Luck

1. Red
2. Lewis Collins
3. Kiev
4. Alberta
5. Leicester
6. Indonesia
7. Japan
8. Despicable Me 2
9. 1960s
10. Mary Magdalene
11. Car boot sale or flea market
12. Jack Dee
13. Austin
14. Ammonia
15. Germany
16. Octopussy
17. Proton
18. Fifth Avenue
19. Melon
20. Sensation

DIFFICULT

Quiz 193: Pot Luck

1. What does the 'A' in the financial acronym EBITDA stand for?

2. The coffee drink mocha takes its name from a seaport in which Arab country?

3. Eve Muirhead led the British team to a bronze medal in the 2014 Winter Olympics. In which sport?

4. Which comedian, radio DJ and TV panel-show regular wrote the 2011 book 'It's Not Me, It's You!: Impossible perfectionist, 27, seeks very very very tidy woman'?

5. Which are the two families that have produced three generations of Oscar winners?

6. What colour is a €20 note?

7. Who won her first Best Actress Oscar for the 1988 film 'The Accused'?

8. The saltwater Hudson Bay is off the coast of which Commonwealth country?

9. In 2007 which band were 'Worried About Ray' and said 'Goodbye Mr A'?

10. Basutholand is the former name of which landlocked African country?

11. Which actor played Mr Pink in the crime classic 'Reservoir Dogs'?

12. In which year was the Football Association founded?

13. Grace Road is the home ground of which English county cricket team?

14. In greyhound racing, what colour vest is worn by a dog running from trap four?

15. Which town on the western outskirts of London is also the middle name of the Hollywood star Denzel Washington?

16. Which gas takes its name from the Greek word for 'inactive'?

17. An object that is fabiform is shaped like what?

18. The mysterious Satoshi Nakamoto is the creator of which digital currency that launched in 2009?

19. In Major League Baseball, each team plays how many games during the regular season?
a) 62   b) 126   c) 162

20. Which radioactive isotope is used to estimate the age of organic matter such as wood?
a) carbon-12
b) carbon-13
c) carbon-14

Answers to Quiz 192: Postcodes

1. St Albans
2. Bromley
3. Chelmsford
4. Darlington
5. Dorchester
6. Blackpool
7. Hemel Hempstead
8. Ilford
9. Kilmarnock
10. Llandrindod Wells
11. Northampton
12. Redhill
13. Swansea
14. Stevenage
15. Swindon
16. Sunderland
17. Southend-on-Sea
18. Telford
19. Tonbridge
20. Walsall

DIFFICULT

Quiz 194: Places part 2

1. Which Belgian city is known in Dutch as Luik?

2. Which country is separated from mainland Malaysia by the Johore Strait?

3. Which European capital is located at the junction of Lake Mälar and Salt Bay, an arm of the Baltic Sea?

4. Home to a pair of large nuclear power stations, the village of Sizewell is in which English county?

5. The village of Stilton, which gives its name to a famous cheese, is in which English county?

6. Shirley, Swaythling, Bevois Valley and St Mary's are districts of which English city?

7. Is New Zealand capital Wellington on the country's North or South Island?

8. Which two seas are connected by the Suez Canal?

9. Dutch Guiana is the former name of which country?

10. The island of Madagascar lies in which ocean?

11. Guadalajara is the second-largest city of which country?

12. Which English city lies at the confluence of the rivers Kenwyn and Allen?

13. A 17th-century promenade known as 'The Pantiles' is a feature of which royal town?

14. The giant Three Gorges Dam is located in which Asian country?

15. Which name is shared by a Yorkshire seaside resort and the largest city on the West Indian island of Tobago?

Answers – page 395

16. Which Pacific Island nation was formerly known as the New Hebrides?

17. Revel is the former name of which Eastern European capital city?

18. Which North American city is home to the largest Chinese community outside of China?

19. Home to the largest tree in the world, Sequoia National Park is in which country?
    a) Australia
    b) South Africa
    c) USA

20. Uranium City is a place in which country?
    a) Canada
    b) China
    c) Russia

Answers to Quiz 193: Pot Luck

1. Amortization
2. Yemen
3. Curling
4. Jon Richardson
5. The Coppolas and the Hustons
6. Blue
7. Jodie Foster
8. Canada
9. The Hoosiers
10. Lesotho
11. Steve Buscemi
12. 1863
13. Leicestershire
14. Black
15. Hayes
16. Argon
17. A bean
18. Bitcoin
19. 162
20. Carbon-14

DIFFICULT

Quiz 195: Pot Luck

1. The Addicks is the nickname of which English football club?

2. Named as a European Capital of Culture for 2015, Mons is a city in which country?

3. What colour is a €5 banknote?

4. Which science book has spent the longest time of any title in the Sunday Times bestseller list over the past 40 years?

5. Which British actor was the subject of a biography entitled 'From Slough to Middle Earth'?

6. 'Ad Majorem Dei Gloriam' (For the greater glory of God) is the motto of which religious organization?

7. In which year were the World Athletics Championships held for the first time?

8. Bulawayo is the second-largest city in which African country?

9. Danish drummer Lars Ulrich was a founder member of which hard-rock band?

10. Which popular TV drama is based on a series of novels by Caroline Graham?

11. '100 Years of Solitude' and 'Love in the Time of Cholera' are novels by which Nobel-winning author, who died in April 2014?

12. What breed was the first dog in Britain to be cloned, after its owner won a TV competition in 2014?

13. The largest earthquake ever measured occurred in 1960 in which South American country?

14. Singers FC was the original name of which Midlands football club?

15. The cult 2001 film 'Y Tu Mamá También' was set in which country?

DIFFICULT

Answers – page 397

16. According to the adage known as Hanlon's razor, 'Never attribute to malice that which is adequately explained by ...' what?

17. Which American airport was formerly known as Idlewild?

18. Which Hungarian-born British author created the fictional character 'The Scarlet Pimpernel'?

19. What is the South American equivalent of football's Champions League?
    a) Copa America
    b) Copa Libertadores
    c) Copa Vittoria

20. Which of the following was the title of the 2014 film starring Tom Hardy?
    a) Bentham   b) Locke   c) Mill

Answers to Quiz 194: Places part 2

1. Liege
2. Singapore
3. Stockholm
4. Suffolk
5. Cambridgeshire
6. Southampton
7. North Island
8. Mediterranean Sea and Red Sea
9. Suriname
10. Indian Ocean
11. Mexico
12. Truro
13. Tunbridge Wells
14. China
15. Scarborough
16. Vanuatu
17. Tallinn
18. Vancouver
19. USA
20. Canada

DIFFICULT

Quiz 196: Alliterative Answers part 2

1. 'Donostiarra' is the name given to a resident of which city in the Spanish Basque country?

2. 'The Human Factor', 'England Made Me' and 'Travels With My Aunt' are works by which English novelist, who died in 1991?

3. 'Bleeding Love' was a 2008 UK number one for which singer?

4. Who was Britain's poet laureate from 1843 until 1850?

5. 'Bluebeard's Castle' was the only opera by which Hungarian pianist and composer?

6. Whom did Karren Brady succeed as an assistant to Lord Sugar on 'The Apprentice'?

7. Neil Buchanan was the host of which long-running, painting-inspired, children's TV show?

8. Which 1990s TV game show featured rounds called 'pocket money' and 'red hot'?

9. Which actor plays Inspector Edmund Reid in detective drama 'Ripper Street'?

10. In the 'Harry Potter' films, what is the name of the professor played by Dame Maggie Smith?

11. Which West Indian batsman was knighted for his services to cricket in February 2014?

12. Who won the Razzie for Worst Supporting Actress in 2014 for her performance in 'Temptation: Confessions of a Marriage Counselor'?

13. Alongside Georges Braque, who was the founder of the artistic movement known as 'Cubism'?

14. Which singer from TV talent show 'The X Factor' won 'I'm a Celebrity ... Get Me Out of Here' in 2010?

15. Which actor provides the voice of Grampy Rabbit in the children's animation 'Peppa Pig'?

16. Who was the first winner of the TV show 'Britain's Got Talent'?

17. Who was the President of Zambia from 1964 to 1991?

18. Who is the famous footballing father of the French midfielder Enzo Fernandez?

19. Who won his first Oscar in 2014 for his performance in the film 'Dallas Buyers Club'?

20. Which film-maker won his only Best Director Oscar in 1987 for 'The Last Emperor'?

Answers to Quiz 195: Pot Luck

1. Charlton Athletic
2. Belgium
3. Grey
4. 'A Brief History of Time' by Stephen Hawking
5. Martin Freeman
6. Society of Jesus (Jesuits)
7. 1983
8. Zimbabwe
9. Metallica
10. Midsomer Murders
11. Gabriel Garcia Marquez
12. Dachshund
13. Chile
14. Coventry City
15. Mexico
16. Stupidity
17. JFK Airport in New York
18. Baroness Orczy
19. Copa Libertadores
20. Locke

DIFFICULT

Quiz 197: Pot Luck

1. Standing some 665m above sea level, what is the highest capital city in Europe?

2. EC3N 4AB is the postcode of which London landmark?

3. What is the capital city of Lithuania?

4. The city of Odessa is located on the shore of which body of water?

5. Which African country was formerly known as the Malagasy Republic?

6. Who was the first Oscar-winning actor to play a baddie in a James Bond film?

7. In 1986, Falco became the first person from which country to top the UK singles chart?

8. Terence Parsons was the real name of which English crooner?

9. What was Abba's last UK number-one single?

10. What colour is a €100 banknote?

11. Matt Helders is the drummer with which award-winning British rock band?

12. What breed of dog is sometimes known as the 'lion dog'?

13. The Sailor King was the nickname of which British monarch?

14. Which English city was awarded a Blue Plaque in 2014 for its pioneering work in the development of postcodes?

15. Miranda, Titania, Oberon and Ariel are moons of which planet of the Solar System?

16. England's Trina Gulliver is a multiple World Champion in which sport?

17. 'Rubus idaeus' is the scientific name for which popular fruit?

18. Who was the last Anglo-Saxon king of England?

19. Robert Gascoyne-Cecil, who served three terms as the British prime minister, was the Marquess of where?
    a) Canterbury
    b) Salisbury
    c) Winchester

20. In which branch of the arts is Juan Diego Florez a notable name?
    a) opera
    b) painting
    c) sculpture

Answers to Quiz 196: Alliterative Answers part 2

1.	San Sebastian	11.	Richie Richardson
2.	Graham Greene	12.	Kim Kardashian
3.	Leona Lewis	13.	Pablo Picasso
4.	William Wordsworth	14.	Stacy Solomon
5.	Bela Bartok	15.	Brian Blessed
6.	Margaret Mountford	16.	Paul Potts
7.	Art Attack	17.	Kenneth Kaunda
8.	Big Break	18.	Zinedine Zidane
9.	Matthew Macfadyen	19.	Matthew McConaughey
10.	Minerva McGonagall	20.	Bernardo Bertolucci

DIFFICULT

Quiz 198: Anagrams part 2

Rearrange the letters to make the name of an Irish county:

1. Gaol Den

2. Ham Rag

3. Not Rye

4. Hang Ref Ma

5. Moms Croom

6. Sam The Wet

7. Bun Lid

8. Wed For Art

9. Fly Oaf

10. Idle Ark

11. Arc Owl

12. Ram Nit

13. Pyrite Par

14. Rick Lime

15. It Miler

16. Ham On Nag

17. Drew Fox

18. Wow Lick

19. Gay Awl

20. Frond Log

Answers to Quiz 197: Pot Luck

1. Madrid
2. The Tower of London
3. Vilnius
4. The Black Sea
5. Madagascar
6. Christopher Walken
7. Austria
8. Matt Monro
9. Super Trouper
10. Green
11. Arctic Monkeys
12. Pekingese
13. William IV
14. Norwich
15. Uranus
16. Darts
17. Raspberry
18. Harold II
19. Salisbury
20. Opera

DIFFICULT

Quiz 199: Pot Luck

1. Which London borough was formed following the amalgamation of the former boroughs of Hornsey, Tottenham and Wood Green?

2. Chek Lap Kok Airport serves which Asian territory?

3. Who is older – David Cameron or Nick Clegg?

4. 'If you want to know what God thinks of money, just look at the people he gave it to' is a quotation from which celebrated American author, who died in 1967?

5. What colour is a €50 banknote?

6. In 1972, Don McLean topped the charts with a tribute to which artist?

7. 'Orbis non sufficit' is the family motto of which fictional character?

8. 'When he was nearly thirteen, my brother Jem got his arm badly broken at the elbow' is the opening line to which 1960 novel?

9. The Jags is the nickname of which Scottish football team?

10. Which bone of the pelvis is also an alternative name for the ancient city of Troy?

11. Which animated Disney dog is known in Finland as 'Hessu Hopo' and in Norway as 'Langbein'?

12. What do the initials JG in the name of the author JG Ballard stand for?

13. Which soft grey metal, discovered by William Crookes and Claude-Auguste Lamy, has the chemical symbol Tl and atomic number 81?

14. 'I've had a heck of a lot of fun and I've enjoyed every minute of it' were the last words of which hell-raising actor?

15. Edinburgh of the Seven Seas is the largest settlement on which remote South Atlantic island?

16. St Vitus Cathedral is in which central European capital city?

17. The words admiral, alchemy and almanac derive from which language?

18. 'Prince Igor' is an opera written by which 19th-century Russian composer?

19. What was the name of the Notting Hill restaurant opened by artist Damien Hirst?
a) Biology   b) Chemistry   c) Pharmacy

20. The Rocky Mountains are not a feature of which of the following US states?
a) Idaho   b) Montana   c) South Dakota

Answers to Quiz 198: Anagrams part 2

1. Donegal
2. Armagh
3. Tyrone
4. Fermanagh
5. Roscommon
6. Westmeath
7. Dublin
8. Waterford
9. Offaly
10. Kildare
11. Carlow
12. Antrim
13. Tipperary
14. Limerick
15. Leitrim
16. Monaghan
17. Wexford
18. Wicklow
19. Galway
20. Longford

DIFFICULT

Quiz 200: Movies part 2

1. Prior to 'Argo' in 2012, what was the last film with a one-word title to win the Oscar for Best Picture?

2. Again prior to 'Argo' in 2012, what was the last film whose title started with a vowel to win the Oscar for Best Picture?

3. 'The Quiet American', 'The End of the Affair' and 'The Heart of the Matter' were films based on novels by which author?

4. Who is the youngest of the acting Baldwin brothers?

5. 'Hatchet Job' was a 2014 book by which film critic and broadcaster?

6. True or false – prior to becoming an actor, Brendan Gleeson worked as a maths teacher?

7. The first British film to win the Oscar for Best Picture was an adaptation of which Shakespeare play?

8. What is the French equivalent of an Oscar award?

9. What nationality is the Oscar-winning director Alfonso Cuaron?

10. Jane Seymour played 'Bond girl' Solitaire in which film?

11. Who is older – Brad Pitt or Tom Cruise?

12. Alois is the middle name of which action star?

13. 'The Great Beauty', winner of the Best Foreign Film Oscar in 2014, is set in which city?

14. The opening line of the original (1977) 'Star Wars' film was delivered by which character?

15. Who won the Best Supporting Actress Oscar in 2014 for her portrayal of Patsey in '12 Years a Slave'?

Answers – page 275

16. The world's oldest film festival is held in which European city?

17. Taking inflation into account, which winner of the Oscar for Best Picture has taken the least amount of money at the box office?

18. What was the first 'Carry On' film to be made in colour?

19. Which film won the Razzie for Worst Picture in 2014?
    a) Movie 42
    b) Movie 43
    c) Movie 44

20. The 2014 Oscar-nominated documentary 'The Act of Killing' is set in which Asian country?
    a) China
    b) Indonesia
    c) Sri Lanka

Answers to Quiz 199: Pot Luck

1. Haringey
2. Hong Kong
3. David Cameron
4. Dorothy Parker
5. Orange
6. Vincent van Gogh
7. James Bond
8. To Kill a Mockingbird
9. Partick Thistle
10. Ilium
11. Goofy
12. James Graham
13. Thallium
14. Errol Flynn
15. Tristan da Cunha
16. Prague
17. Arabic
18. Alexander Borodin
19. Pharmacy
20. South Dakota

DIFFICULT